BITTER WIND

Joe McGowan

First published in 2009 by: Aeolus Publications

All photographs by the author unless otherwise
stated

The author wishes to acknowledge and thank
all those writers whose verse or prose is
included in this book.

© Joe Mc Gowan / www.sligoheritage.com
Email: joemcgowan@sligoheritage.com

ISBN 978-0-9521334-5-2

Design and Typesetting: Martin Corr
Typeset in Eason

This publication has received support from the
Heritage Council under the 2009 Publication
Grant Scheme

'The old brown thorn-trees break in two high over Cummen Strand,
Under a bitter black wind that blows from the left hand;
Our courage breaks like an old tree in a black wind and dies,
But we have hidden in our hearts the flame out of the eyes
Of Cathleen, the daughter of Houlihan...'

W.B. Yeats
Red Hanrahan's Song about Ireland

To John Fowley and Kevin McGrath; to the storytellers herein, memory men and women, last of their kind.

Contents

Part 1: THE DROWNING WAVE

Part 2: BANISH MISFORTUNE

PART 1

THE DROWNING WAVE

1

IN SEARCH OF EADÁILS

Except wind stands as never it stood, it's an ill wind turns none to good.

Thomas Tusser (1527-1580)

The ill winds of winter blew a rich harvest for some. When they ferociously raged, men of the village converged on the shore before the sun threw its first wan rays into the eastern sky. Silhouetted scarecrows of the pre-dawn, one here, two there, they moved steadfastly along the cliffs. Out on the fathomless ocean Mannanán Mac Lir madly rode his tumbling sea horses; whipped their stinging mane across the men's weather-beaten faces, lashed spray and foam across the sodden fields.

They stumbled on. Ragged rows of flickering, firefly lights from candle-lit cart lamps traced their path. The hypnotic call of the sea, luminescent in the half-dark, lured them. Eerie morning shadows in the dim-lit dawn they made their way along the bleak, boulder strewn shores of *Cromadach* or *Lugashanny*, *Pollachurry* or *Pollnaweegoge*. In favourite places well known to them they explored the waves, ledges and inlets for '*eadaíls*' driven ashore.

'E*adáils*' were remnants of cargoes: logs and planks, barrels and rafts, washed off the decks of ships at sea. Sometimes it was wreckage from craft that had sunk far out beyond the horizon. Old men recall huge logs drawn from the shore that required two ass carts to draw, one in front and one behind. The term '*eadáil*' is a survivor from the Gaelic. I was a grown man before I realised the commonly used word *eadáil* was not an English word at all, but an Irish one meaning 'riches' or 'plunder'.

Spectres of the half-light, bent into the teeth of the gale, making no sound against the roar of wind and wave, the seashore gatherers moved resolutely onward. Life hung precariously along this great abyss where land and sea so violently collide. Its treachery was well known to these men; a fear that was bred in their bones. Misread the ocean's mood and the deep would rise to claim them. Poised between solid earth and treacherous sea they keenly scanned the waves' curling mountains and hungry green underbelly. Toppling with a furious noise the rollers sucked viciously at the land, receded, joined the next inward bound monster and, returning, rose higher still to crash again and yet again shredding into wind-blown spume on immovable rock:

'*Wave after wave, each mightier than the last; till last a ninth one, gathering half the deep, and full of voices, slowly rose and plunged Roaring, and all the sea was in a flame.*' [1]

Mindful of the risk, they appraised carefully the scene before them. Their lives depended on their wits. That churning, twisting maelstrom was an ally, but could be an unpredictable adversary too. Knowing it, they never trusted it; they feared and respected it. 'Never turn your back to the sea', they said, echoing a warning as old as Plato's advice that the 'sea makes a dangerous neighbour'. It was the first and oft repeated lesson on a novice's introduction to the shore. Faces always turned to the threat, the wise man was ever alert to the ocean's whims. 'A man who is not afraid of the sea will soon be drownded,' an Aran islander once told J.M. Synge, 'for he will be going out on a day he shouldn't. But we do be afraid of the sea, and we do only be drownded now and again.'

The waters are influenced by many factors: phases of the moon that dictate spring or neap tides; storms at sea that throw up treacherous groundswells; wind directions that influence tides; ocean currents that create rips and undertows. Depending on high water or low, turbulence can be determined, but not accurately. Bigger breakers come in a recognisable order, but not always: three big ones, then a lull of six or so less powerful. There is an order, but it is a changing one.

The ocean provided the gatherers with food and bounty — it

[1] *The Coming of Arthur*, Tennyson

would equally take their life. When they looked on its face they looked into their graves, one foot on the edge.

> ...*In time I surrender my drowned,*
> *My appetite speaks for itself,*
> *I could swallow all you have found*
> *And open for more,*
> *My green tongues licking the shores*
> *Of the world...*
>
>

The Sea, Brendan Kennelly

In this wild and rugged landscape the earth was rarely at peace. Here on land and sea the winds incessantly blew. On long, black winter nights when it roared in the chimney and fusillades of hail rattled a sharp tattoo on doors and windows, men rambled to neighbours houses. Huddled around the turf fire they piled on the sods; flames danced and smoke hurried away up the chimney as they spoke of many things: of drowning and shipwrecks, of close shaves and narrow escapes.

My father might relate quietly of the night his boot got caught between two boulders while in search of *eadáils*. An incoming tide crept, advancing slowly, very slowly, inch by unbearable inch, threatening to drown him. Heartbeat by heartbeat the torturous minutes — or could it be hours — went excruciatingly by; his foot swelled, each wave inched higher and still higher as he prepared to die. Stretching, choking, inhaling seawater he went under, again and yet again, and still the boulders held him fast. The sounds of wind and wave faded away, faded slowly; losing consciousness his body relaxed, a great peace enveloped him.

Afterwards he would swear that just before his eyes closed for the last time he saw what looked like a mermaid — for her appearance fitted descriptions he had heard — sitting on a rock combing her hair as she watched him. He held out his hand to her as the mists closed in and the roar of the sea faded away. His eyes closed and he moved swiftly, smoothly from the horror.

Suddenly it was a bright summer day. He emerged to a placid, sunlit landscape. The sun glittered on a tranquil sea. He was free, floating, light as air, a part of the scene, and yet not. He was in a surreal parallel world. He saw everything clearly as if from a height, but yet heard no sound. There was a strong scent of roses. He saw a prone body, his own, lying by the shore. The mermaid sat by the body, watching, smiling. The strange creature hovered for a moment, moved to the water's edge, slid into the sea and disappeared beneath the waves. The light darkened, the dream faded and suddenly he was lying above the high water mark, barefoot, soaking wet, exhaling seawater from his lungs and gasping for breath. Pulling himself up on hands and knees he looked around: the sea still raged among the boulders, the wind blew fiercely as ever but there was no mermaid, nothing to show that anything unusual had just happened.

Next day he went back at low water and found one of his boots wedged in the stones; he never found the other one.

On another occasion, a night of driving wind and rain, near the Sailor's Hole at *Dreimire Buidhe*, he was surrounded by multitudes of rats attracted to the light of the cart-lamp. More curious than threatening the bizarre procession followed him as he made his way along the shore: a reluctant 'pied piper'.

Here along these barren places among the mist and sea fog strange things happen. Country people feared to bathe in such quiet places on a Sunday. Mermaids came up on the rocks on that day and might take them away. If you looked out on the sea you might be mesmerised, drawn into it and away.

Johnny Cummins had been listening intently:

'Them things can happen' he said. 'Sometimes if you saw a mermaid it was a sign someone was going to drown. My brother Francie was going along the shore under Classiebawn one day an' didn't he see one, like a woman with a fishes tail, that's the truth, I wouldn't tell ye a word of a lie. She was up on the rock,

Francie stood looking at her an' she went into the water again. The next day, the grandest day that ever was seen, and no ground swell, there was three people drowned over on the back Strand behind Cliffoney. Fr. Rattigan that was going on for a priest that time, he was with them. They couldn't be saved. That finished the bathing there. There's fierce holes over on that strand. They were pulled out and a wave came then and pushed them in again. I often think about it.'

The night wore on and one story of the sea followed another. They might talk about close shaves, or marvel at how lucky they were to be alive. It was a comradeship of the deep: men thrown on this earth in a barren, frugal place to live by chance and their wits. Wild and scenic it might have been but you 'can't eat scenery' my mother replied to visiting cousins. And indeed you couldn't, and the land provided a poor living. Appreciation of the landscape was a long way off and would come only many, many years later when a sense of the aesthetic was sharpened by a full belly and improved living conditions.

Sometimes the men worked with each other to recover heavy logs or timbers. More often than not there was great rivalry to capture the prize of barrel, bale, raft or block of tallow as it was swept ashore. They took great risks, edging ever closer to the 'green hells of the sea, where fallen skies and evil hues and eyeless creatures be'.[2] Dwarfed by the breakers that might snatch them, they stretched every muscle to throw the iron grapnel further and be the first to claw onto a floating prize.

The gods looked down on man's puny efforts and one day laughed as they tossed the dice for Johnny Barry at *Oileán Mór*. Swept off his feet by 'a wave so huge it had washed among the stars and put them out' he was carried away on the swirling tide. Each receding wave pulled him here and swept him there — for cruel sport it seemed. When his companions had given him up for lost, breathless and dazed, he was washed close to the shore by another capricious surge. Despite the belief: '*Bíonn a cuid féin*

[2] G. K. Chesterton, *Lepanto*.

ag an bhfarraige' (The sea must have its due), his neighbour Paddy Callery took off his coat, handed one end to Michael Duffy and holding the other end himself reached for Johnny and pulled him to safety.

Custom held it was unlucky to save a drowning person. "Are you mad?" said the peddler in Sir Walter Scott's *The Pirate*, "you that have lived sae lang in Zetland to risk the saving of a drowning man? Wot ye not, if you bring him to life again he will be sure to do you some capital injury?"

This same belief of a life for a life was found among others who squeezed a living from the waters: the St. Kilda islanders, boatmen of the Danube, French and English sailors and beyond Europe even among the most primitive of tribes. When a man is drowning it is the intention of the gods that he should die. You cannot cheat Fate out of a life. A place in the sea was destined for a corpse — someone must fill it. The rescuer shall, in time, forfeit his own life in place of the life he saved.

Many years later, Johnny saved me from a similar fate when, fishing from the rocks, I lost my footing and was suddenly plunged into a whirling, green undersea world. Setting aside the custom, for my rescuer, and for Johnny's, the gods gave dispensation.

Media reports carry news each year of people swept from shore and drowned by 'freak waves'. They are a dangerous and uninformed exaggeration. Such waves do exist but are not as common as reported. Waves that sweep people off rocks or breakwaters are almost always from regularly occurring groundswells, high seas generated by depressions at sea.

In the early morning hunt or late at night this knowledge served the sea scavengers well. Especially prized on their trips were bales of raw rubber, cast up in greatest abundance during the war years of '39 to '45 and for several years after. Weighing about one hundredweight, they were carried from the shore, hidden and by cover of darkness brought by secret ways to merchant

Frank Sweeney in Grange. He bought them in surreptitious deals by candlelight for five pounds each — a small fortune in those pinched times. Bales of cotton were sold for one pound.

Gardai and Customs officials were regarded with dread. They slept warmly in their beds while the huntsmen risked death, drew their treasure home and hid it from prying eyes. Their law was the natural law. Items recovered from the sea belonged to the rescuer. It made sense. Anything else was bad law. But law, good or bad, was law and the statute books stated clearly that anything recovered from the sea was the property of the State.

The men in uniform were tireless in enforcing the regulations. They gave no quarter as they diligently searched houses, turf-stacks and hayricks for contraband. Villagers were equal in their determination to thwart authority and hold on to the items they had worked so hard to acquire. Similar legislation on the Isle of Lewis allowed the 'Admiral Deputy of the Western Isles' lay claim to everything washed ashore. Officers of the department marked the letter 'S' in red paint on all moderately sized driftwood making it extremely difficult to use for islanders who depended on this flotsam to roof their homes. Houses were searched and any such timber, even if blackened with soot and age, was confiscated.

Visiting Government officials, in uniform or out, never brought good news: Gardai nosing about for unlicensed dogs; 'Pension Officers' with long noses and sharp pens anxious to cut the family stipend; rent and rate collectors claiming the last piece of paper money in the house. A visit from these officials meant ever only one thing: Trouble. An honest days pay for an honest days work was fair enough but busybody officials were an unwarranted and unpopular imposition! Ploughman and mower had to wait for their money. But that grinding taskmaster, Authority, must have its pound of flesh on demand!

Not greed but sheer necessity was the motivation of men who gambled their lives and dared the sea. Their very survival depended on it. There was no question of right or wrong. Practical home use seemed a worthier end to the ocean's bounty than confiscation into the maw of an obscure, faceless government. They believed the sea's gift to be as much their ancestral right as the herring they netted, the ballan they fished, or the seaweeds they gathered along those same shores. What gave the State a right to it? If they were interested in reclaiming 'State property' why didn't they take their place along the shore and reclaim the goods by honest toil like everyone else?

In January 1947, following a particularly extended spell of stormy weather, excise men, accompanied by Gardai, came to Mullaghmore to search and confiscate. Informers had been at work. My father, Petie Mc Gowan, was on their list of men reported to have acquired a bale of rubber. The customs man, refusing to believe his protestations of innocence strode into the hay-garden. Squaring up to the rick the strong arm of the law plunged his steel probe deep inside.

'Ye have the rubber, I know it and I'm going to find it,' the Revenuer challenged.

'Ye're wrong, there's no rubber,' was my father's emphatic reply.

'Ye fooled me about the dog before,' Guard Burns chipped in, referring to another one of his unsuccessful missions checking on unlicensed animals.

'Never mind the dog,' my father replied, 'it's rubber ye're after now.'

They probed and searched and dug, but found nothing. The raid was anticipated and the bale of rubber cradled safely in the bosom of a friendly neighbours turf-stack.

Centuries of hiding gun and pike in thatch and rick had bred a crafty, resourceful people. Many a moonlight deal was done for bales of rubber, and many a cache of timber dug up by lantern light and brought by circuitous routes to Johnny Mc Cann's or Eddie Harkins sawmills. Here they were cut and fashioned into carts, wheelbarrows and other essential farm implements by these canny men.

Many of the old tellers of stories prefer to remain anonymous, so in the course of this book I will respect their wishes by using assumed names.

Brian K—— was an old man when I spoke to him. Working a small farm, hunting rabbits and searching for *eadáils* provided for him the elemental fabric of existence. He remembered the poverty of the time: the despair on the death of a farm animal, the joy and excitement of a successful hunt. Recalling a particularly good haul of timber from one outing he remembered how he could scarce believe his luck when plank after plank came floating in on the tide. Carrying his treasure from the waters edge he stacked it above the high water mark. Later, bringing his cache home he dug a hole in a corner of his field and buried it.

Afterwards, when he thought about it, he suspected that a neighbour — a neighbour that experience had taught him not to trust — had spotted him hiding his catch. There was camaraderie and co-operation in small town Ireland but at least among some, there was jealousy and begrudgery too. That bard of country life, Patrick Kavanagh, missed nothing! Noting this failing of rural Ireland in *Temptation in Harvest* he wrote:

> '…The sides of the ricks were letting in; too hurried
> We built them to beat the showers that were flying
> All day. "It's raining at Shancoduff now,"
> We'd speculate, half happy to think how
> Flat on the ground a neighbours stooks were lying…'

That night when Brian went to bed he couldn't rest. The thought preyed on his mind. He tossed and turned. Eventually he got up, put on his clothes, dug up his catch and re-buried it in the cow byre. Two days later the Gardai arrived with spades. They went directly to the place where he had first buried the planks. Did they have information, confirming Brian's hunch about his informing neighbour, or did they, being keen of eye, observe that the ground had been disturbed? No matter, his cache was safe and some days later Brian brought the planks to Eddie Harkin's sawmill where the planks were sawed into boards and made into a new horse cart. The authorities viewed his new chariot with some suspicion but there was nothing they could do and Brian had scored another small victory for the underdog!

The day when a hogshead (50 gal.) of whiskey was washed ashore at Ros Caoireach on the Sligo coast is still recalled with affection and glee! Cupped hands were used to sample the liquid on the spot and creamery cans requisitioned to divide the prize. Some was doled out in bottles and cans to friends and neighbours but most of it was brought to pubs in nearby Bundoran, Co. Donegal to be converted into cash.

In later years I learned that sea-borne booty was common and prized all along the western seaboard. Blasket islander, Maurice O' Sullivan, recorded in 1943 the delight of his neighbours when a ship was wrecked. The quay and the strands were a 'grand sight, big timbers lying here and there and not a curragh with less than a hundred planks.'

'By God,' they said, 'but war is good.'

'We should thank God and have a holiday in his honour,' said Mickaleen Liam of Mughinis island in Conemara when a barrel of rum was rescued from the sea on that coast. 'One hundred and sixteen gallons. Made in Jamaica 1916', was printed on the side. 'My soul from the devil, but the Germans have done their share in helping the poor, sick and aged, causing this rum and other good things to come to us,' Mickaleen said.

Blasket islander Tomás O Crohan in his book, The Islandman recounted a wreck on the White Strand in the Blaskets during the famine. The islanders tried their best to save the crew, but failed. Thousands of sacks of wheat torn from the ships hull were tossed ashore by the waves: 'If it hadn't been for her, not a soul would have survived on the Island, and you may be sure that the old hag said that it was God who sent her to the poor.'

Tea was first introduced to the Blaskets as an *eadáil* when a ship foundered there in the late 1800s. Dozens of tinfoil-lined boxes were washed ashore. Most of the men, not recognising the strange substance, emptied the contents and used the wooden tea chests for firewood. One woman, noticing the deep colour when the tea was steeped in water, made a complete success of dying her petticoats with it.

Continuing her experiments she discovered the pigs liked it. A jealous neighbour went to visit in order to find out what she was up to. The woman told her she had two ravenous pigs that were dying of hunger. Since she started boiling the stuff for them, mixed with a handful of meal, they lay at their ease, belly upwards in the yard, "and pretty soon they'll be fine and fat," said she.'

Her friend, who had two famishing pigs of her own, 'ready to eat the children with hunger — all skin and bone though they're nearly a year old', went home in a rage to her husband. He was one of the men who had dumped the contents and kept the box. They got into a big fight and she 'made him so savage in the end that the neighbours had to come and separate them.' He rose early the next morning on the pretext of going into Dingle to buy food for the pigs. Some relations paid his fare and he was never seen again.

Tea arrived on Inishmurray Island, Co. Sligo in 1865 by a more conventional route. It was introduced there by 'Macy' Heraughty who had acquired his nickname from having worked for a time in Macy's of New York. The substance was somewhat of a wonder when Heraughty arrived home with it.

Some time afterwards it happened that a station Mass was held on the island. The priest's breakfast after Mass was always a big affair. Only the very best in the house was good enough for this important guest. If there was anything new and fashionable the improving woman was going to be ahead of her neighbours in

providing it. Wanting to impress the celebrant, Fr. Malachai
Brennan, the woman of the house borrowed some tea from 'Macy
Heraughty'. When the leaves were well boiled she put a knob of
butter on top and served them up to the priest. He smiled and:

'*Déan arís é is tabhair dom an sugh,*' said Fr. Malachai. ('Make it
again and bring me the juice.').

Chests of tea that washed ashore were a puzzle to the Shetland
islanders too. Donald Mc Donald in *Lewis: A History of the Island*
relates that a cargo of tea from a wrecked vessel in the late 19th
century was spread there on the fields as manure! It was used as
bedding for the animals too until somehow the women discovered how to infuse it to make a drink. According to accounts
they kept the secret from the men and hid the pot when they
were home.

At the outbreak of World War 1 there were many shipwrecks
off the southwest coast of Ireland, among them the Lusitania on
May 7 1915. 'There was good living in the Island now,' Maurice
O'Sullivan remembered. 'Money was piled up. There was no
spending. Nothing was bought. There was no need. It was to be
had on top of the water — flour, meat, lard, petrol, wax, mar-
garine, wine in plenty, shoes, stockings and clothes.'

Islanders of the Inishkeas did not wait for the gods of sea and
wind to bring good fortune. They went out on the ocean and attacked ships from their curraghs. It was a risky form of piracy as
their crafts were tiny and raids often took place twenty miles
from land. Having no weapons they intimidated the crew by carrying stones, 'which they shower such a volley on the deck that
the crew are driven below.' The Coastguard recorded that, 'from
the whole of the shores of Broadhaven, Blacksod Bay and the Islands of Inishkea the currachs assemble in great numbers.'

The speed and organisation of the piracy astonished the authorities when the schooner *Mans* was plundered on the 16th
April 1847, the worst year of the famine. The men, threatening
the crew with axes and stones, demanded flour to eat. Having

previously recognised that 'people must plunder or starve' officials anticipated such robberies and tacitly accepted them.

Vessels found in trouble on the Scottish Isle of Lewis were regarded 'as a sign of Divine favour'. When the 'William and John' of Colchester was salvaged by the islanders after being driven fully laden on to the rocks near Stornoway, serious rioting broke out. The captain, who had abandoned the ship when she went ashore, was furious about the seizure. He collected a hundred of his fellow Englishmen who went rampaging through the town threatening to kill all Scots unless the ship was handed back. Eventually it was.

Rights of salvage did not escape the attention of the all-encompassing Brehon Laws — ancient even when St. Patrick first arrived in Ireland — in which codes had long been established for appropriate behaviour when rescuing goods from the sea. They decreed that when a vessel was washed ashore and merely damaged it was the duty of the inhabitants of the area, and the owner of that section of coast, to do all in their power to save the vessel and help the crew. If the boat was washed ashore and wrecked beyond redemption, the debris could be recovered and divided. This was done in strict measure according to the articles of law. Rescued crew members were fed and sheltered for as long as was needed, 'for the district on whose shore the vessel is cast is bound to keep, protect, feed and make provision for such parties'. [3]

Nine waves was a critical element in mythology and folk belief. According to the old laws any person recovering an article that was nine waves or more from land could claim it no matter to whom it belonged. If it was less than nine waves from shore the owner's permission was necessary to rescue it. Anyone retrieving an item so close to land without the owner's authority, could not claim it.

The theme of nine waves recurs again and again. *Morann,*

[3] A *Social History of Ancient Ireland*, P.W. Joyce, Vol 2. p524

mythical judge and son of *Cairbre Catcheann* (Cathead), was born with a blemish so disfiguring that his father ordered him to be taken away and put to death. His friends prevailed on the old man to seek the advice of an inhabitant of the fairy hills. Morann should be held under water until nine waves passed over him, the fairy healer declared. The waters would then make him whole. The remedy was tried and the blemish washed away by the cleansing waves.

In one fierce battle of pre-history when Milesian invaders fought the Tuatha De Danann for possession of Ireland the attackers succeeded in gaining a foothold on the shore. The defenders, by a ruse, tricked the Milesians into re-embarking. According to legend, when the enemy went out beyond nine waves the Tuatha de Danann's magic was restored upon which they immediately raised a storm that almost destroyed the Milesian fleet. The Milesians however regrouped and eventually won the day.

Ferleginn, head of St. Finbarr's School in Cork, fled with fifty of his pupils, in A.D. 664, to an offshore island to avoid the yellow plague that ravaged the country. The pestilence, he believed, could not cross over the required nine waves. As far as we know he and his students survived the threat.

Walk today along a storm-tossed shore, look across the rocks and ledges of *Ros Caoireach*, *Dreimire Buidhe* or *Leac na Mealdha*. Shadows you may see there, or ghosts long gone, but seek and you will seek in vain for any evidence of the importance of these places to past generations: the industry, the fury, the life and death struggles.

Yet, '*on all these shores there are echoes of past and future: of the flow of time, obliterating, yet containing all that has gone before, of the sea's eternal rhythms—the tides, the beat of surf, the pressing rivers of the currents—shaping, changing, dominating, of the streams of life, flowing as inexorably as any ocean currents, from past to unknown future.*'

Rachel Carson, *The Edge of the Sea*

2

LUGGERS, SLUGGERS AND CADGERS

I must go down to the sea again, to the lonely sea and the sky,
And all I ask is a tall ship and a star to steer her by;
And the wheel's kick and the wind's song and the white sails shaking,
And a grey mist on the sea's face, and a grey dawn breaking...

John Masefield
I Must go down to the Sea

On land, as we have seen, the struggle was to glean whatever Providence delivered to the shore. At sea the battle was often for life itself.

Such was the drama that took place in the closing days of 1951 during the epic fight of a heroic captain to save his ship. Under the command of Captain Heinrik Carlsen, the *Flying Enterprise* left Hamburg on December 21st 1951 bound for the U.S.A. A three deck ship of seven thousand tons she carried a cargo of thirteen hundred tons of pig iron, nine hundred tons of coffee and ten passengers.

On Christmas night, four hundred miles west of Lands End, the ship was forced to heave to in gale force winds and mountainous seas. Despite forecasts of improving weather the storm didn't abate. Endless day faded into bitter darkness as heavy seas relentlessly battered the vessel — then a sixty-foot wave, bigger than all the rest, almost finished her off when it cracked the hull. The ship heeled to port, her cargo shifted and she could not right herself. Developing a forty-five degree list, heavy waves broke over her decks knocking out the engines. On December 28th realising his situation as hopeless the captain transmitted an SOS signal.

A rescue ship arrived but due to the atrocious conditions lifeboats could not go alongside. The ten passengers aboard and forty crewmen had no alternative but to don lifejackets, jump into the boiling sea and hope to be rescued. When all were pulled safely from the water Captain Carlsen decided to stay with his vessel. Thus began the epic struggle of one man and his ship against the worst that the forces of Nature could throw at him.

Although the storm increased in ferocity, by some miracle the craft stayed afloat. By January 3rd 1952 the tug *Turmoil* had reached the *Enterprise* but again found it impossible to connect a towline. Further unsuccessful attempts were made the following day; now, close to sinking, the ship's list had increased to an angle of sixty degrees.

On those short, dark days when the sun, even at its best, never managed to dispel the gloomy shades of winter, men and women in villages and towns all over Ireland gathered anxiously around the 'wireless' to hear the latest. The blasts that tore at the stricken *Enterprise* swept savagely around their homes too. It shook fragile thatch, tossed the hayricks in the haggard, threatened their boats in the harbour. Seafarers themselves, my father and the men of the village knew too well the tremendous powers faced by Captain Carlsen. Hadn't they confronted similar dangers in frail fishing craft themselves when caught at sea in sudden squalls? This was the universal battle of man against the elements. Day after day the drama unfolded. Would he live or would he die? Would his ship survive, or would it sink beneath the waves and he with it?

With grave faces, men and women discussed the crisis in hushed tones. They had never met Carlsen, probably never would, yet he was no stranger; he was a sea-faring soul mate. Although not known to them he was their kin and comrade. In spirit they willed this courageous mariner to triumph and mentioned his name when the family rosary was said at night. Newspapers each day carried pictures of the ship showing the latest degree of list as she leaned more and ever more to the seabed. The latest on the tragedy was read and re-read and the newspaper passed on to neighbours.

On January 5th the weather had settled somewhat. A cable was attached and a tow commenced to Falmouth one hundred and twenty miles away. By January 8th the storm had again increased. Ship and tug were forced to heave to. On January 9th in a northwest gale with driving sleet and snow and a thirty-foot swell running, the towline snapped. There was no time to lose now, and no option left but to abandon ship. On January 10th Captain Carlsen, and Kenneth Dancy, who had joined him from the *Turmoil*, walked along the ship's funnel, which was now almost horizontal, and jumped into the sea. Picked up by the tug they watched the final moments of the *Flying Enterprise* as her bow rose in the air, held for a few moments and then slid beneath the waves. Captain Carlsen was brought ashore at Falmouth, England to a hero's welcome.

Carlsen had stayed with his ship for twelve glorious days. Daily press coverage of the heroic salvage effort had made him world famous. Listeners and readers in simple country homes shared in the elation when it seemed he would succeed. They despaired as the ship listed further and still further. Their hearts sank when the towline broke, but everyone rejoiced in the end that such a gallant seafarer, who had fought so valiantly against all the odds, had come home safe. The sea is an unforgiving master and the end not always a happy one!

The day after the rescue Meman's son was going down our road with his ass and cart to get a load of turf from the bog. Michael was his real name, but there were several Duffys in Mullaghmore so this name distinguished him from all the others. His father was known as 'Meman' — but not when he was within earshot. A harmless enough title, as these names go, but nevertheless it wouldn't do to risk giving offence. Quarrels started over less. The name stemmed from his habit of ending sentences with 'me man' to emphasize a point.

Back then giving people nicknames provided fodder for sharp

but idle minds. Michael had two sisters: Mary Kate who was known as the 'Ballinalee', after Michael Collins's armoured car, and Brigid who was known as the 'Scout'. I don't know where 'Scout' came from but I suppose where you have an armoured car you just might have a scout. These were names you definitely did not use when the two ladies were within earshot as everyone knew Brigid kept the iron tongs nearby and Mary Kate was quite skilled at delivering instant punishment to miscreants with the iron crook that hung in the chimney. Both of these implements were always ready to hand when everyone had big open country fireplaces and, where the Meman's were concerned, many a sore and sorry head could testify to their lethal effect! Indeed it may have been in Mullaghmore that the practise of 'zero tolerance' began decades before the term was invented!

In every town and village there seemed to be one family who were teased and taunted beyond endurance, their only failing a swift reaction to provocation. A countryside full of young people roamed the roads then with time on their hands and mischief on their minds. A spirited response to a practical joke was just the thing they were looking for. If there was danger in it so much the better; it heightened the excitement, made the adrenalin flow. A stone thrown at certain doors guaranteed an instant reply. It was predictable. The door flew open. Out stormed two furious women and one man, crook and tongs in hand and the chase was on. When the culprit was captured he was thoroughly abused, both verbally and physically. More than one young fellow carried the scars of an encounter with these star performers of the tank battalion. Sometimes it was difficult to know who to feel sorry for, or who was the real victim, as the Duffys were judged well capable of looking after themselves. No matter what the outcome of the encounter there was no sympathy for the offenders and these episodes made good story-telling the next day. Reprisals didn't deter other chancers and the thrill of the chase enticed them to run the gauntlet another time.

Once a prankster got the bright idea to steal the linchpin of their cart. This was the metal piece at the end of the axle that held the wheel in place. Without it the cart was useless. Days went by, the cart lay idle, the work undone. Tempers frayed; vengeance was in the air. The mischief-maker, Dinny Cummins, added another twist to the plot. He told a neighbour where the missing item was hidden. He had thrown it up on to Duffy's gutter, he confided. It was still there under the eaves. Would the neighbour be good enough to tell them where it was, the joke had gone on long enough? This added another twist to the plot. The miscreant knew that whatever good samaritan was foolish enough to tell the pin's location would be instantly blamed for stealing it in the first place. How else would they know the whereabouts of the stolen item? The messenger was going to be shot.

Sure enough when the whereabouts of the missing pin was revealed the outraged owners 'nearly pulled the head' off the informant creating even more entertainment for everyone on the hill road in Mullaghmore.

Michael sped down the road as fast as the ass would allow. Normally people didn't go to the bog this time of year but the previous summer had been a bad one; Michael's turf were wet at the end of the season and still in storage clamps on Cloonty bog. The centre of the stack might have dried sufficiently by now for him to get the makings of a few fires.

The Meman's didn't have a radio — not too many people did — so Michael stopped at Bartley Gillen's to get the latest news on the *Flying Enterprise*.

'I'm afraid she's gone down,' Bartley said.

'Ah, for Chrissake,' said Michael, 'that's a holy terror after all the poor divils went through. Was there anyone lost?'

Like everyone else he was bitterly disappointed to hear the ship had sunk. The incident brought back memories of times he and his comrades had themselves gambled with death. The ass was happy enough eating grass on the side of the road and Bartley a willing listener, so Michael, propping his elbows on the stone ditch began to tell his story:

'I used to fish in the Rosebud. T'was Petie Mc Gowan was skippering her at the time. We were held up a week below in Teelin one time with a storm. A week! And you mightn't believe it but a better week I never spent.

Thady Conway was in it with us, and 'Big' Dan Gallagher an' Tom Cartin. Petie came in to my house one day with a report of a big fishin', herring there just for the takin' across the bay in Teelin. That's how it started. We got the boat ready, loaded the nets in, and off we went. No sooner did we land in Teelin than be Jasus the storm started. We were above in Gallaghers shop, Jack Gallaghers. Jack is dead now but I think the family still have a shop in Killybegs there in the main street.

'What about going to the ball', one of them says to me.

'Where is it?' says I.

'Kilcar'!

'Jasus', says I, 'The clothes I have is not fit for going to a ball'.

No matter. Into the punt in Teelin with us anyway and away across the bay to Kilcar. Landed at the Ball in Kilcar. We had great sport with Big Dan Gallagher, he got a few drinks in him and up with him on to the stage and gave a sermon that was a public show to God! There was no dancing at all only Gallagher prachin'! He was well shot from a five naggin bottle of whiskey that we got in Haughey's in Teelin that he brought down to the boat first. Drank the whole five naggin bottle!

Anyway, next day the storm settled and we headed out of a Thursday evening, and we shot the nets. Bejasus, we got a great shot of herring. Away for Killybegs with us. We sold the herring there anyway. Joe Molloy [Willie Joe] bought them and we took about twenty cran of mackerel to bring home.

There was a great boat in Killybegs, the 'Pimpernel' but the Rosebud'd sail her anytime so long as she was fit to carry the sail!

But if the Rosebud had to put in the reefs, she wouldn't bate her. The Rosebud had a crooked mast and, whatever was about it, she'd sail the devil when she had a full sail.

I was fishing in the *Drostin* too', he went on. 'A couple of weeks after that we went out of Mullaghmore after herring wan night and it was the worst night ever came. I'll never forget it anyway. Me an' Tom Duffy that's dead beyond in America and Jamesy Duffy, Bernie Rourke, John Rogers and John Callery. That's the crew we had on her an' Bernie Rourke's father, Mickey Rourke. Two luggers went out that night, the Rosebud and ourselves.

Going out by St. John's Pt., across there at Donegal, there was two drifters laving Killybegs, the *Harvest Star* an' the *Gola*. Rourke wanted to follow the drifters out — if he had to get his way we were all lost! There's no getting out of it! We shot the nets anyway an' before we had the third net shot the back rope broke with the gale of wind that was in it, from the north. We hauled all the gear into the boat at that and away for Mullagh as hard as we could.

When the two boats landed at the breakwater we couldn't see it with water breaking over it. We could see nothing, it was that dark. No lights on the Quay, no nothing! We went out about a mile off land towards Bundoran and threw out two anchors anyway, out of the *Drostin*. The *Rosebud* was a bit above us and she threw out the anchors too. We didn't know how we were goin' to get through the night but there wasn't a hate else we could do. Well, I never put in such a night in me life. Pitch black, be the Jasus, an' the sea breaking over the boats. We never thought we'd see the light of day again. We were sure we'd be put up on the rocks any minute!

When day broke our boat smashed the chain on one of the anchors and the other one started to drag. The wind was from the north, fair on St John's Point. A livin' hurricane! There was nothing for it but to put the sail on her an' away for Bundoran. There was seven foot of water in her on the lee side. 'Twas going into the hold on her, an' the mast was the same as my elbow there now, bent like that. The Rosebud started to haul anchor too. They ran her up on the strand right away.

When we got half way to Bundoran we brought her about an' she came 'round like a top. We headed for the quay, make or break. When we came to the breakwater her side struck it on the way in, we came that close on it. With that, between the two quays, the sail busted in pieces. We threw out th' anchor an' wasn't it bad when she brought the anchor with her. Now wasn't there a quare gale in it, an' no sail on her? The sail down in bits an' she dragged th'anchor even at that. She finished up there on the wee strand at the boathouse. It settled some time after that an' we took the Rosebud off the other strand an' floated the Drostin as well.'

It was a good story, so good that a local woman immortalised the event in verse:

Ode to Rogers

Come, fill your glass and sit awhile
we'll talk of storms at sea
and we'll drink a toast
to the Spanish ghost
that saved big John and me.

The night was black, the sea was mad,
we were heading round by Teelin;
I was gripped with fear
and I cursed the beer
that caused that sickly feelin'.

I tried to haul the main sail in,
it damn near broke me neck,
Big John he cursed
as he went head first

across the rolling deck.

The captain's face was white as foam
as we fought the raging sea;
he smelt the fear
'cos death was near
for him, Big John and me.

T'was then I saw de Cuellar's ghost,
his feet ne'er touched the floor,
I tell no lie
he steered us by
the head of Mullaghmore.

The 'Dark One' was the picador
and his bull the raging sea.
Let us drink a toast
to the Spanish ghost
that saved Big John and me.

In a companionable silence the two men looked out over the
stone ditches and rectangled fields, looked out beyond to the
sea, the hungry sea, the treacherous sea, a sea so deceptively
calm now. Bartley had a story too: he told Michael about the
night he lost his roof in a northwesterly gale. But the day was
short and Michael had to get to the bog and Bartley to feed his
cattle. Having swapped stories each man went his separate way
feeling a comradeship that only men who have endured the
brunt of uncaring Fate and survived could feel. Theirs was a
fragile existence, primeval even, close to nature, close to hardship and close to God.

The Zulu luggers, that Michael and his comrades sailed in,
were decked sailing boats of from forty to seventy five feet long.
One of their more unusual features was a huge mainmast two

feet in diameter and up to sixty feet high unsupported by any rigging that might get in the way of nets or lines. Used mostly for trawling or drifting for herring these magnificent sailing boats had their heyday in the decades around the turn of the 20th century. When motor power was popularised in 1892 by Rudolf Diesel's invention of the 'internal combustion engine', it was only a matter of time before these picturesque craft became a thing of the past.

Another smaller boat, the Drontheim or Greencastle yawl, an open, double-ended sailing boat was the workhorse of every fishing port in Ireland. Averaging twenty-four feet in length they were a reliable, versatile workboat. Powered by two spritsails, sometimes a jib, they rowed and sailed well. Greencastles were so highly regarded that by the year 1900 the Congested Districts Board had large numbers built for fishermen all along the west coast. Crewed by six or seven men, each member was responsible for the baiting and shooting of his own line although on occasion the job of digging 'slugs' (lugworm) for baits was given as a permanent task to one of the crew members.[4]

One by one, as gently as falling leaves, these old long-line fishermen passed away. They were vital links, living connections, to a lost way of life. Now there is no one left to tell what it was like sailing and working in the Greencastles and Zulus. The romanticism portrayed by photographs of the old craft never extended to life on board. It was grinding hard work. Anyone listening to their stories would never feel envious they hadn't experienced it.

Waterproof clothes were practically unheard of. Apparel differed very little from what was worn ashore. Leather, iron-shod boots and tweed trousers designed for working the land were poor protection against ice-cold salt water that seeped off fishing gear and slapped viciously across the gunwale. Food was mostly farls of bread or cold potatoes with a bottle of tea wrapped in a sock to keep it warm. It never did — at least not for very long.

[4] *In the Shadow of Benbulben*, Joe Mc Gowan. See chapter entitled '*Last of the Windjammers*', p229 for more on Greencastles and fishing.

Cold tea gave poor comfort to drenched and weary bones.

In contrary winds or when the breezes failed altogether, fishermen had to resort to oars eighteen feet in length to pull the boat to the fishing grounds or home. 'If ye weren't used to it and hadn't the practice, even if ye were as strong as a horse, ye wouldn't stick it', one old veteran declared.

At the end of a long row home, ballast and masts had to be lifted ashore and stowed on the pier. In tidal harbours the stones used for stability at sea could smash through the boat's timbers as she grounded at low water. Fishing gear was brought home and readied for another day. Bait was procured for the next day's fishing — and all this in addition to the multitude of tasks involved in working small farms.

While they were alive these old seamen could be coaxed to tell of the drudgery involved in digging 'slugs' and baiting lines. Finding slugs often meant long trudges of up to seven miles. Wearing heavy iron-shod boots they walked the Sligo shore, good weather or bad, to *Poll Bréan* in Moneygold, to Dernish Island or further. Spades on strong shoulders, tin cans in hand they sought the juicy lugworm to bait the hooks. Each man needed sufficient bait to prepare 400 hooks for the next day's fishing. Consequently, competition for places along the shore was fierce.

As if that weren't enough these 'Mullaghmore sluggers', as they were called, were forbidden to dig along the sea's edge in places where the landlord held sway. Smaller property owners with foreshore rights didn't like the sluggers either. They were keen to prevent the diggers from their activities believing their 'slugging' damaged the '*famluc*'(bladder wrack). This was a valuable commodity used by farmers to fertilise crops and meadows. Slug digging meant turning sand over on to the 'famluc' thereby retarding the growth of the weed or even rotting it. '*Báirneacs*' (limpets), which were easier to gather, were not as effective a bait as slugs but could be used to supplement the supply.

Following strenuous hours of digging these men walked home to spend further tedious hours baiting hooks by the hundred. When several days of bad weather intervened the bait rotted on the hooks, fresh lugworm had to be procured, and the whole time consuming process repeated. It was not unusual, in extended periods of bad weather, for the routine to be repeated, three or four times, before the weather cleared and the boats could put to sea.

There were good and rewarding days too. When the boats came home full, lines of 'cadgers' (fishmongers) waited on the quay with horse and ass carts. Prices were agreed and cod, ling, pollack, skate or mackerel transferred from boat to cart without delay. There was no refrigeration. Travelling door to door for miles throughout the countryside the fish hawker's fresh, cheap and wholesome product from an unpolluted ocean was sold on to a welcoming countryside.

In the '40s and '50s, things started to change. The Zulu luggers and Greencastle yawls became fewer and fewer. Eventually they lived on only in the colourful stories of the old men. The age of sail was passing. It gradually gave way to the early, unreliable and cantankerous prototypes of the now reliable diesel engine. The fishing industry soon passed from the small ports of Ireland to become concentrated in just a few big fishing centres: Killybegs, Dingle, Howth, Dunmore East. 'Mackerel Millionaires' and 'Supertrawlers' replaced local fishermen, luggers and yawls. The boat builders of the small ports lost out too. Contracts for the bigger boats went overseas. Fibreglass and steel took the place of larch and oak.

The sun was setting too on the horse and ass-drawn carts that trundled their big iron-shod wheels over rough and stony roads. Central distribution, motorised transport, and supermarkets evolved rapidly to cater for an increasingly choosy market and busy lifestyle.

For fishermen, fortunes were few and tragedies inevitable:

'A man of the sea never had a good life and never will,' Blasket islander Maurice O'Sullivan's grandfather advised him.

'I have gone through as many perils on it as there are grey hairs on my head, and I am telling you now, wherever God may guide you, keep away from the sea.'

'I'd sooner ate praties an' salt than have anyone belonging to me take up fishin", Kate Sweeney of Mullaghmore said.

In 1890 a Greencastle yawl and its crew of eight Mullagh men was smashed into matchwood behind the big hills at '*Carraig Fhada*' when a wave broke over it. How? Why? They were experienced fishermen. Did they risk all and haul too close to the rocky shore with a ground swell rising? In a brave or foolhardy attempt to save their lobster creels, all hands were lost. An oar broke on them, some said, unbalancing the boat. There was a man by name of Moohan aboard and a Duffy and others.

Most of the names are forgotten now, but the disaster is remembered, grief-etched, in a timeless sort of way as if it mattered not whether it occurred last year or last century. Macabre details still fresh in the mind: the flesh on the hands of one of the bodies torn to the bone in a desperate attempt to claw his way up the rocky shore to safety. Steel tacks and toe plates torn off the boots of another drowned man in a similar desperate attempt to clamber ashore. We can imagine the panic and desperation in his heart, the black pit in his stomach, as he strove to escape; see in our mind's eye the rollers crashing down on him, tossing him, clawing him into the deep as he desperately sought to survive, to live for another while, to return to his home and family, to escape the clutches of the merciless sea.

Close calls there were many: Hughie Cawley's boat and crew driven ashore by a sudden squall at *Traigh Ghearr* while out fishing handlines; skippers Jamesy 'Charlie' Gallagher and Bernie Rourke, lost with their crews in a fog that lasted twenty four hours. Villagers gathered along the shore shouting to give a direction home. Worry and fear turned to relief and joy when the fog lifted and they were found safe and well.

Mc Canns of Milk Harbour shipped merchandise between Sligo and Killybegs, Co. Donegal in their double-masted Green-castle yawl. One trip almost ended in disaster — but this story has a funny side to it as well.

They had a commission to bring a load of periwinkles across the bay to a fish merchant in Sligo. The boat was heavily laden on the way home, the sails full, and the trip routine. Suddenly a squall blew up from the Northwest. Waves slapped against the gunwale, spilled over and slopped into the boat. Normally this posed no danger as the water could easily be bailed out of the bilges with an old bucket kept for the purpose.

This time things were different. The water came in but couldn't be bailed out. The winkles were drinking it! The boat sank lower, and lower. The winkles were in winkle heaven — but what was the skipper to do? To get rid of the water he would have to dump the winkles! His choice: throw the cargo overboard or lose his boat, and maybe his life. In the end he compromised by throwing a few bags overboard and made for a landfall in Mullaghmore. It was a serious incident with a funny side that had a happy ending. This time.

It was not always so! Even yet, despite the advent of sophisticated and modern equipment: autopilots, satellite navigation, sonar and radar, every port in Ireland has its tragic tales of shipwreck and drowning. The Killybegs, Co. Donegal, trawler, *Evelyn Marie*, was pounded to bits in 1975 under the Rathlin O'Beirne lighthouse close to its home port. All hands were lost and a pall of tragedy cast over the town and nation. A year later the *Carraig Una* was wrecked on the same rocks.

> '... *They guided this trawler for one year and some days.*
> *What ill fate befell them within the freak waves?*
> *A call to their comrades, "Mayday at the sea.*
> *Assist us this moment with the Evelyn Marie."*

"*Assistance now coming - Summer Star and its crew.*"
Saying, "*With God's help we'll make it, your trawler is new.*"
A *disaster it was then. They just saw her stern*
As *she sank near the rocks outside Rathlin O'Beirne…*'

The destruction of the modern, well equipped St. *Oliver* on Duck Island near Rossaveal, Co. Galway in 2004 baffled the seafaring community. Four lives were lost. The list of tragedies at sea grows ever longer. The unfathomable ocean, wicked and kind, fierce and gentle, but always unpredictable, can be a friend but also an adversary against whom the sailor must be ever vigilant.

Most that go to sea know the smell and taste of fear. They have felt its icy grip when routine turns suddenly to misfortune, order to disorder. Time itself is paused: a minute becomes an hour and an hour a minute. The bane of the lobsterman's occupation is the rope attaching the creels to the main line that curls and whips along the deck as the traps go over the side and into the sea.

Once on a routine fishing trip I lifted lobster creels, baited them and watched carefully as they slipped one by one over the gunwale back into the depths. In an instant, quick as a flash, a bight of rope curled, snapped, and gripped my ankle. Knocked off balance, the line dragged me relentlessly towards the gunwale to follow the lobster pots to the seabed ten fathoms below. In the blinking of an eye, a normal day had turned into a struggle for life or death. In an instant all that mattered in the world was reduced to survival on that deck at that moment. Now, in a few heartbeats, a man would live, or die, alone — and what did it matter to the Creator or to the greater plan any more than if it was a sparrow or a seagull?

Panic swelled within, but on another plane the thinking was ice cold and clear. There could be only two outcomes. I was going to be pulled beneath the waves — or I was going to survive and it was going to be just another day at sea. A desperate tug of war ensued as the rope tightened and pulled tighter and ever tighter edging me towards the gun'ale. The boat ploughed heedlessly on. Fishermen always carried a knife. Now the importance of this practice was brought home to me. Reaching for it I slashed desperately, the rope was severed, and Death thwarted, one more time.

There were other life and death incidents. In a freshening northwesterly gale the screw became hopelessly entangled in rope, and the boat, powerless, drifted towards Bomore rocks. I remember still hanging over the boat's stern hacking at the rope with a knife jury-rigged to the end of a boathook; the taste of fear, the swelling of muscles, the cotton-dry mouth, the knotted stomach, the overwhelming sense of relief when the screw was freed.

There were days of calculated risk when the creels were shot on a 'bolg'. Bolgs are reefs and natural homes for lobsters and crayfish. In settled weather a good haul can be expected — but when a groundswell comes up suddenly that's where the sea is going to break first. Although the traps may have been set in good weather a sudden change, from low-pressure systems far out to sea, would bring mayhem and a hell of green-crested breakers crashing down on the reef

What then when you arrive on the fishing ground in the morning and all is changed. The placid waters of the day before have been transformed and become a menacing hell of heaving ocean. What to do then? Turn around and leave traps and nets? Better safe than sorry! Or take a calculated risk: is the swell rising, is the tide going or coming? If it's coming there's less risk; going, there's more. Is it a spring tide or a neap tide? More risk with a spring, less with a neap. Right then, every ninth wave is the big one — maybe. Wait for it. Now the lull: throttle up, dash in, adrenalin flowing. Turn the pot hauler to full speed, wrench ropes and lobster pots into the boat, all the while watching,

watching, a sharp knife ready to cut the leader line and get out quick if the curl of the breaker gets too high, if a thousand tons of water rises curling from the deep.

It wasn't all brinksmanship and danger. There was magic on the ocean too: magic in an early morning summer sunrise over Barnes Gap on the faraway Donegal shore; in the sun's bronzed path across a tranquil sea with all the world asleep; in the thrill of hauling a creel in the dawn light, or any light, and finding three, maybe four lobsters flapping about inside; in the exuberance of a school of curious dolphins at play around the boat.

Or in close encounters with the natural world.

On one wild and storm-tossed day crewman, Pádraic Callery and I released two young dolphins caught in our salmon drift net. Being air-breathing mammals they drown just like humans. Disentangling them we stroked their soft, silky skin in admiration before returning them to the sea. That was to become one of the best fishing days we ever experienced. Within an hour we pulled salmon from the meshes as fast as we could go along the net. To this day Pádraic swears it was the dolphins, grateful for their freedom that rounded up the salmon and drove them into the net. Perhaps it was! There's a hint of mischievous camaraderie when man and dolphin meet.

Gathered around the fire in the warmth of country kitchens when the nights were long and the sea raged on the shore, close calls and mysterious happenings on sea and land were recalled. These men who knew the ocean depths and often faced its dangers told of spine-chilling encounters of their own or unexplained and mysterious happenings. There were funny stories too of remarkable characters they knew. Sometimes a good storyteller might need to be prompted. He had to be sure it wasn't just politeness that prompted the request. That was the custom. Whether it was singing a song or telling a story no one accepted a first offer. They had to be persuaded. Michael Duffy was no exception:

'Michael! D'ye remember the one ye were telling me about the day ye got Big Dan Gallagher in the bunk an' tied him. He had a fierce appetite, didn't he?'

'Ah, sure I'm no good at telling a story,' Michael shrugged, 'if James Rourke was alive or Jamesy Charlie, them's the men that could tell ye!

'Go on Michael, I heard ye telling it before and it's a good one.'

'Ah some other time maybe, it's getting late now.'

'No time like the present Michael, go on now. Sure that clock is fast anyway. It couldn't be more than ten o'clock!'

Martin, the persuader, felt the same about time as the Tailor did when he declared to Ansty in *The Tailor and Ansty* that 'the best clock any man ever had was his belly. That tells him when it is time to eat. And when there's no one sitting by the fireside then it's time to go to bed. And the time to get up is when you're tired of being in bed!'

The Tailor had a clock but didn't trust it as he had a notion that it was a day wrong but wasn't sure whether it was a day fast or a day late.

Michael was laughing all the time and twisting himself round to a more comfortable position in the chair:

'Well, to tell you the truth, Big Dan'd ate the shirt off his back. I seen him ating about fourteen pound of beef. As sure as I'm sitting here an' I wouldn't tell ye a word of a lie. He was a big man well over six and a half feet, or more.

Me an' James Rourke an Jamesy Charlie Gallagher an' Big Dan Gallagher left the quay one time with six priests that wanted to go across to Teelin for the day. Six priests! Wasn't it some crew. Jamesy's boat we were in. It was a Sunday, a grand day with a nice air of East wind.

When we were out middle way in the bay the priests took out any amount of stuff — they took out more beef, the best of beef, than was a holy show an' God knows ye wouldn't see much beef in them times! Me and James Rourke and Gallagher started to eat first an' Jamesy was steering. We ate our fill — an' Gallagher was still eating. James Rourke started to steer then an' Jamesie Charlie came to eat an' the priests had to open another three tins of beef. As sure as the priest said Mass on Sunday this is no lie! Jamesy finished eating an' still Gallagher was eating!! Stuffin' it into him, an' he claned th'other three tins of beef!!

'Wasn't he a holy terror!' said the listeners, 'that was some appetite'.

'Hold on a minute,' James Gorman said, beginning to hum a tune 'There was a song, Johnny McEldoo I think was the name of it, could've been written for Big Dan. I forget the beginning of it but it went something like this:

"…*Johnny McEldoo turned red, white and blue*
As a plate of Irish stew he soon put out of sight
He shouted out "Encore!" with a roar for some more
That he'd never felt before such a keen appetite
We ordered eggs and ham, bread and jam, what a cram
But him, we couldn't ram, though we tried our level best
For everything we brought, cold or hot, mattered not
It went down him like a shot and he still stood the test

He swallowed tripe and lard by the yard, we got scarred
We thought it would go hard when the waiter brought the bill We
told him to give o'er, but he swore he could lower
Twice as much again and more before he had his fill
He nearly supped a trough full of broth says McGrath
"He'll devour the tablecloth if you don't hold him in"
When the waiter brought the charge, McEldoo felt so large
He began to shout and barge and his blood went on fire…"

'Will ye be quiet for a minute and listen 'til ye hear the end of the story', Martin said.

Everyone laughed, Michael cleared his throat, spat into the ashes piled at the side of the fire and continued:

'Well! We landed in Teelin anyway,' he went on, 'an' Gallagher was mad for porther an' whiskey. Someone had to mind the boat so we cast lots to see who'd stay. It fell on Gallagher. Me an James Rourke an' Jamesy went away up to Harkins. We had a couple of drinks there an' I went into Jack Gallaghers shop. Who comes up only Joan Carr of Rosses an' says to me:

"There's a chum of yours below in our house."

"Who is he?" says I?

"Big Dan Gallagher", says she.

"Don't let on ye saw me," says I

"No I won't," says she.

I had another drink an' changed me mind and went down to where Big Dan was. Joan got two loaves and put them on the table. Now this is as true as I'm telling you! Then she put down a pair of eggs for aich of us, of course I wasn't fit to eat. Gallagher claned three big mugs of tay, the most of the two loaves an' he claned the two eggs, and my two as well — after ating that feed on the boat on the way over!'

We headed away home after awhile and landed on the quay in Mullagh anyway safe and sound. Mrs. Hannon was alive at the time so into Hannons Hotel with us, an' the priest stood a couple of drinks. Gallagher took the looseness, made a bust for the door an' he went in along the side of the road where the pump is now. When we went home Kattie the wife was coming down looking for him an' he was still there at the pump, couldn't pull the trousers up on him. She got him home eventually an' he didn't go to bed the whole night with the shkither, way down in the field he was the whole night.'

Michael was slightly asthmatic and at this point burst into a turkey-cock gulder of laughter that tapered off to a chesty wheeze. His humour was infectious and everyone joined in, one man's laugh feeding on another's. There were no toilets in houses then of course — and no pollution either — and the mental image of Dan's discomfiture hunkered in the long grass was too much for them.

'I could tell ye plenty more,' said Michael with tears of laughter in his eyes, 'but that's Big Dan and the feeds for ye anyway.'

Pádraic Callery wanted to hear more: 'What about the night ye tied him in the lugger?'

'Oh, Chrisht, I'll never forget it! 'Twas me that tied him. It was in the *Rosebud*. Petie Mc Gowan was steering it. Gallagher was that big he could go into no bunk only the one was on the *Ita*; it had the biggest berth. He went into bed and the two feet was up in th'air. Petie says to me: "Pull out a board of the partition an' let his feet go through it. It's th'only way he'll fit."

Gallagher fell asleep in the upper bunk. There was a big cast iron stove near the bunks, every man was hungry, an' we put on a big feed of bacon, sausages an' eggs. Didn't I take a notion an' tie a rope round Big Dan's two feet so he couldn't get out of the bed. We made the tay anyway, ate the lot till there was nothing left but the tea leaves. When Gallagher got the smell he tried to get out of the bunk an' he couldn't get out!

"Loosen me," he'd shout. "Loosen me. I'll murder ye if ye don't let me outa here!"

The smell of the grub was putting him mad an' we had no heed for him at all.

When we had all et we were down near Teelin an' Petie says to me:

"You might as well loosen him now".

I took the rope off his feet anyway. Well, when he got free, he caught the board an' he made a shot at me an' it went round me jaw like a bullet. I had to cut like hell for the deck or he'd have murdered me for sure. There was a whole pile of stones near the mast that was used to sink the nets, with strings tied on them. I fired the shot of the stone, there was a Sacred Heart badge on the bulkhead an' I struck the badge alongside his head. When he went to the kettle for the tay there was nothing left but the tealeaves an' we were lucky he didn't kill us all. I can hear that roar in me head yet:

'*Loosen me! Loosen me!*'

More gales of laughter followed this story. In the companionable silence that followed Jamesy Charlie Gallagher brought up about the ghost of the landlord and priest-hunter Soden from Moneygold, who some years ago had wrought great mischief when the boats were out fishing herring at night. They marvelled at the power of the priest who, following appeals from the frustrated fishermen, banished the devilish spectre to Bomore's bleak and barren rock.

Soden had gone mad following a confrontation with the local curate, a Fr. Rynne: 'he ate his own flesh and nothing could be done with him' Jamesy explained.

Following the incident Soden was locked in a disused Revenue Police Barracks in Grange, Co. Sligo known as Lang's shed that until recently had barred windows and doors. A Loughlin family from nearby Caiseal, charged with his care, fed him his meals through the bars at the end of a pitchfork. Once a week they tied him to a lone blackthorn tree in a nearby field 'in order to scrape the lice off him'. The tree still stands.

Following the landlord's death, reports went out of a 'huge black dog with fire coming out of his mouth' seen at Hood's gate near Soden's property. People went around by the fields at night rather than pass the spot. In the daytime, passers-by hung rosary beads on the handlebar of their bicycles for protection. Horses pulling sidecars or traps reared up and stood trembling when they came to the haunted spot. It happened to the O'Connors of Moneygold. Mrs O'Connor had the presence of mind to say a prayer and: 'Go on, in the name of God', she said to the horse upon which the horse calmed down and went ahead.

Locals called on Fr. Rynne to do something about the spectre, upon which he exorcised the unquiet spirit to the open sea a few miles away. The phantom dog disappeared following Fr. Rynne's intervention — but that wasn't the end of it. The following winter fishermen from Mullaghmore went to the priest with a strange story. Something, they believed it was Soden again, was interfering with their nets and tangling them as they fished herring at night. Could he do something to help them?

The priest performed the exorcism again, this time banishing the tormented and tormenting demon to the bleak and barren Bomore Rock, ten miles out to sea. Legend has it that he is allowed to return once every seven years.

There are those who have witnessed the homecoming and on a flat, calm summer's day, with no living thing to be seen, or enough wind to stir a leaf, have heard noises like 'a herd of elephants or horses' crashing through the woods on the old Soden estate. They believe it's the phantom landlord making his way to his old haunts from where he was originally banished.

'A ghost is compelled to obey the commands of the living', W.B. Yeats once wrote. 'The stable boy up at Mrs. G——'s there met the master going round the yards after he had been two days dead,' an old countryman told him. The lad said, 'be away to the lighthouse, and haunt that; and there he is far out to sea still, sir. Mrs. G—— was quite wild about it and dismissed the boy.'

The placing of a curse on their oppressor was the only resort left to the persecuted who felt they had been wronged. There are many examples in folk tales of harm coming to tyrants by mysterious means. In this case the priest was the avenging agent. Among other methods of revenge employed by victims were the 'Widow's Curse' the 'Fire of Stones' or a ritual visit to the 'cursing stones'.[5]

How deeply the fireside storytellers loved their countryside, how intimately and profoundly they knew it. No time or date ever accompanied their narratives, such details being considered of no consequence; enough to know the story happened once. Chronology was irrelevant and all thoughts connected only to

---

[5] For more on cursing see Mc Gowan, *Inishmurray: Island Voices*, Chapter 14 'Cursing Stones and Ritual Voodoo'.

emotion and place.

'The past is at its best when it takes us to places that counsel and instruct,' William Chapman wrote in *Wisdom Sits in Places*, 'that show us who we are by showing us where we have been, that remind us of our connections to what happened here.'

The spirit of a locality radiates from inanimate things. A place that ever was lived in is forever stamped by that living; by the joys, the anguish, the human struggle. It bears an imprint like a persons soul, an *animus* of the earth that can never be extinguished. Its being is intact, forever pulsing within it have we but the faculty, the instinct to draw from it as water from a well. 'Whenever we travel in this country of the past,' Chapman said, 'instructive places abound'.

Walking by the seashore, warmed by a summer sun, we admire the golden sands, blue skies, green sea, rolling sand dunes. How much more is revealed and the landscape transformed when we learn that this here is the spot where the *Drostin* went aground on that stormy, terror-filled night, all those years ago. And is this Hood's Gate where the demon dog once frighted an entire countryside? Right here is a place once known as *Port na hEorna*! What meaning lies hidden in the name? Let's ask: *Port na hEorna* means the 'Barley Port' we are told. Yes, the old people say, Mullaghmore, that big hill, was once an island. People long ago loaded their turf on boats at *Denis's Hill* just across the flats there. They landed them here, right here at the Barley Port. Our curiosity is aroused. These few stones here: were they once part of a harbour wall? This area must once have been a hive of activity— boats to-ing and busily fro-ing from one port to the other. Did our ancestors load barley here too? And aren't we blood of their blood, heart of their heart. Was the grain intended for the *poitín* industry that once thrived in the countryside? And isn't that mound there, in this quiet and haunting place, isn't that the spot where they buried suicides and unbaptized children: those who had known too much and those who had known not enough of this life?

The old familiar places have not left us, we have left them; they have not betrayed us, we have betrayed them; old friends that we have walked away from, without a thought, a care, a backward glance. W.B. Yeats believed that *'barbaric people receive influence from the anima mundi more visibly and obviously, and in all likelihood more easily and fully than we do, for our life in cities, which deafens or kills the passive meditative life, and our education that enlarges the separated, self-moving mind, have made our souls less sensitive.'*

Go back to those forgotten places now grown strange; talk to the stones. Go on; don't be ashamed; talk to them; they will answer; yes, they will answer. Get to know them again. The old gods look out from the rocks and hills, the secret places. They have things to tell us. But only if we listen. Let the wordless conversation fill your mind; come alive the quiet field. Expose your being to the *anima mundi*, the soul of the earth. Revisit that time and place in the stone wall where you once filled the tank with a bucket from the stream, the silver chattering stream, for the cows to drink. Over there is that Big Ditch of solid fieldstone; each and every rock and quoin specially chosen by an unknown ancestor, lifted, caressed by a human hand, judged and placed with care in its own unique position — for eternity maybe. In idle moments a child's inquiring hand found the builders broken, blackened clay pipes discarded in the crevices and imagined the gaunt faces, the calloused, work-worn hands that once held them. Here, at milking time, you drove the cows for shelter from the driving rain, the soft driving rain. The wall doesn't seem so massive now; not so tall and strong as it was then, and now it leans just a little crookedly, tiredly. And over in that other field wasn't that where you saw John C—— mount the heifer stirk, in the shed, on a hot summer's day? That shocking hot summer day. In such scorching weather cattle curled their tails over their backs and fled in terror from the fly that laid its eggs on knee joints; eggs that hatched out and burrowed along their intestines to emerge as fat ugly maggots the size of a little finger along their backs a few months later. In the still autumn evenings, when the milking was done and the calves fed my brother Mick and I squeezed the juicy, loathsome slugs out of their skin-bound holes and squished them with a stone on the ditch. And yes, over there, there's the hill where as a child you rolled and tumbled, climbed up and rolled down again in the long, timeless, sun-filled summer hours. Years later, home from school, you kept watch from that friendly height as you herded the cows on the roadside's 'Long Acre', hour after monotonous hour. You had a visitor one day, a young man of the village. "Do you want matches', he said, and of course I did. If I had them I could pull heather and light small fires to pass the time. I wasn't allowed to have them at home, or comic books. There was a catch. He opened his trousers and put them through his pubic hair. I could have them if I fished them out. Reluctantly I snatched them, one at a time. 'Go on' he urged, 'take them all'. When his mounting excitement frightened me I ran away. Later he warned me not to tell. I still see this man, old and withered now, with wizened face and grizzled hair and think within me if through his dull eyes and flaccid face he remembers as I do. If behind the evading glances he wonders deep within him whether I remember. Unspoken memory. I do not hate him: was he too not made in God's image and likeness? Over there in Barry's field I see the Duffy sisters spreading bag after bag of carrageen moss out on the grass to bleach and dry before carrying it home to sell in the shops. It was Brigid that once on a dark night on the Hill Road near the old stone tower met Michael Callan and bet him a pound note he couldn't urinate. His staff was well known and often exposed to the local girls; in the chapel on Sunday Michael's voice was raised several decibels above everyone else's when he led the Rosary and Litany of the Saints. He took the bet and lost when Brigid lifted her skirt. A man's abilities allow only one function at a time. There's our Big Garden — and the Wee Garden, and over there is *Geata* where the mushrooms came in abundance when the wetting mists rolled in from the sea in late August, little white upside down saucers nestled in the mossy, close-cropped pasture; others domed, creamy-white fairy huts.

'I remember well,' an old Kerry man once told Robin Flower, 'how once, when we were digging a grave, we found shaped stones below the earth, and there were the marks of lime on the stones. It was said that Pierce Ferriter had his castle there, a place that he could fly to when the chase was too hot upon his heels.'

And that cave we see there, high on the cliff face? Is that where Ferriter, the poet and rebel hid when the King's soldiers in their red coats scoured the countryside looking for him? Yes, that's it, 'the place where he was often lonely in it in days of storm and wild weather.' A fine dry place with a little stream of spring water and a drip from the roof overhead

> 'Hast thou no pity, O God, that I lie this way,
> Lonely and cold and hardly I see the day;
> The drip from the heart of the stone never stilled in my ear,
> And the voice of the sea at my feet ever echoing near?'

Now we have freed the yearning spirit to draw sustenance from the earth. At once the landscape we thought we knew has changed. Now we have a *sense of place*, a realisation of what we are and from whence we came. We are part of it, it is part of us, and we will never see the cave, this hill, that hollow, the same way ever again.

Go talk to the stones. Seek too the old people, old men, old women, memory men, men of words, they who will never be young again, whose likes we will never see again. Ask them what they know. Now! Before it's too late and they take their wisdom to the grave, that dark abyss of lost knowledge and wasted dreams!

3

CRANGLE'S NIGHT

God's son of hosts that none can tell, the fury of the storm repel!
Dread Lord of the sacrament, save me from the wind's intent,
Spare me from the blast of hell.

Rumann, (8th cent. poet)

Grinding tediously on its cold and stormy way the oppressive gloom of winters' short-nipped days and long-drawn nights was hard to bear.

'Nothing lasts forever' my mother said breezily as she stripped Christmas decorations from wall, dresser and window. Nothing ever seemed to bother that woman:
'Ye can see a stretch in th'evenings already. Every day getting' longer now by a cock's step in the duncle'.
'A cock's step in the duncle! What is she talking about?' I thought as I looked despondently at the bare walls. Bleak, undecorated, impassive, the cheerless kitchen mocked me. Christmas candles, bright decorations, a visit from the mummers, good-humoured exchanges of greetings, all had raised our spirits briefly. For a while, time itself was suspended and our minds lifted above the drudgery of winter chores, most of which centred around foddering cattle: pulling hay from the rick, drawing water from the well, hand slicing bucket after weary bucket of mangolds, scalding and slicing potatoes. The list was endless. A latter day Sisyphus, had I offended the Gods? Our cattle byres too were the Augean stables, and I no Hercules.

Experience taught that worse lay ahead. The desolate and barren months of January and February had yet to be endured. There was much to fear in the unknown where sky joined sea on the dark and foreboding horizon beyond Bomore Island where the ghost of Soden lived out his dreadful punishment. Atlantic depressions and gales were the bane of those who lived along the wild and rocky western fringe. A glance at the map of Ireland shows a coastline battered and indented by millennia of wind and wave, a torturous collision of land and sea.

Along this wild shore staggered the ill-fated ships of the Spanish Armada in 1588. Making their way to Spain after disastrous naval battles with the English, three ships took shelter behind Inishmurray Island in Sligo bay: the *La Lavia*, *La Juliana* and *Santa Maria de Vision*. Eleven hundred men died cruelly there when their ships were driven aground on the mainland at Streedagh. One of the survivors, Francesco de Cuellar, wrote an account of the catastrophe. Anchored 'half a league' from land his memoir recalls the horror:

'... On the fifth day at anchor there sprang up such a great storm on our beam with a sea up to the heavens, so that the cables could not hold, nor the sails serve us. We were driven ashore upon a beach shut in on one side and the other by great rocks. Such a thing was never seen for within the space of an hour all three ships were broken in pieces, so that there did not escape three hundred men and more than a thousand were drowned...'

Wounded, half naked and starving with hunger, De Cuellar's troubles were not over when he reached the shore. Resorting to *Staid* Abbey for refuge he, 'found it deserted, and the church and the images of the saints burned and completely ruined'. Sir Richard Bingham's soldiers, 'went about searching for us to make an end to all of us who had escaped from the perils of the sea.' Inside the abbey he found twelve of his comrades, 'hanging within the Church by the act of the English Lutherans'. Fortunately for us he and a few other survivors made their way back to Spain where his account of the incident provides us, not just with the horror of the shipwreck, but a detailed description also of the living conditions of the inhabitants of the area at that time.

In September 1701 Richard Crofton of Achonry, Co. Sligo reported to Kean O'Hara that all the harvest in his fields had blown away following a fierce storm: 'I expected we should have met before now in another world, for most of us in this country was of the opinion that the last hurricane we had was ordered from the heavens to raise the dead as well as the living, and convey us to another world.'

He described the 'strange things that happened on the seashores in Tireragh and several other places of this county': More than twenty tons of herring and thousands of seabirds were cast up dead more than a mile inland from the shore. Houses and fields disappeared under thousands of tons of sand. In other places houses were knocked down or blown away altogether.[6]

Savage as the Asian tsunami of 2005 the fierce blasts that swept the land on January 6th 1839 are still remembered as *Oiche na Gaoithe Móire*. Stories of that fearsome 'night of the big wind' yet chill the blood. The violence of the storm, its sheer brutality, horrified those who lived through it; they counted it the most extraordinary experience of their lives. So imbedded was the experience in minds and folklore that when the old age pension was introduced seventy years later a recollection of the night was sufficient qualification for those who had no birth certificates.

Contemporary accounts say the day began well enough. It was 'Little Christmas' or *Nollaig na mBan* (Women's Christmas). Indoors was hustle and bustle as everyone looked forward to the evening's festivities. Outside the children played in the snow. At about three o'clock in the afternoon it fell unnaturally still. So calm, they later recalled, that voices floated between farmhouses more than a mile apart. Something strange was happening but no one knew exactly what. It was just as well they didn't, for the storm that was soon to break would be the most terrifying ever experienced.

Families cowering under frail and trembling roofs said later that the carnage outside sounded like 'an army of devils' dragging chains along the road. The Sligo Champion reported a noise

6 Swords, Liam, A Hidden Church.

resembling the 'deafening roar of a thousand pieces of artillery'. Fishing boats were, 'smashed to pieces along the coast, and many houses carried away altogether'. Roofs were shredded and blown away; embers from the hearth fires set the thatch ablaze. Along the western seaboard, people convinced that the end of the world was at hand, made their peace with God.

The following morning the sun rose on a wasted land. Familiar things were unrecognisable. Known landmarks were gone. The country came to a standstill. People dazed and bleary from lack of sleep and nervous exhaustion wandered about.

The storm was an ecological disaster. Nothing was where it should have been. The produce of the land was blown into the rivers and what should be in the rivers was in the fields. Along the shore much of the harvest ended up in the Atlantic. Boats were put out on lakes and sea to gather hay. Grain was killed by frost or eaten by birds or grew unheeded where it fell.

In retrospect, the relief effort was a dry run for the famine experience a mere nine years later. A foreign Government, sitting far away in Westminster, did nothing to help. Neither did succour come from the landlords sitting in their castles. Worse still many contracts between landlord and tenant required the tenant to make good on any storm damage. It was a crippling blow; all assistance was down to self-help and charity. Schools were opened as shelters, soup kitchens were set up and straw, when it could be found, was distributed for thatching by those who could spare it.

'Crangle's Night' the event was named afterwards in memory of the foolhardy captain of the *Andrew Nugent* who left Sligo harbour despite being warned not to sail. Too proud and foolish to heed local counsel he did not live to tell the tale. The story is well documented:

On January 6, 1839, the ship, owned by Scott and Patrickson of Sligo, waited for the flood tide to proceed to Glasgow with a cargo of bacon, butter and other goods. Evening fell, the wind increased and local seamen implored the captain to postpone sailing until better weather. 'If the ship was blown to hell and in spite of God or the devil I will set sail,' Captain Hugh Crangle swore! Scorning their pleas he hoisted canvas and 'set keel to breakers, Forth on the ungodly sea...'

Pressing his ship past Raughley headland he plunged madly through wind and wave. Soon, realising his position as hopeless he attempted to turn around — but could not! As he reefed the canvas to bring her about the craft was taken broadside by huge waves. Several crewmen were swept overboard. Buried where they were found on the shore at Knocklane, the graves of the drowned crewmen can still be seen. Damaging the rudder in the manoeuvre he was forced to bring the boat back on course again, or perish on the shore. The die was cast; his fate was sealed; now he had no option but to go on!

In a desperate fight for life the chastened captain set sail for Aranmore Island in Co. Donegal. Here he hoped to find a safe landfall in the lee of Rutland Island. Watchers from the Donegal shore, observing the stricken ship, realised that a grounding on Keadue Bar was imminent. Lighting beacon fires on Poolawaddy Hill and on Eighter Island they sought to direct him to a safer landfall. Two Aranmore pilots, Coll and Tom O'Donnell, put to sea. Despite great danger to their small boat O'Donnell boarded the *Andrew Nugent* and brought her to a safe anchorage at Calf Island. But it was not enough! The storm was relentless. Dragging her anchor during the night the ship struck a rock at Duck Island and was broken into matchwood. The captain, sixteen crew and passengers including the pilot, Tom O'Donnell, were lost.

Next day a reporter from The Sligo Journal visited 'the spot on which the body of poor Crangle was found, he had on only his trousers, vest shirt and stockings, no shoes or jacket, but, extraordinary to say, his cap was on his head. He could not have been long dead...'

There were many other such awful occurrences, some of which were calamitous enough to warrant a mention in The Annals of the Four Masters:

'The Age of Christ, 1478. A great tempest arose on the night of Epiphany, which was a night of general destruction to all by reason of the number of persons and cattle destroyed, and the trees and houses, both on water and land, prostrated throughout Ireland.'

Such upheavals of nature caused dread in ancient times. In picturesque imagery the ancients said that *Manannán Mac Lir* the Celtic sea-god rode the waves on his white-maned steeds on such wild and tempest-filled nights. 'White horses' some call them; '*Graubias*' the old people said they were. Look there even yet among the chaos and the fury and you may still behold the chariot of the mighty sea god dashing madly.

Worshipped by the early seafaring Celts, the wind was seen as the personification of the god Vintius. Druids claimed the ability to control it and, according to the early Christian writers, did so with the aid of demons of the air.

Only the Vikings could inspire more terror in early Christians than the threat from wind and waves. A quatrain written in Irish in the margin of a 9th century manuscript, the St. Gall Priscian, records the comfort that the writer found in a storm-tossed ocean. Contemplation of the scriptures were untroubled when storms protected against the plunderers:

> '*Fierce and wild is the wind tonight,*
> *It tosses the tresses of the sea to white;*
> *On such a night as this I take my ease;*
> *Fierce Northmen only course the quiet seas.*'

Ruman, the 8th century poet, at the bequest of the Dublin Norsemen, composed a song in honour of the sea for the 'Viking sworders'. Styled the Homer and Virgil of Ireland, bards of a later age memorialized the words he wrote:

> *'Tempest on the great seaborders!*
> *Hear my tale ye Viking sworders:*
> *Winter smites us, wild winds crying*
> *Set the salty billows flying,*
> *Wind and winter, fierce marauders.*

> *Lir's vast host of shouting water*
> *Comes against us charged with slaughter;*
> *None can tell the dread and wonder*
> *Speaking in the ocean thunder*
> *And the tempest, thunder's daughter.'*[7]

These storms inspired fear — they still do! Slates and tiles give good protection now. Not so very long ago roofs made of rye straw, tied down with hand-twisted oaten ropes were a fragile defence. Our neighbour, Bernie Kelly, although small in stature, lacked nothing in grit and steel. Like the coastline, his weather-beaten face traced the weathering of many a gale. Time, experience and observation had instilled practicality:

'All the months of the year curse a good February,' he told me, 'that's what the old people used to say.'

In bleak, windswept days Bernie took comfort from the thought.

'If ye have February good,' he elaborated, 'ye'll suffer for it the rest of the year.'

When gales threatened, my father and his neighbours held counsel. Jaws set, craggy faces grim, they looked out to sea, scanning the elements for some sign of what might come. Peaked caps turned front to back, in their way, was a surer indicator than any barometer of the severity of the coming storm. With knowledge rooted in generations of experience they read the signs: weather galls in the western sky yesterday, a ring around the

---

[7] *The Irish Tradition*, Robin Flower, p51.

moon last night, red skies this morning and now mares tails above. When these signs came together they shook their heads, knowing without speaking there were sleepless nights to come.

Palmerston, twice Prime Minister of England, was absentee landlord of North Sligo. He 'squared the land' in the mid 19th century bringing rectangled order to the rundale field systems. Moving his tenants from the sheltered 'old town' on the eastern slopes he assigned new plots to them on the bleak and inhospitable western hill road. The change was catastrophic. A century later the old people of the village still spoke with bitterness when they recalled the anguish of their ancestors. Their removal to the windswept, newly built highway, they believed, was just another ruse designed to make them quit the land to make way for sheep and cattle.

Charles Mc Glinchey of Inishowen in *Last of the Name* recalled the upheaval when their land was similarly re-apportioned in 1841. His neighbour, Paddy Mór Harkin, 'lost the good bit of ground he had and his family before him. They were given a bare bit of heathery ground and lived under a rock till they got a sod house built for themselves. The bailiffs got the pick of the good land; and in those days if you met a bailiff and didn't touch your cap, you'd find yourself out of your farm or maybe in jail.'

Centuries of warfare tempered a beleaguered but still defiant people. Having survived the persecutions of the 17th century and emerging from the rigours of the 'Penal Laws' the Irish peasant was relieved to have even a small piece of ground on any terms. Tenant refusal meant instant retribution. Move they must and move they did. On bog, moor or windswept hill they used with ingenuity materials scavenged from the land to build simple dwellings on the ground allotted to them: stone from the fields, lime mortar from the mountains, scraw (*scraith*) from the plains, fir from the bogs and straw for thatch and bindings. Clearing the ground of stones they used them to build sturdy 'ditches', separating pasture from meadow, meadow from tillage. Serving as a barrier to break the force of the restless Atlantic winds that ever seemed to blow, they gave a measure of protection to exposed pastureland. Cattle sheltered and were milked there.

One hundred years on, against all the odds, the descendants of Palmerston's tenants clung still to the stone built houses erected by their forefathers. A kitchen in the middle and a bedroom at either end provided refuge and comfort. The side facing west to the sea and prevailing wind was windowless the better to seal off the interminable driving wind and rain. On the opposite wall, along the new-built road, three small windows, one in the kitchen and one in each bedroom provided light. Views and comfort were for their masters in the 'big houses': the privileged classes in the luxurious mansions of Lissadell House or Classiebawn, Hazelwood or Templehouse, whose power and grandeur then stretched everywhere

On a January night in the 1950s men of the village studied the signs with stern faces. Yesterday the mare's tails and goat's hair of cirrus cloud foretold it, a red sky this morning warned it, now a ringed and hurrying moon confirmed that a storm was indeed imminent. Those that had boats hurried to secure them with strong ropes and chains or move them to the sheltered side of the harbour. Swells would soon sweep around the peninsula. Crashing, white-crested across the breakwater wall the tons of water would smash the unprotected fishing craft of the careless.

On such lowering days the old men recalled a January in 1868 and the enigmatic reply of a visiting ship's captain. Scorning the advice of the locals who advised him to move his ship to a protected part of the harbour and dismissing their weather 'signs' as local superstition, the captain of the '*Idwal*' replied with haughty indifference that he 'always took as much of another man's advice' as did him good! Next day his body, along with that of his crew, was taken from the wrecked ship. It had broken its moorings. During the night it was wrenched from the harbour and smashed to pieces on the jagged and desolate Leitrim shore three miles across the bay. Almost a century and a half later his exact words are still quoted as a cautionary exemplar.

As the wind increased my father looked anxiously at what he knew from experience to be the Achilles' heel of otherwise indestructible stone houses: the straw covering. Raising the ladder he climbed to the roof to check for weak spots. Finding them he pushed in 'keepers', forked sticks of sally or hazel, to secure netwire and thatch to the underlying sod. Ropes and chains with large stone weights or lumps of iron attached to the ends were secured across the hay-ricks. Old quernstones having a hole in the middle, and therefore easy to tie on, were ideal for this purpose. These devices were called 'slingers'. Suspended just above the ground the weights would soon dance to the tune of the gale.

The storm, as so often happens, broke on the flood tide. Softly it started. The first fretful gusts twirled the nervous leaves dancing them along the street. Wisps of hay scudded by, jittered uneasily in sheltered corners. Buckets and barrels left unsecured rolled about as the intensity increased. Night fell. Away to the west the twinkling stars blinked out to vanish behind billowing black clouds. The force intensified, slowly, inexorably. Soon it was impossible to walk except by leaning into the wind, body slanted at a sharp angle to the ground.

Darkness deepened; now someone must keep watch. I had just entered my teens and on achieving small successes often overheard the neighbours say with some pride to my father:
'That young fella of yours is coming on well, he'll soon be man-able now!

Being 'man-able' meant being able to do a man's work. In a world of hard physical labour a man-child was especially prized in the farming community. My time had come. The night vigil fell to me. A teenager on the brink of manhood this night would prove to be a crossing over, a rite of passage.

Reluctant to leave such an important job to a new hand my father was the last to retire. Walking outside we checked byre, house, haggard and rick. As we walked an uneasy moon lit and quenched, lit and quenched, weaving swiftly through black clouds on an ominous stage — now bathing the countryside in a pale light, suddenly dousing fields and buildings into a sea of blackness. As we walked he impressed on me the importance of constant vigilance. If the wind lifted a section of thatch and it was spotted immediately, the roof could be saved:

'There'll be no sleeping tonight, ye can sleep tomorrow if we're alright' he said. Seeing the worried look on my face:

'Ah, don't worry about it' he said mischievously, 'there's no storms in it now like there used to be. I remember me father telling me about a gale o' wind 'way back when he was a young fella. He said it blew the crows out of the trees all the way to Ballyshannon and they had to walk home!'

We both laughed at the mental image of crows being forced to walk instead of fly. And indeed, given the weather that was our lot they were lucky to hold on to their feathers!

Midnight came. The family went to bed. I was alone. Their safety was in my hands.

The details of the scene are clear to me yet; like an 'out-of-body' experience: Prepared for a lonely vigil, wrapped in an old army overcoat a boy, not yet a man, sits in the chimney corner on an old kitchen chair. It's very old. One leg, long broken, is neatly fastened with a binding of copper wire. He has no sense of purpose in being there — it's what his father ordered and what he, unthinkingly, must do. A prisoner of the night, and of his father's wishes, he huddles into the great coat, settles down and day-dreams. The chair is painted 'Light Oak' and he wonders why; it looks more a creamy yellow than anything resembling oak. He knows it's his mother's favourite colour since she discovered it on one of her infrequent trips to Sligo town. The front door is Light Oak too and so is the 'furm' (long stool), and the dresser.

She had a few shillings left over that day and impulsively splashed out on a bright green scarf she fancied. Such impetuosity was rare as she was a thrifty woman who knew she had nothing to spare for such indulgences. Full of good humour she put it on when she came home and:

'How d'ye like it?' she asked my father as she waltzed into the middle of the kitchen floor and posed, smiling, good-humoured and happy with her small extravagance.

He looked up from his contemplation of the fire.

'Well, God blasht the like!' was his curt reply.

She never forgot his answer, and often recalled the incident, especially when she got older and was more given to reminiscing:

'"*God blasht the like*"', that's what he said — well wasn't that an odd thing to say?'

She puzzled over the unexpected retort. He was an uncommunicative man so she must never have asked him the reason for his blunt response. She could have been resentful but she wasn't. Was it because he thought green was an unlucky colour, she mused? Many country people believed that. No point in tempting fate. A cow might get sick or crops fail. You never knew what might happen!

The boy stirs; piles turf on the fire, watches the spiralling smoke give way to darting flames, and waits. A pale yellow light from the oil lamp illuminates the kitchen with a feeble glow. *Solas na bhFlaitheas agam* ('The light of Heaven shine on me') the old folks recited when they lit it.

More picturesque than practical the big open fireplace draws draughty airs across the stone-flagged floor and sucks them into the chimneys vacuous maw. Like an oversize pipe organ it thunders a spirited response to each gust. The warm glow of the fire gives little more than an illusion of comfort. Warmth as well as smoke is sucked fiercely skywards. The leaden hours, minute by dreary minute, drag monotonously slow and slowly by. Outside, barrages of wind hurl against the sidewalls of the house in vicious assaults, whip wickedly around the gables and fade into the distance with a banshee wail.

Darkness adds extra dreaded dimensions. It invests the storm with new terrors, real and imagined. Inside was an oasis of quiet shielded from the violence outside — but there was something eerie about these dead hours of the night.

Something infinitely troubling.

An unearthly quiet lay heavy on the room. No living person disturbed the silence; there were no familiar footsteps on the road outside. Even the cattle were asleep, oblivious. An unnatural feeling pervaded the air. This was a time reserved for the otherworld. The boy was trespassing on time that rightly belonged to the supernatural, the phantasmal realm of ghost and faerie. He had heard the old people speak about them. Like Hamlet's ghost these gnarled oldsters,

> 'could a tale unfold whose lightest word
> Would harrow up thy soul, freeze thy young blood,
> Make thy two eyes, like stars, start from their spheres,
> Thy knotted and combined locks to part,
> And each particular hair to stand on end,
> Like quills upon the fretful porpentine.'

He had heard them speak of James Mc Govern and his wife who once lived in a small wee house at the other end of the village. Following a long illness James lay dying. Two neighbours decided one evening to visit and offer help to his wife. On their way to the house, near where Pat Charlie Gallagher lived, they were surprised to meet the sick man on the road. It was a moonlit night so his features were clearly visible. Delighted to see him in such good health they thought it strange when he hastened by without responding to their greeting. Pleased to see he had recovered anyway they decided to continue to the house. On arriving they were astonished to discover that James had passed away a short time before. His corpse lay before them stiff and silent on what had been his sickbed a short time previously.

Having no family James' wife lived alone after the funeral. As time went on neighbours visits became less frequent so she was delighted one night to hear a knock on the door. Opening it she froze in terror at the sight of her dead husband standing there. She stood for an instant and, not knowing what else to do, slammed the door shut. A few nights later the same thing happened again. Desperately afraid she went to the parish priest, Father Malachai Brennan in nearby Cliffoney, to have her husband prayed for and to ask the priest what she should do. He advised her to keep a bottle of holy water on the dresser. When the spirit returned she should invite him in and ask if there was any way she could help him.

A few days later the knock came to the door again but this time, even though she was deadly afraid, she was prepared. Knowing the holy water was in the house, she felt secure. When she opened the door it was her dead husband again. This time things were different; he seemed agitated. She addressed him anyway as the priest had advised:

'James' she said, 'won't you come in.'

'How can I come in,' he responded angrily, 'when you have holy water in the house.'

Losing her courage the woman slammed the door, shutting out the terrifying vision. The appearances happened repeatedly until the poor woman could take it no longer. She moved to the neighbouring townland of Carnduff. She was aghast when the visits continued.

She never did any good after that, Annie Callery who knew the family well remembered. Even though the neighbours were kind and sympathetic to the troubled woman, there was nothing they could do to help her.

The story has no happy ending; James' widow could not placate his tormented spirit or discover why he kept returning. Her health deteriorated from the strain and she joined her husband in death soon after.

This house, these walls, those blackened rafters were ancient. How many had been born by this fire, died here, cried and laughed here, been waked in that kitchen bed? The walls were heavy with ancient memories. Did phantoms of long gone ancestors lie hidden in the shadows — or maybe outside the door, listening, watching? Had they too in their time sat in this chair? Perhaps they were an unseen presence beside him. Would the door open and a silent spectre float in? Or would it just materialise in the gloomy light down by the dresser — hardly seen, or a figment of his frighted imagination.

It had happened many years before in the half-light of an evening when he was very young. A shadowy form had materialized from the solid stone wall by that same kitchen dresser, emerged fleetingly and was as quickly gone. 'Don't be daft!' his mother dismissed when he told her. No point in arguing. But he knew. He knew. He had seen it clearly.

What if it happened again? Was that creature, that phantom, still hidden in the wall in some strange spirit-peopled nether world, unseen, barely known, but close to us?

Without the animating daylight the pictures on the wall seemed pallid, still, cold and indifferent. Comfortless and solitary now was the red glow of the Sacred Heart lamp on the wall. Above the flame, with his heart exposed, Jesus' pleading eyes seemed inanimate and powerless. The longer he thought about it, the more he pondered, the heavier with foreboding became the air. Fear rising within, he willed his mind to think of other things. Scraping his chair closer to the fire he broke the silence, picked up the besom, swept the ashes into a tidy pile at the side and put the kettle on. This small activity, the little familiar noises, restored a sense of the normal, chased the spirits to their shadowy lairs, cleared the dark imaginings of his mind.

The wind changed direction. Veering west, it intensified in strength. The howl of stronger gusts was terrifying, a fear that lives within him still in a scarred subconscious. Now he had to venture out. Rain and salt spray driven across three thousand miles of churning ocean stung his lips and face. Foam, whipped from the shore, flew by like outsize snowflakes. Swirling, they danced a frenzied dance. A jagged streak of blue light sundered the dark, freezing for a split second a surrealistic outline of house and haggard, and was gone. Like a broken flight of starlings Bartley Gillen's thatch streamed into the night; skeleton ribs of rafters and purlins were revealed in a snapshot instant, then darkness fell again with a rolling crack of thunder.

The flashlight's thin beam tunnelled through the blackness showing all the items his father had taught him to inspect. Roof and thatch were holding fast. The ricks shook and danced in the garden as if shaken by a giant hand, but they held. Preparation was rewarded; now props and slingers served their purpose well.

Chilled to the bone the boy/man, returning to his fireside watch, poked the coals and built up the fire. Dutifully he listened to the wind, gauging its menace. The little warmth coming from the fire soothed him and he relaxed, heavy-lidded, but no, he couldn't — he mustn't sleep.

> '...Hour by hour with sleepy light
> Glimmering. All without this lair
> Was darkness and the noise of night,
> Where the wide waste of ocean roll'd
> Thundering with savage crash, and air
> In one tremendous torrent stream'd
> Across the rocks, across the wold,
> Across the murky world. It seem'd
> There never could be daylight more
> From earth to sky, on sea or shore...'

Author unknown

What harm then if he closed his eyes? He would still be awake; he could rest just on the edge of sleep; it would be safe there. His lids flickered and fell but still he heard the bellowing, moaning chimney, the hammer blows on the walls; his head dropping to his chest, he jerked awake; his eyes fell again, opened and fell once more; the storm sounds receded, receded slow and slower and stealthily faded away, away, away... Falling into a disturbed sleep he fell, tumbling, paralysed, down a cliff face, tumbling and falling endlessly...

Jarred awake by a wind that struck the walls with sledgehammer blows I jumped up, startled. Panic-stricken and racked with guilt I rushed outside to a sky that danced in madness. The noise, a rending upheaval of nature, swirled high and low demonstrating how vulnerable are the things that man has made. On nights like this the Norsemen believed their God, Woden, tore through the sky with his fierce women, shrieking curses and hurling destruction.

The lamp's beam lit the thatch flying in streamers off the barn; the roof heaved and bulged in the grip of the gale. Overwhelmed by a sickening dread of failing my watch, I raced for the ladder. What would my father say? How could I face judgement in the morning? With strength born of fear and a cotton-dry mouth I clawed my way on to the roof, again and again. Everywhere the thatch ballooned and flapped I pinned with heavy flagstones until at last the heaving ceased and the wind tore vainly at the battened straw.

It was a close call but the damage was curtailed and only a small section was stripped. Explanations would be called for in the morning when an account of my stewardship was due. It could have been worse, a lot worse. The indentations left by the flagstones would draw the rain and eventually rot the thatch underneath, but for the moment the damage was contained. Leaning against the ladder, legs shaking and heart thumping I vomited from fear and exertion. The mocking wind caught this too and threw it in my face.

Looking out to sea, from which direction all this torment came, there was no reprieve. All the vicious winds released from Aeolus's leathern bag filled the dark and boding sky on the horizon beyond Bomore Island. The 'black butt' the old men called it, and felt the black pit of dread in their their stomach when it churned there. How much more violence lay waiting to be loosed? Heaven help the seafarer on a storm-tossed ocean this night.

Listen! What was that, faintly heard in the rushing wind?

There it was again! Weak but distinct; rising and falling; a wailing cry. Could it be the screams of drowned sailors carried on the air — or does 'wandering in these desolate seas and listening to the cry of wind and wave bring madness'?[8].

There was nothing more to be done. Away from the chaos and safe inside again I listened to sheets of rain beat like spikes of steel against the walls. Water seeped with whistling splutters through the cloths my father had packed painstakingly into the crack between door and jamb. This he did with meticulous care each time the wind changed direction: the front door was sealed when the wind blew from the east, the back door when it came from the west. On the sheltered side, in good weather, the door was left open to admit extra light.

Many years later I was to learn that this method of draught control merited J.M. Synge's attention during his stay on the Aran Islands in the early 1900's! Although many of his observations contain the patronising overtones of the outsider who tries to understand without the humbling grind of experience, his observations on this phenomenon are worth repeating:

'Nearly all the cottages are built with two doors opposite each other,' he noted, 'the more sheltered of which lies open all day to give light to the interior. If the wind is northerly the south door is opened, and the shadow of the doorpost moving across the kitchen floor indicates the hour; as soon, however, as the

[8] Dectora in *The Shadowy Waters*: W.B. Yeats

wind changes to the south the other door is opened, and the people, who never think of putting up a primitive dial, are at a loss.

The system of doorways has another curious result. It usually happens that all the doors on one side of the village pathway are lying open with women sitting about on the thresholds, while on the other side the doors are shut and there is no sign of life. The moment the wind changes everything is reversed, and sometimes when I come back to the village after an hour's walk there seems to have been a general flight from one side of the way to the other.'

Wind direction influenced the kitchen routine too. Most hearths had capricious chimneys that refused to draw with certain 'arts' or directions of wind. You didn't have to look outside to determine which way the wind blew, or if it had changed direction. You knew. Huge puffs of smoke billowed down when the wind went north in some houses, east in others. Different chimneys, different habits. No tinkering with turf or burning embers or any other remedy worked. The chimney's smoking habits had to be placated. There was only one thing to do. Open the door — or the window if it wasn't stuck with age and paint. No matter what the weather!

In wintertime our back door, the one that faced the prevailing west and northwest winds, had an additional storm door attached. On that January night the driving rain soaked through the storm door; trickling on to the floor it gathered in an expanding pool. Overflowing, it pushed out along the joints in the stone floor and made its way, snakelike, pausing, building up and then pushing in little short rushes towards the fireplace. The craftsman that laid the flagstones, probably an ancestor now forgotten to memory, had misjudged his levels. The incline should have been away from the fire, not towards it.

Wearied from my exertions, but alert now, I watched as the water crept slowly forward. No need for concern, there were no carpets, no rugs, mats or parquet to be spoiled. Instead, a sense of tremendous relief as the arrival of the rain meant the storm would soon abate. This was a tremendous relief as usually these storms lasted for days. Rain released the venom of the wind as a lance purges a boil. Experience had taught us that this was the order of things. The weather charts of the Met. Service would eventually show us why. Understanding the shifting patterns of weather systems that swept over us belonged to a later time. There was no facility then to illustrate warm fronts, cold fronts, isobars, anticyclones and depressions. From observation grew knowledge.

The storm gradually eased. Lulled by the sound of the wind as it gradually receded I dozed fitfully on the chair. Drumming on the back door the undulating, rhythmic throb of driving rain now accompanied the dying breezes. The chimney played softer now; the lowering sky purged itself; water splashed merrily and copiously from the thatched eaves making music on the cobbled street.

Night passed into waterlogged day. A thin dawn light struggling at the windowpane soon stirred me to consciousness:

> 'Another night is fled,
> Another morning rises red....'[9]

Away in the distance a straggle of *eadaíl* seekers bent their way to the shore. Who knows what treasure the sea might bring! In the next field, oblivious to the night's hardship, a watery sun revealed a ragged group of crows bathing in a pool formed in a grassy hollow. Squabbling and flapping they splashed joyously in showery sprays. Two jackdaws watched with interest. Oystercatchers and seagulls, driven from the windswept coast, probed the flattened grass for an early breakfast. As we cosseted humans shiver off into the oblivion that seems an inevitable consequence of 'global warming' perhaps it is they who will inherit the earth!

The windowpane reflected a haggard face looking back at me

[9] *Description of Morning*, James Clarence Mangan,

from the new day. It was time to rake the fire. Shovelling ashes and sods of turf onto the few remaining red embers, I turned my steps wearily to bed.

4

THE ENCHANTED WAVE

'He took out his knife, held it to the wall of water and it split in two, one half goin' one road and one half the other. They turned the boat an' he says to them, "Now" he says, "row like buggery for the shore, if there comes another one on us we could be drownded."

Mickey McGroarty

'This is not as aisy as it looks, ye know', Paddy Leonard would growl wild-eyed at his audience. 'I often put up a cover for bucks here an' they'd start the first of it alright. But that was it. Bejasus, before they'd be finished the last meash, it was that big a lobster'd go out through it. What good is men like that!'

Thinking ahead to summer days fishermen spent long nights making nets for lobster creels. For today's fisherman, net covering for the creels or traps comes readymade in a roll easily cut to size and stretched over ribs of plastic or coated steel. Only the 'pipe' where the lobster enters the creel requires skill in the making. In Paddy's time everything was expertly constructed by hand. An entire creel was fashioned from a ball of twine, a few laths and some supple rods. Ribs were made of hazel, ash, rhododendron or whin saplings that were carefully selected in the woods for suppleness and strength. When Paddy had a hundred or so suitable rods gathered he tied them to the handlebars of his bike, wheeled them home and with infinite skill twisted and bent them into the required shape.

The kitchen/workplace itself was the essence of simplicity: On one gable a big open fireplace with soot stained brace and a hearth that always had a blazing fire of turf and wood, dominated the room. Blackened cast iron three legged pots, kettle and teapot stood around. Spaced at the ends of the mantelpiece were two brass candlesticks and two china dogs. Along its length were thrown a well thumbed pack of playing cards, a few smoke-stained, dog eared postcards of Long Island and Miami Beach sent by a sister in America, a tin tea-box, and a collection of old letters brown with age. Tucked cosily behind the chimney corner was the kitchen bed beside which was placed the 'furm' (long wooden stool) that could be used for seating — or a leg-up into the bed.

Pride of place on the opposite gable was the wooden dresser along which hung a row of cups suspended by the handles. Displayed on the shelves were delft mugs, bowls, blue patterned ironstone plates and serving dishes. Underneath in a space next to the floor, mice rummaged through the hay that had served as a nest for broody geese the previous spring. Between the door and the window, a pine table took up the space along the side-wall, over which hung a paraffin lamp. Over that again, attached to the roof timbers was a sheet made up of whitewashed flour bags. There was no conventional ceiling but a 'cathedral' ceiling long before they became fashionable. This one was of bog oak and earthen sods. Under the table, driven into the space between the wall and the floor was an iron ring used to tie the newborn calves for their first few weeks of life. The table was moved first of course and a bed of hay put down. Two simple wooden chairs in front of the fire completed the furniture.

Underfoot, a stone-flagged floor quarried along the seashore, laid by some forgotten ancestor and worn smooth by successive generations of Leonards, too many to count, served its purpose well. It was a sundial too: the doorpost acting as gnomon to the joints between the flagstones marking the hours and minutes. A hard and unremitting master was the sun! When Paddy and his father came in from the meadow for dinner the shadow from the doorjamb sped across the floor. It was the only time of day it moved so fast! In Co. Monaghan, when Patrick Kavanagh went once to Pat the Hack's house to rouse him for the fair at Carrick in Co. Monaghan Pat was unperturbed. He looked at the dresser.

'It's not six yet," he said. 'It's not six till the sun shines on the second of them blue plates.'

Every area had its own variations on the theme!

Hanging on Paddy's seaward wall a glimmering, red-globed Sacred Heart lamp illuminated an image of Jesus, a Jesus that never flinched at Paddy's blasphemous outbursts. Heart exposed and bound with thorns, he promised eternal salvation to 'the house in which the image of My Sacred Heart shall be exposed and honoured.' Paddy in his tirades meant no disrespect to the Lord so we can be sure a forgiving Saviour took that into account. Other holy pictures of lesser saints and martyrs: St. Anthony of Padua, St. Theresa of Lisieux, Blessed Martin de Porres and such, hung randomly nearby.

Paddy and John Rogers were among the last fishermen in Mullaghmore to 'knit the covers' for the creels in the old way. Tools were simple: an auger, hammer and fisherman's needle. A six inch nail driven into the windowsill held the first mesh as, night after night, with infinite patience, Paddy stooped over his work, converting spools of twine into netting, deftly and patiently adding mesh to mesh by the dim light of the oil lamp. Unpredictable, quick to laughter and quicker to anger, his movements were as energetic as his conversation was lively.

Hazel rods, pine laths and wood shavings that smelled of summer and open woodland cluttered the busy floor. Talking while he knitted, he told stories of great fishing trips long ago or hard days spent at sea:

'There's no lobsters in it now compared to when I started, long 'go,' he'd declare. 'Ye could shoot a dozen and a half o' creels an' ye'd get a dozen and a half o' lobsters. I seen me gettin' six lobsters in one creel! But it wasn't like that all the time an' when ye weren't making money it was hard to keep a crew. The day ye'd get a couple of dozen lobsters they'd be all smiles but the next day if ye only got eight or so they'd be cryin':

"Ah, I'd be better off working than at this game," they'd tell ye.

There was wan oul' whinjer at this one day: "Arra, go t' fuck," says I, "an' go workin', see if I care!"

They were hard to listen to sometimes ye know, but when ye're fishing ye have to take the good day with the bad day.'

His favourite story, often told, was about a close call he had some years before when he was fishing longlines. The boat was an open, twenty-one foot, Mc Cann built, Greencastle style 'double ender'. Owned and skippered by John Rogers, a spritsail and jib drove her when there was wind; oars and manpower when there was not. 'Last of the windjammers', my father said with a smile as we watched the St. Patrick tack back and forth across the bay in later years from our vantage point in the hayfield high up on the hill. A fisherman in his younger days he still had a lingering affinity with the sea. The ribs and skeleton of his beloved Zulu lugger[10], the *Rosebud*, lay mouldering near the bridge at the harbour. Pausing sometimes in his work he would look pensively at the boats as they sailed out to the fishing grounds.

Marriage brought added responsibility so he left the sea when he took a bride to give his full attention to the family farm. It had fallen to his care when his only brother Patrick emigrated to New York. Those were the hungry times — the days of the 'American wake', and Patrick would never see his native fields again. There was a living to be made in America, but no fortune, he realised, when he lost all his savings and almost his house in the crash of '29. Much later, when things improved, a cheque often came to our house in the American letter. I wonder if he and his wife, Grace, ever realised how much it meant to us who had so little then.

Wedding pictures came and as time passed, images of his children, Mary and Peter, my cousins, as they grew up. Far away, distant and unreal they seemed. Electricity and telephones hadn't even been thought of, not in rural Ireland anyway, so my father, with much prompting from my mother, would don his glasses to sit by the window and write an answering letter to the brother

[10] Carvel built two masted boat having three sails, designed in Lossiemoth, Scotland in 1879. Named after the war waged by the English against the Zulu tribes in Africa at the time.

that he would never see again. Although the spade, shovel and graip were his tools of daily use he had a fine handwriting style. A child's uncaring eyes could not see the pain in his heart that was surely there as he reached out in inadequate, inanimate words to the brother with whom he had shared a cot, that he had played, laughed and grown up with. They must have been close as when the war against the English came they were comrades in arms too. When freedom arrived, the country that Patrick had helped set free had nothing to offer so he and many, many others who had fought on the Republican side had to leave. There was nothing here for them. The impoverished New Ireland turned its face impassively, was maybe glad to see them go. Out of sight, out of mind.

Later I would learn from my cousin Mary, Patrick's daughter, of how it was on the other side. She knew my father, Petie, was her uncle who lived in a faraway place and missed never really meeting or knowing him. Her dad would talk about him when a letter or picture from Ireland came. It opened a chink on the brothers past lives on the ocean and the farm.

'Close relatives were missed as so many friends had these and I did not' Mary remembers. 'There was a far away quality to my father that would show itself when he was alone or with his cousin from home, Jim Mc Lean. They would sit in the kitchen talking for awhile and then would sit together staring at an empty space.'

Perhaps the space wasn't empty, Mary. Perhaps in those transcendental moments the life and friends they left behind played like a familiar movie in their mind's eye. Perhaps in these stolen minutes their spirits escaped and wandered again across the ocean, lingered awhile among some well-loved hills and fields, or walked the haunting places they were forced to leave and would never see more. We will never know. For my uncle these spiritual visitations, if such they were, were the only trips to his childhood home he would ever make.

Paddy Leonard swore as he knitted, waved his arms to make a point, and warmed to his story. The crew of five were fishing longlines off St. John's Point on the Donegal coast. *Bun na Truffin* was a sheltered port across the bay and *Cas an Sowh* less sheltered, but nearer, on the Point peninsula. With darkened brow and fierce glances Paddy confronted his audience. No one dared say a word. Winds howled and seas crashed through the kitchen as he recalled how close they came to a watery grave:

'We were away at daybreak,' he began, 'there was five of us in it, an' a nicer morning ye never seen with a nice wee air of wind for sailing. When we got to the Point Head we had the lines shot away in no time. We worked away anyway an' about the middle of the day when we were hauling didn't the wind start to come up fresh from the south. It got stronger and stronger, comin' in big puffs, and Rogers shouts at us:

"Get them lines in as quick as ye can an' we'll head for Mullagh."

There was no fish in it! A half box is all we got, a coupla dozen whiting, a few herring and a few wee codling. Well when we had the lines all in, it was blowin' a gale an' we knew we had no hope of makin' it to Mullagh. Some o' them wanted to try to make it to *Bun na Truffin* but me father was with us an':

"Were ye ever in *Bun na Truffin* or d'ye know anything about it?" he said, rale cross. They didn't know what they were talking about, ye see!

We put her head for *Cas an Sowh* anyway an' we rowed till we nearly got blind in th' eyes. She took one shear away on a big sea an' I shouted to Rogers,

"Go down and steer that boat or the bastard'll [naming the steerer] drown us before we see land.

"I'm sayin', I will," says Rogers — he was a great man in a boat.

She started to fill with water an' it was as much as we could do to keep her baled out. Before we got to Cas an Sowh the sail was tore to bits — she was runnin' with the bare fucken masht. We

ran her up on the shore an' only we had plenty of help we would-
n't be fit to draw her up outa the water. The Point men was all
down tying down their boats afraid they'd blow away. We were
nearly all lost — it blew a fecking hurricane after that, it was days
before we got home.'

Paddy was passionate in all things and a lover of dancing too.
On special nights he cleared out nets, twine, shavings and rods.
The floor was swept, the gramophone put on the kitchen table
and word sent out that there was going to be a dance.

Prior to electronic gadgetry there was no shortage of ways to
pass away the long winter nights. Sometimes it was pranks that
were often cruel in nature; like lacing the tea with a strong laxa-
tive in a house where a dance was being held and then tying the
doors so no one could get out. There were no toilets in the
houses then and the dancers of course were mixed, men and
women. Very funny for the jokers but a mortifying embarrass-
ment for the victims!

Others 'rambled' or 'ceilidhed', sitting around the fire in neighbours houses. The Oxford English Dictionary defines rambling
as: 'wander in discourse, talk or write disconnectedly' also: 'a
walk without any definite route or other aim than pleasure'.
Rambling in Ireland was indeed both. Although not having
recognition as such these gathering places were cultural institu-
tions of a kind too. It was here that local news was exchanged
and the old lore passed on before the arrival of 'mass media'. The
door was always open or at least unlocked. Everyone felt welcome and a visitor never had to knock: they just walked in. They
were pleasant evenings, although from time to time subject to in-
terruptions from practical jokers who might tie the doors from
the outside and climb up to put a sod or slate across the chimney,
filling the house with smoke.

Men mostly, and sometimes women, chatted and told stories;
they played cards, recited poetry, sang songs or gave out riddles
and brainteasers. People then lived according to nature's

rhythms; stories of the *seanchaidhe* took place in an infinite 'now'; no great distinction was made between past and present. Time was not chronological. It was connected not to clocks or calendars but to sun, tide and seasons in an ever changing 'present' that was cyclical and ageless. 'The past is a foreign country; they do things differently there,' the writer Leslie Poles Hartley once said That is true now — but it wasn't true then, for people farmed and worked as their forbears had done for countless generations. The prodigious changes of the late 20th century had not yet occurred. The past was as familiar to them as their present, as familiar to them as it is alien and remote to us.

Women rambled out to the homes of their friends taking their knitting, sprigging or crochet with them. Chatting as they practised their craft they turned out socks for the men, warm jumpers for the children or lace items for the market in an era when there was great interest and pride in such handcrafts — and financial necessity too.

'On a winters night, about seven or eight o'clock the men'd all meet at a crossroads an' they'd start for our house or some other rambling house,' Maggie McGowan recalled. 'There was no one to bother them. They'd start whistling a tune when they'd be walking along the road an' they wouldn't have it finished until they'd land at our house. An' it was an Irish tune mind ye. That's a thing died out altogether, whistling. Did you ever hear whistlin'? Well it was all the go in my day.

When they'd come in to our house me father'd say:

"I suppose it's time for me to go now".

He'd go out rambling to a neighbour's house an' that left the house free for us then. All the old men used to go in to the neighbour's, to Hughie Dolan's and Pat Tivnan's and Paddy Dolan's. They'd have the gossip of the day. 'Twas a cleaner way to spend the time — not as dirty as the television that's going now anyway. After a while the house'd fill with young people, the table was brought out an' we'd all start the cards.'

Musicians were especially popular at any gathering. In Selacis, Co. Donegal, Mickey Mc Groarty never went out, to bog, fair or rambling house without his mouth organ. People knew this and gave him a special welcome. They invariably asked him to play a tune and, 'the women would throw down their 'sprigging' and go out and dance a reel.'

Itinerant fiddle players like Johnny Doherty from Fintown, Co. Donegal, were welcome wherever they went. A night's lodging and board was theirs for the asking; the house where Johnny stayed deeming it an honour to have him. A gifted musician, he also composed tunes. Often he combined both of these talents with a good story. The Black Mare of Fanad, another tale of near-tragedy at sea with strange consequences, was one of these. Mickey Mc Groarty learned it from Johnny himself and this is how it went:

'A travelling man and his brother down at Dungloe used to go and fish in the harvest time with the local people and one of them told this story after. That man was Johnny Doherty. They were out fishing this nice calm day a long way out from the shore. They were facing east to the rising sun when one of them chanced to look back and when he did he warned the others that there was a storm a-getting up.

"We better head back," he said, "There's a big cloud risin'."

It's always a sign something could happen, a freak wave or a storm or something that could capsize the boat. They decided anyway to haul in the nets and go ashore with whatever few fish they had. It's better to save your life than to be drownded.

On their way back didn't this big wave rise up behind them and was going to swamp the boat. Oul' Johnny Doherty, taking quick stock of the situation, knew right away what to do:

"Men," he says, "we're going to be drownded if I'm not fit to split this wave."

He took out his knife, held it to the wall of water and it split in two, one half goin' one road and one half the other. They turned the boat then an' he says to them:

"Now" he says, "row like buggery for the shore, if there comes another one on us we could be drownded."

They made the shore of it anyway and it was still early in the day, everyone was out workin' at hay. Johnny went out with the farmers to help them tramp a couple o' cocks o' hay. When he was finished it was comin' close to nightfall. He was very fond of smokin' a pipe and:

"I'll go up to the shop up the road there," he says to the ones was with him," and get a couple of ounces of tobacco."

"That's alright," they says, "but be back before bedtime."

Away up the road with him anyway an' it was kinda turning dark this time. He was well on his way when he found the galloping of this horse comin' up behind him.

"In all the times I was on the road," he thought to himself, "I never found a horse coming galloping without the noise of a cart or something behind it as well!

A man that he had never seen before, riding on a black mare, pulled up beside him an' says to him:

"Are ye goin' far?"

"I'm going to such and such a townland," says Johnny.

"Well get up behind me," says the stranger, "I'm going the same way."

So up he got behind the stranger on the black mare an' away wit' the two o' them like buggery. When they came to the crossroads, Johnny wanted to get off but the stranger said to him:

"Now" he says, "I'd like ye to do me a favour. There's a girl sick in the house an' I'd like you to cure her for me."

"God," says Johnny, "Sure I never cured nobody."

"Don't worry about it," says the stranger, "You'll do!"

So he went on with the stranger anyway till they came to a big house. The stranger tied the black mare to the gate and the two of them went into the house. The stranger brought him to a room and he was surprised to see the finest girl ye ever left two eyes on lying on the bed.

"I want ye to cure me," she says to Johnny.

Johnny explained to her that he had no power to cure anybody. "D'ye see that knife there," she says to Johnny, pointing to her hip. "Is that your knife?"

Johnny looked at it and got the surprise of his life when he saw the knife he had split the wave with earlier that day stuck in the girl's side.

"I'm bleeding to death," she said to Johnny, "and no doctor can cure me or no man save me except the man that drove the knife in me. Will ye pull it out?"

So Johnny reached over and pulled the knife out an' she explained to him then that she made the wave to bring him to her, that she had always great admiration for him an' that she wanted him to be her husband.

"You saved my life just now," she says to him then, "now I'll grant you a wish."

"Right," says Johnny, "I wish that every time I go out fishin' I'll get back to shore safe and always get plenty of fish."

"Right," she says, disappointed I suppose that he didn't wish for her. "That's granted, now be away, the black mare'll take ye back to the shop you were going to before my brother picked you up.

Johnny did that, got his tobacco, went home and told the story. When he was finished he made up a bit of a tune in respect of what happened that day. From then on he always played it at the end of the story. The name of that tune is the *Black Mare of Fanad.*'

E. Estyn Evans recorded a similar version of this story in *Ireland and the Atlantic Heritage*. He had taken it down following a personal conversation with Johnny Doherty. The Evans version has three drowning waves instead of one. Neither does Johnny claim to be the man who split the wave but relates that it was a man named Byrne.

Evans's version is that, following the removal of the knife, the stranger invited Byrne to take food and offered him a bowl of porridge:

'It was the best porridge he ever tasted, and he asked where the oats that made the meal were grown. "The grains were all the top pickles of the corn", said he, "grown at Mullaghmore in the County Sligo."

Then Paddy Byrne knew for sure that it was the fairies was in it, for it is their custom to steal the top grain of every head of corn. Sure everyone knows this is why the top pickle is always missing at harvest!'

This is the tune that, according to Mickey, Johnny Doherty composed:

The Black Mare of Fanad   J.D.

5

THE DROWNING WAVE

When ye, therefore, shall see the abomination of desolation, spoken by Daniel the prophet, stand in the holy place.

Matthew Chap. 24, Verse 15

The sea is our master. In 1640 a huge wave broke completely across Aranmore Island devastating everything in its path. It can and will happen again. Experts warn that the west and south coasts of Ireland lie directly in the path of a tsunami that could be triggered by an eruption of the Cumbre Viejo volcano on the island of La Palma in the Canary Islands. It has been the most active volcano in the region, erupting at least once or twice a century. Tremors there could cause a massive slab of rock, twice the volume of the Isle of Man, to collapse into the sea. This collapse would trigger huge tidal waves, travelling at up to 600 miles per hour that would come crashing on to these shores within four to five hours of the occurrence.

Cumbre Vieja's last eruption in 1949, and accompanying earthquakes, opened a fracture two and a half kilometres long, about 1/10th of the exposed length of the Cumbre Vieja. Parts of the western half of the ridge moved about 1m sideways and 2m downwards towards the Atlantic Ocean. Other than that the eruption was uneventful — but it may not always be so.

Thousands died in a massive wave that occurred on All Saint's Day 1755 as a result of an earthquake off the coast of Lisbon in Portugal. A devoutly religious people, they struggled to understand why God had chosen a holy day to punish them. Bedlam ensued, and believing the survivors to be in league with the devil, priests caused many innocent people to be executed.

Tidal waves radiating from Lisbon swamped Cork Harbour causing the collapse of Coranroo Castle on the south coast of

Galway Bay. On the Sunday after the earthquake the effect was felt at Kilmore Quay. At low water the, 'inner dock was crowded with small sailing craft and quite dry. In less than five minutes every boat was afloat and we had high water; in five minutes more, the water ebbed again to the lowest spring tide'.

According to the Annals of the Four Masters a fierce storm and deluge occurred in, 'The Age of Christ, 799 [recte 804] ... There happened great wind, thunder and lightning, on the day before the festival of Patrick of this year, so that one thousand and ten persons were killed in the territory of Corca-Bhaiscinn, and the sea divided the island of Fitha into three parts. A night of general destruction to all by reason of the number of persons and cattle destroyed, and the trees and houses, both on water and land, prostrated throughout Ireland."

The island of Fitha mentioned in the text is Mutton Island off the coast of Co. Clare. Scarcely more than rocks, Inismattle and Roanshee are all that survive today as additional small islands. The nearest mainland village is Quilty.

A few miles north, near Lahinch, the Atlantic Ocean now swells over what was once dry land. It was submerged when a tidal wave engulfed the village of Cillstifiann and its people. The ghost town of Cillstifiann, its monastery and clustering houses, can still be sometimes seen in the clear waters of the bay south of Lahinch. When this happens it is an evil omen and signals tragedy to those who have witnessed it.

Such an event occurred on a fine summer's day to a boy who, with his father and two neighbours, went out fishing. The sea was calm and the child admiring the cloudless sky, 'when the young man in the stern called out suddenly, 'Cillstifiann! Cillstifiann! Oh God, have mercy on us'. His eyes were riveted on something in the depths of the sea and his face was the colour of clay.'

Before anyone could act a huge wave rose up from the depths. It seemed as big as a mountain and the little group thought themselves lost as it approached with an eerie silence. Breaking across the boat and almost suffocating the occupants, it fell away as quickly as it had risen.

The crew, when they recovered and could see again, beheld the bay as calm as it had been before the drowning wave hit. They were safe but there was an empty space at the stern where Matt, the young man who had apparently seen the sunken village, was sitting. They summoned help and searched for his body for hours and days but it was never recovered. 'The rest of us saw nothing that day but the rocks and the seaweed. Matt did, I know it. His sudden prayer to God for mercy was the result of his glimpse of Cillstifiann.'

On that day in 804 A.D., when the Clare island of *Fitha*, was sundered, St. Caológ knelt in prayer on a hilltop at *Cill Ciaróg*, which was his monastery at *Ballyteampaill*, near the village of present-day Mullaghmore in the County of Sligo. Miraculously, this account, found concealed in a souterrain under the site of the old church, survives:

'The Vigil of Patrick, Apostle of Ireland, at the canonical hour of *nones*[11] and our monks deep in prayer for the conversion of the pagan. The sun growing dark we looked to the west and saw ravening clouds, the burial clouds, in black masses spreading out behind the island of Bomore and the bigger island of the blessed Patriarch *Muiredach*. When we felt the ground tremble beneath our feet, an uneasy dread came over us. The sky grew darker, the animals became restless, a nervous whinnying from the horses, the pigs squealed and jostled each other. Eyes bloodshot, wild and rolling, they milled about nervously. Rats and wolves slunk from their lairs and ran blindly across the pasture. The wind fell away; it died altogether as we penned the cows. An eerie silence fell in which voices travelled for miles. A pale sun rolled low over the southern horizon. The air itself stood still; the very birds fell silent.

From *Ben Gulban* in the south to *Sean Gleann* in the northland of O'Donnell a great mass of cloud erupted, rolling fearsome as it

[11] The fifth hour of the daily religious services of the Catholic church, originally fixed for 3 pm.

advanced. Down near the sea families poured out of their cabins. Their cries tumultuous rose to me on the hilltop. Blessing themselves with the sign of the Saviour they hurried uphill to the monastery. Some went to their boats, others hastened to the high ground at Ostann na Bríona.

And then I saw it! The waters receding and drawing up, up, right out to the deep. Like the parting of the Red Sea, huge hills of water tumbling one over another. On the eastern shore the ocean went from around Carraig Ordóg; a steep pinnacle arose leaving only a deep pool at Poll Domhain. I tell no lie, the waters ebbed out and out until you could walk across the bay, past Muirlean to Tulachfinn in Leitrim where holy St. Patrick blessed the wells and cursed the river Dubh. Plaice, conger, Pollack: all kinds of fish flapped about in the mud gasping for life.

Away to the west from Cnoc na Taoisigh to Ros Caoireach the waters fell away, almost to the horizon it seemed. They piled up to the sky. Banc Cuirlieroidhe and Banc Eoghainagrath rose up from the seabed. The like was never witnessed before, lobsters and crab crawling on rock ledges no human had ever seen.

Then a deep rumbling — the ground shook as it did when our blessed Saviour died on the cross. Racing like a devilish beast the ocean turned and rushed toward the land. Faster than a bird could fly. Thunder rolled across the sky, jagged flashes of lightning hurtled from the clouds. Inis Muireadh and Bó Mór vanished from our sight. A great wall of water crashed on to Mullach Mór and, foaming, swept up and up. A deluge of rain and the winds increased to a fury, tearing at the straw-covered botháns. Even though we watched from high on the hill at Baile an tSeampaill we all prepared to meet our God.

A great tidal bore, it was like a high, crashing wall, rushed around the peninsula. Herds, flocks and husbandmen, all swept away from the fields in one dreadful inundation. Breaking with a mighty roar across Oilean Cleasaí Bán, on the east of the peninsula, it demolished the bothán ósta[12] and cabins of the poor peo-

[12] Drinking cabin

ple there. Matchwood it made of the boats at *Port na hEorna*, many perished. The waters swelled and raged all around *Mullach Mór* right up to *Cliathmhuine* and *Craobhcael*. The cell of our brother at *Cill na mBochtán* was swept away and the monks drowned, every one. Wind and water battered the houses. They were either blown down or washed out to sea; people buried beneath the rubble, cattle swept away. Desolation deepened everywhere, hour by hour.

Two great waves, no, mountains, one from the east and one from the west, met in a maelstrom of fury just under *Teampaill Buí* at *Clíathmhuine*. Great lakes were formed at *Bundubh*. They stand forever in testament to the day when the anti-Christ ruled the heavens, the very laws of nature challenged. Great hills of sand were thrown up at each end of the channel, one at *Trágh Bundubh* and another at *Trá Bhaile*. Now it is a wasteland of white; to this day you can gather seashells on dry land where boats once went. It is a sign that you can believe what I tell you.

The Lord is righteous. He saw that the people had violated his commandments and afflicted us in the day of his great anger. It was a sign from above and many pagans were converted to Christ in the following days. We give thanks to God that our monastery, *Cill Ciaróg*, was left untouched. Numerous were the prayers we offered to the Son of God for sparing our lives for we heeded his word: "When ye, therefore, shall see the abomination of desolation, spoken by Daniel the prophet, stand in the holy place." May He be forever praised.'

There is a place at Mullaghmore today, not marked on any maps, known as *Port na hEorna* (Port of the Barley) as mentioned above. Giving credence to this account the old people will tell you that the peninsula was once an island, that turf from near the mountain was once brought by boat from Denis's Hill at Upper Bunduff and landed at *Port na hEorna*.

One of the great drowning waves of Irish mythology was named after Clíona, a goddess of the Tuatha Dé Danann. *Clíona*

Cionnfhionn (fair-haired) was the daughter of Gebann, chief Druid of Tír na nÓg, the dwelling place of the sea-god Manannan Mac Lir. In the time of Fionn Mac Cumhaill, Clíona fell in love with *Caoimhín* a warrior of the Fianna. Some time previously Caoimhín had been expelled from the Fianna because of his penchant for women. Through time, 'the Fianna got to be tired of him because there was not a woman of their women, wed or unwed, but gave him her love. And Fionn had to send him away at the last, for he was in dread of the men of the Fianna because of the greatness of their jealousy'.

Missing his old comrades, *Caoimhín* wandered about until at last he made his way to *Tír na nÓg*. Old habits die hard and, wouldn't you know it, it wasn't long till he struck up with up *Clíona* the virgin, 'that had never given her love to any man, but when she saw *Caoimhín* she gave him her love.'

His past was of little concern to *Clíona*. Soon, eloping together in a curragh, they fled *Tír na nÓg* altogether. When they landed at *Trá Théite* in Glandore, Co, Cork, *Caoimhín* went ashore to hunt for deer leaving his woman in the boat. Hell hath no fury like an angry father and soon, 'the people of Manannan's house came after them, having forty ships. And *Iuchnu*, that was in the curragh with *Clíona*, did treachery, and he played music to her till she lay down in the boat and fell asleep. And then a great wave came up on the strand. Sweeping her away it delivered her back to her father and to her kingdom. And the wave got its name from *Clíona* of the Fair Hair, that will be long remembered'

6

THE SHIP-SINKING WITCH

I tell you, men of Ireland, we
Are of the people of the sea
And restless, wind tormented still
Have no will but the water's will.
As the great sea-flood comes and goes
The tide within us ebbs and flows...

Robin Flower, *Sea Children*

Fishermen worked close to nature and the primal elements. They held the sea in reverence and fear. Care was taken not to offend spirits that although unseen were ever watchful. Taboos were rigidly observed: to stick a knife in the boat's 'taft' or mast invited bad luck; meeting a red haired woman on the way to a fishing trip was an evil omen; bread went unbuttered for fear of bringing misfortune; whistling was forbidden, it 'whistled up the wind': 'there'd be 'a bad smell off ye' if ye whistled in a boat. Ye could play music or sing, but there'd be no whistling'.

In Urris, on the Inishowen peninsula in north Donegal, when fishermen turned their boats around they always 'turned the nose of the boat round with the sun'. Care was taken that no white stones were used for ballast; these stones, usually quartz, were for use by the *sidhe*; humans should not use them. When pointing at a boat the whole hand was used; using a finger in the normal way might sink it! Water and fish blood lying in the bottom of a boat was good, it had great power over the spirits of the sea.

Far removed from nature today we may scoff at such simple beliefs — but was there any basis in fact to these superstitions? Thomas Boyle worked as a fisherman in the early 1900s and he believed there was. Hadn't he experienced it himself?

'Hughie Cawley and Jimmy the brother, Dan Mc Govern and

meself were going down to fish mackerel early on a summer morning. At the eye of the New Quay there was always a rat seen running; he used to come to the edge of the quay and run down in between two stones. This morning I decided to have a go at him, lifted a stone at the Iron Gate, and fired it. I tumbled the bugger anyway and he disappeared. Thinking no more about it we hopped into the boat and away.'

When the fishermen returned in the evening they tied up the boat and stowed their handlines under the gunwale in the spot where they normally fished when at sea. Care was taken to remove the 'drove' of mackerel bait from the hook so as not to attract rats or seagulls when the boat was unattended.

Next morning, after the rat incident, the skipper and crew got ready to put to sea as usual. Our storyteller noticed immediately that his handline was cut:

"Had you the drove off the handline?" says Cawley.

"I did," says I.

'We used to take the droves off the handline the night before, as the rats would eat the drove of mackerel and cut the line along with it if you didn't.

That was alright; we arrived the next morning and it was the same thing, two cuts in the line and no gear but mine was touched. The third morning the same thing happened. The Cawleys and Dan Mc Govern weren't a bit happy about it and told me that I'd have to go altogether, that whatever it was I fired at, it was no rat.

Well this went on for awhile, but to make a long story short, it quit eventually anyway, but I can tell you that I fired at no more rats after that. I nearly lost my place in the boat over the head of it!'

Seafarers encountered other hazards too: 'The old people could point out the *ród sidhe* or the fairy road, where the spirits always travelled,' Charles Mc Glinchey claimed in his book *Last of the Name*. 'It was three waves close together one after the other, and it was dangerous for a boat until the third wave passed. It was the *rod sidhe* that put down an Isle of Doagh boat in 1847, when the whole crew was lost. In one of the houses that night, a hen crowed twice and someone struck her with a stick and killed her. They say that the first two crows got the boat over the first two waves of the *ród sidhe*, and that if they had let her crow the third time the boat would have survived the third wave. The women thought it was the spirits of the sea that took the men away and that they might return.

Every night for a long time they put roasted potatoes in the saltbox for the men in case they happened to get back home for a night. But whenever blood appeared on the men's old shoes, that was a sign they were done for good. People setting out to sea at the present time don't pay as much heed to signs like these as they did in days long ago, but that doesn't say they are any the wiser for it!'

Embedded in old tales are nuggets of past worship and beliefs, Gordian knots of mystery and enigma. Such was the case with the amazing ship-sinking witch of Bruckless and a mass drowning that happened on the shores of Donegal Bay many years ago.

Fishing was poor along the Sligo coast when news reached there of great catches of herring across the bay in Bruckless, Co. Donegal. There was no dole then or state subsidy; you got nothing for nothing. Fishermen had small plots of land where they grew their own food, but they still needed cash to pay the landlord and to buy the few essentials that could not be grown: tea, sugar, tobacco, flour.

It was usual for seafaring men to take great risks. It went with the occupation. It wasn't that there was any such thing as choice in employment. There were no jobs. You took a penny where you got it. Craft were frail, equipment patched and barely serviceable. Bruckless was a long way from home, but the men made their boats and nets ready, said goodbye to their families, and set sail.

When the Mullaghmore men got to Donegal the herring fishing was as good as they had hoped. The weather was fine and they worked all through the night, landing their catch in the mornings. Each day an old woman came and asked the men for herring. They knew her as Biddy. She had very little money but gave whatever few pence she could. When she had no money left the Donegal fishermen refused to give her any more fish.

It was not because they were miserly. To give goods away without receiving anything in return, they believed, was to 'give away your luck'. There was no question of taking a chance with such things. Luck, good or bad, meant success or failure, poverty or survival; the belief ran deep in the orthodoxy of rural communities. In their life's cycle many forces, mysterious and unpredictable, sinister and benign, were at work. Customs, pagan or Christian, sanctioned by generations of experience were sacrosanct. They protected against evil and the unknown. No, they couldn't just give the fish away; they had to get something in exchange.

Any small amount would do, but the poor woman had nothing at all. Evening after evening she came to the boats and each time was turned away. Eventually she was given fish by the crew of a Streedagh, Co. Sligo boat who took pity on her. Taking the gift, she went off up the road threatening those that refused her that they would have cause to remember their meanness. There would be a story to be told soon, she threatened.

The Streedagh fishermen lodged in the same house as the Donegal men. When they went out to shoot their nets the next evening a Donegal boatman donned a sweater belonging to a man named Bruen from Streedagh, Co. Sligo by mistake: a happy mistake that would later save his life.

The next day, Friday the 12th of February 1813 started normally like any other day. A rosy dawn broke bright and clear over the Bluestack Mountains and Barnes Gap as the fishing fleet finished

The mankeeper: 'Burns, whether by fire or scalding water, were cured by people who had acquired the remedy from licking the belly of the 'mankeeper' (newt) three times while saying certain prayers.'

Gerry Cribbin of Tooraree, Ballyhaunis, Co. Mayo, holding the animal legs that, hung in the byre, acted as a preventative against disease, primarily blackleg. (Inset animal leg in place)

Blessing with stones at *Tobar na hAingeal*, Co Donegal on the eve of Bealtaine. 'Each stone is put 3 times around the head, arms, legs and body…'

Elfstones: 'The cure was to dip the elf-stones, which had been gathered in the fields and carefully kept over the years, in the water of a three-mearing drain, to treat the sick animal.' (average size 2cm across)

Ballintrillick stone head: 'for relief from toothache go there at midnight, kiss the stone head three times and ask to be cured.'

The Fairy Rock at *Dostann na Bríona*. At this threshold was left a 'wee crockery jar of whiskey' as a votive offering for favours received and ailments cured.

Mass at Staíd Abbey, Streedagh, Co. Sligo celebrated in 2007 over 400 years after the building was destroyed by the English under Sir Richard Bingham. Spanish Armada survivor Francesco de Cuellar in seeking refuge there found twelve of his comrades 'hanging within the Church'.

'The placing of a curse on their oppressor was the only resort left to the persecuted…' Here tenants carry an effigy of their landlord Col. J. O'Callaghan, Bodyke, Co. Clare, July 1887. The sign reads: 'Praise the Lord for the tyrants hand was paralysed.'
Photo: Courtesy Nat. Library of Ireland

Last moments of the U.S. freighter *The Flying Enterprise* January 10th 1952
(Inset: Capt. Kurt Carlsen)

Hulk of the trawler *Gulmarin* driven aground on the Leitrim coastline in 1989 in the same spot where the Idwal was wrecked in 1868.

A small version of the Zulu lugger c.1910. Photo: Courtesy of Ulster Museum
(Inset: Greencastle yawl)

John Rogers in his Greencastle yawl the St. Patrick 1959:
…*Farewell to you, Kildoney lads, and them that pull an oar,*
A lug-sail set, or haul a net, from the Point to Mullaghmore ;
From Killybegs to bold Slieve-League, that ocean-mountain steep,
Six hundred yards in air aloft, six hundred in the deep…
(The Winding Banks of Erne, Wiliam Allingham)   Photo: Courtesy of Padraic Callery

The author gathering *sleabhac* at *Leac na Meala*

Mick McGrath harvesting periwinkles on the shore.

Rafts of *feamain dubh* (*Ascophyllum Nodosum*) at Kinvara, Co. Galway. *Feamain dubh* is harvested along the shore, built into rafts or *cleimín* at low water and poled to land when the tide fills.

End of an era: Picking herring from gill nets aboard the *Kilkilogue* at Mullaghmore Harbour, Co. Sligo c1982.

their night's work. Preparing for her revenge the old woman watched from a cabin window on a hill overlooking the bay. She filled a milk pan with water. Placing a bowl to float on it she asked her daughter to keep watch from the window and tell her what she observed. Staring at the pan with a fierce concentration she splashed the water about in the vessel causing the bowl to dance about.

'What do you see,' she asked the girl,

'Oh a breeze has sprung up, mother,' she replied

The old woman continued to agitate the water.

'What do you see now', she asked.

'The breeze has turned into a gale,' the daughter replied. 'The men are reefing the sails. I think the boats are in danger.'

The witch, for that is what villagers later claimed she was, continued to cast her spell while questioning her daughter:

'What do you see now? Are they still afloat?'

'Yes, mother, but some have sunk and others are trying to make it to land.'

She continued to dash the water about in the pan until the girl told her mother she could no longer see the boats. Crying out in delight Biddy ceased her stirring. The storm abated but the fleet was completely wrecked. Some were swamped at sea, others driven ashore and broken to matchwood on the rocks. The old woman's words had come true. Most of the Donegal boats were lost and their crews drowned — except for the man who was wearing the Streedagh man's jumper! He came safe from the old woman's curse and lived to tell the story.

It's a remarkable tale, but is it true? Newspapers of the day do indeed carry accounts of the tragedy. It happened at Bruckless, Co. Donegal on Feb. 12th, 1813. According to these reports, no accurate estimate of casualties is known. The approximation of forty-five men drowned, leaving 'thirty widows and one hundred and two orphans,' is regarded as conservative.

How was the sinking accomplished? Was it a natural disaster, a vindictive act precipitated by the old woman's curse, or a mere coincidence? Who can say? We do know that tales of ship-sinking witches are nothing new. Fifteen hundred years ago the Greek play 'Alexander Romance' described a similar ship-sinking rite performed by the Egyptian pharaoh Nectanebus!

When news of the Bruckless drowning reached Mullaghmore, families feared the worst. Villagers lined the shore by day anxiously scanning the sea for sight of the absent boat. They lit fires on the cliffs at night to guide the fishermen home. Hoping against hope that their men would return they prayed for a miracle but steeled themselves for a tragedy.

We can only imagine the jubilation of the watchers when word eventually went out that the Mullagh boat was sighted beating against the wind and waves as she made her way home. Hard pressed and storm driven the crew couldn't make it to the harbour and were forced instead to head for shelter. They beached their craft at *Trágh Ghearr* south west of the peninsula under where Classiebawn Castle now stands.

Watchers lining the shore counted seven men on the boat as she sped along the coast behind the hill known as *Cnoc na Taoisigh*. They were relieved to see that everyone was safe, but surprised to see a woman sitting at the helm alongside the skipper on the 'stern taft'. This created a stir and a few giggles. Maybe one of the men had met a woman over there and there might be a wedding in the offing. When they went to help the fishermen draw their boat to safety they found only seven men, but no woman. The fishermen shook their heads when they were asked about the stranger on board. No, there were only seven men on the boat at any time. There must be some mistake. No, there was no woman. The inquirers shook their heads in disbelief. Sure hadn't the whole village seen her clearly with their own eyes as the boat went by the headland!

Following the incident, villagers discussing the strange visitation speculated that the woman they saw in the boat was the spirit of a dead relation guiding the fishermen safely home from certain death — or perhaps a woman of the *sidhe* who took the boat and crew under her protection.

The mystery of the extra passenger has not been decisively resolved to this day. The individuals who witnessed the incident are long dead, the details barnacled and dimmed with time. The story itself just barely survived. It was passed on by the recollection of one old man of the village; passed on faintly through a lucky conjunction and a fortuitous 'echo-harbouring shell' of recall.

The story has another curious twist! Some time after this extraordinary deliverance, the fishermen and their relations made a pilgrimage to a place known locally as *Dostann na Bríona* near Classiebawn Castle. There they left a 'wee crockery jar of whiskey' as an offering and a thanksgiving. Why? To the uninitiated *Doras na Briona* looks like nothing more than an outcrop of rock. To whom or what then was the offering made? There was no church there, nor even a ruin, so we can be certain it was to no Christian God!

'People used to go to the Fairy Rock, or *Dostann na Bríona* as some call it, for lots of reasons with bottles of whiskey and poteen,' Thomas Boyle told me. 'It was a regular thing long 'go. The offering was left at a small round hole at the top of the rock in thanksgiving for some blessing or at set times like Hallowe'en. They used to pour the whiskey on the ground or break the bottle and let the liquid soak into the soil. It's not so long ago that Mountbatten's wife, Edwina Ashley, used to write notes and leave them there in a crack in the rock! She must have believed in them too.'

'Quare things happened there,' Thomas went on. 'There was this fella one time delivering a keg of poteen to Classiebawn. 'Twas a nice day and he was taking his time. When he was going up past the Fairy Rock he sauntered over to the door to have a close look at it. He got an awful hop when he heard a voice saying to him:

"Pssshth! Give us a drop of what you have there in the keg with you."

He jumped back and made for Classiebawn as quick as he could. Before he got to the top of the avenue the keg fell and smashed on the ground!'

As it spilled away he swore he heard a voice hissing:
'Good enough for him!'

Thomas took a long pull out of his pipe. Looking at me quietly for a minute he ventured an opinion: 'Don't ye think he'd be as well if he had to take the cork off it and give them a taste. I'm thinking if he had, he'd still have had the poteen!'

In olden times when poteen was brewed it was customary to give a drop to the fairies. 'Oh! You couldn't run it at all if ye didn't do that,' Michael Heraughty of Inishmurray Island declared. 'We used to say, "*Seo chugaibh! Seo chubaibh! Seo chugaibh!*" and tell them if they hadn't their fill they could come to the keg and drink more. Welcome to them all!'

The fairies will have their due!

If you stand today on the Fairy Rock and look to the east, ten miles off, in a clear line of sight across sea and valley, a similar place of worship exists. It is marked by a standing stone in a hill fort above the old churchyard in Finner, Co. Donegal. Those seeking victory before a hurling match on nearby Tullan Strand brought their liquor to *Flaithbheartach's* Stone in a jar or bottle. The vessel was broken on the pillar, 'spilling the liquor on it and letting it flow down the sides of it, on the ground. And happy is the party of *camán* players or any other match, who is there first and pours the libation; they are sure to win the day...'[13]

Offerings left at the Fairy Rock and many other such places throughout Ireland were commonplace at one time. Perhaps in this concluding detail we have precious gems buried in an old story. Were these tributes on a hillside, fragmentary remnants of ancient worship — sacrificial offerings made in witching spots at

[13] Donegal Vindicator, June 8 1889, quoted in 'Where Erne and Drowes Meet the Sea', P. Gallagher, p34

a time now lost to memory? Did our ancestors gather at these special places long ago with the sorcerers of the Tuatha de Danann or maybe with Druid priests?

There are things on this earth that are not given to us to understand: 'A little north of the town of Sligo, on the southern side of Benbulben, some hundreds of feet above the plain,' Yeats once wrote, 'is a small white square on the limestone. No mortal has ever touched it with his hand, no sheep or goat has ever grazed grass beside it. In the middle of the night it swings open, and the unearthly troop rushes out. All night the gay rabble sweep to and fro across the land…. Sometimes a new-wed bride or a new-born baby goes with them into the mountain….'

I have never seen Yeats' door in Benbulben, nor have I looked for it — but I know the place where the fairies come and go in Mullaghmore. Did Yeats *sidhe* visit their kin at Mullaghmore's Fairy Rock? I'm sure they did! Perhaps they still do. Like me, the great poet was a believer. He laid store by Socrates judgment when he was giving a learned opinion about a nymph of the Illisus: *'To be curious about that which is not my business, while I am still in ignorance of my own self, would be ridiculous: the common opinion is enough for me'.*

We may never resolve the mystery of the Fairy Rock. A brooding hill, it stands today silent and enigmatic, guarding its secrets. Perhaps in an age of unbelief we don't deserve to be brought further into ancient knowledge. The old people have pointed out to us the portal where the *Sidhe* come and go. Let it rest so until such time as the wheel turns and the old gods return to their ancient places.

No one relates these stories around the fireside anymore. Indeed it would be difficult now to find a hearth fire — and television has replaced the storytellers. But if you want to touch the magic, and you look hard enough, and if you are very lucky, you may still find old men and women who will tell you of the Bruckless Disaster and the mysterious spirit woman who vanished when her work was done.

To the incredulous they will show the fairy footprints embedded in the rocks by the seashore at *Tragh Ghearr* under Classiebawn. They will tell you all about the ship sinking witch and transport you on enchanted wings to an age when life was simpler; a time when things were possible that are now inconceivable. If you are favoured by fortune and find such a magic moment, treasure it. All you have to do is sit, and listen, and believe.

> '...*Faeries, come take me out of this dull world,*
> *For I would ride with you upon the wind*
> *Run on top of the dishevelled tide*
> *And dance upon the Mountains like a flame.*'

W.B. Yeats *The Land of Hearts Desire*

PART 2

BANISH MISFORTUNE

✳

7

THE PIPER OF THE FIREPLACE

…The poetry of earth is ceasing never;
On a lone winter evening, when the frost
Has wrought a silence, from the stove there shrills
The cricket's song, in warmth increasing ever,
And seems, to one in drowsiness half lost,
The grasshopper's among some grassy hills…

John Keats *On the Grasshopper and Cricket*

In the first half of the last century country kitchens were spartan affairs: such luxuries as couches, armchairs or carpets were a long way off. At one end of the kitchen a big open fireplace commanded the room. Providing heat for cooking and warmth, light for reading and, on long winter nights, inspiration for story-tellers, it was the working centre and life-giving heart of farm and family. The 'flame that never died' was covered over with ashes every night and kindled back to life every morning. The very fabric of farm and family, leisure and living, work and play was woven around it.

Raking was an important function in homes with an open fire. This was done by smothering, or 'smooring', the live coals with ashes on going to bed at night and placing a few sods around. Some placed a pot lid on top to deflect downdraughts from the chimney. Raking preserved live coals until morning when a new fire was lit from the embers. In this way the hearth fire was kept alive for generations, as long as the house stood, without ever being extinguished. On moving house sufficient coals were taken to start the new fire thus preserving the continuity. The tongs was used to make the sign of the cross on the fire before retiring following which it was left lying across in front of the coals to preserve the house. Flame would not pass iron!

When the sole surviving member of a family passed away thoughtful neighbours took home a live coal from the last fire in the deceased's home and raked it with their own. In this way the dead family's fire was perpetuated and integrated with a living fire thereby entwining the spirit of both families. A true eternal flame![14]

Central heating may now be more efficient and toil free, but gone is the friendly face of the welcoming hearth where warmth, light and laughter came, hurrying after the leaping flame. It was the very stuff of inspiration for *seanchaidhe* or storyteller. 'Beautiful it is to see the strengthening gleam,' the American writer, Nathaniel Hawthorne wrote, 'the deepening light that casts distinct shadows of the human figure, the table and the high-backed chairs upon the opposite wall, and as twilight comes on, replenishes the room with living radiance and makes life all rose colour. Afar, the wayfarer discerns the flickering flame as it dances on the windows and hails it as a beacon light of humanity, reminding him in his cold and lonely path that the world is not all snow and solitude and desolation.'

Beside the hearth, nestled in the alcove, was the 'pooch' or 'hag' bed reserved for the man and woman of the house. 'The old people used to spend the night in that beside the fire, with an old stump of a clay pipe going,' Tomás O'Crohan of the Blaskets recalled, 'or two pipes if there were two of them living, and smoking away; he would have a wisp of straw for a pipe lighter. A good fire of fine turf smouldered away till morning; every time they woke they took a light from the fire and puffed at the pipe... The old man would stretch across to give her a light from the wisp; then the smoke from the two old pipes would drift up the chimney and you would imagine that the couple's bed was a steamship

---

[14] Professor Seamus O Cathain in his book *Festival of Brigid*, observes that in some places the raking was accompanied by a prayer:

> Coiglimse an tine seo mar a choiglionns cach,
> Brid ina bun agus Muire ina barr;
> Dha aingle deag d'aingle na ngrast,
> Ag cumhdach mo thi-sa go la.

(I rake this fire like everyone else, Brigit below it with Mary on top; twelve angels of the angels of the graces, protecting my house till dawn.)

as they puffed away in full blast...'

The old man's choice of pipe lighter may seem irrelevant, but hidden in such details there is much that tells us of a lifestyle where frugality was, not just a necessity but a virtue as well. In modern times no one thinks twice about purchasing a box of matches or a newspaper. Yet not so long ago these commonplace items bordered on the luxurious. No one cracked a match if they were sitting by the fire; they used a piece of paper or an ember to light their pipe or cigarette. The fire itself was raked at night and was rekindled from the live cinders in the morning. Newspapers were rarely bought and passed on to neighbours when they were read.

Chairs there were some, but not many. Alongside the hag bed was a 'furm' or long stool that could seat four or more people; on the other side of the fireplace another 'furm' or a plain wooden chair. Set into the wall at the opposite end of the room was an open dresser, displaying cups, saucers, bowls, delft basins, and big ironstone dinner plates. A cantilevered length of wooden trim at the top concealed the farmer's small store of tools: builders' level, bicycle pump, pincers, hoof-parer for the ass and some few other essentials. Underneath, two compartments closed off by curtains or doors served as storage areas, and often doubled as nests for broody hens or geese.

One of my informants, Hugh Pat G——, remembered the kitchen nests: 'There was two foot long recesses in the bottom of the walls for geese,' he recalled. 'It's there at Regans yet. There's where they used to hatch the geese. I saw them in our house. We closed them off one time the station Mass was coming. The space under the dresser was used for nesting too. I knew a brood of goslings to be hatched in our house at home. The goose died an' would ye believe it, the gander went in an' hatched the eggs — that will happen. Did ye know that if ye pet the goslings, take them away from the goose, ye could go to the bog an' the whole lot'd folly ye. They're very aisy petted, an' pigs the same.'

Hugh remembered the 'long kitchen' too that fell into disuse in the early 1900s. 'I saw Martin Frank Gallaghers up there when the kitchen was a big long room with the cows tied in at the lower end. There was no partition between the kitchen and where the cows were. The sink was the lower side of the door as ye came in and 'tying' for 3 or 4 cows. It was very warm, they couldn't rear the children without this heat. The heat of the cow with the insulation of the thatch kept them cosy and healthy. All the houses was like that at one time. There was an outshot bed in the kitchen too, that was for the oul' fella an' oul' lassie to sleep in. It was grand and warm beside the kitchen fire.'

Me: 'Wasn't the outshot bed a very practical thing Hugh!'

'Of course it was! But d'ye see what happened was grandeur passed out the people. I'm tellin' ye now! Grandeur passed out the people!'

'Didn't some houses have settle beds?'

'That's right, they had that in lots of places. Two people or two or three childer could sleep in it at night an' it folded up to make a lovely seat in the daytime. The mattress that was used in the settle bed was made in the same way as the mat that was used for the ass and creels. An' on top of that was a feather tick. When I was a-rearin' every bed had a feather tick. An' the blankets'd be all made in Lisbellaw in Fermanagh or in Foxford below in Mayo. The back door would be lined with these straw mats too for the winter months against the storm. Sheaves of straw in behind it for insulation, but this made a nice front, the mat hanging down. In cold weather when there'd be heavy frost or snow there'd be one for each window too, hung on the inside.'

A sturdy wooden kitchen table, an oil lamp to illuminate, and a Sacred Heart picture to preserve and protect, rounded off the list of items indispensable to a simple but functional working kitchen. Above all, smoke-blackened and ancient, bog-oak timbers and wattles rose in a sturdy pyramid to support sods covered by thatch on the outside.

Just as much a part of this setting as the people, the fowl or the furniture was the 'piper of the fireplace': the cricket. While much is written about the disappearance of the corncrake from the fields and meadows of Ireland, the humble cricket, once a resident of almost every rural hearth has, unnoticed and unsung, all but vanished from the Irish countryside. They were imbedded in folklore and farm life. Where people and warmth was found there you would find crickets. Indeed it's almost unfair to label them as insects, they seemed to have so many human traits.

Warm sunny days enticed them out to the ditches and hedgerows for a brief fling in the summer sun, but they always returned to the security and warmth of the kitchen with the onset of winter.

'They sit up on me shoulder and sing to me at dusk in the evening,' Jimmy Flynn said. 'They never did a hate wrong to me in the world, they make lovely music in the summer, all night long, like on a French fiddle[15]. Sometimes that's a sign of rain coming. They're a lucky thing to have in the house, the priest'll tell ye that!'

Jimmy, born and reared in Laghey Barr, a small townland near Kiltyclogher in Co. Leitrim knew everything anyone needed to know about crickets. Gentle guardian and protector of a thriving brood of these musical insects, Jimmy lived alone in a house where there was always a welcoming fire — for cricket or neighbour. One evening, as we sat listening for the sound, he pointed to a cluster of newborns under a turf:

'In the month of May, if ye see them flying out the door it's a rale sign of good weather,' he said.

Crickets evoked only two emotions in people: a great affection, or intense dislike. Both of these sentiments were firmly held in our home. The disparity of feeling was because of their deeply rooted, and ambiguous, place in Irish country lore which held that they brought either good or bad luck, depending on your point of view.

[15] Mouth organ or harmonica

On a quiet harvest evening long ago our kitchen was a scene of domestic bliss and tranquillity: my father sitting on one side of the fire by the outshot bed reading the Irish Press; my mother on the other side, knitting an Aran jumper, her busy needles working in unison, click-clacking an unceasing rhythm. Books spread out on the kitchen table, I sat with ink-stained fingers and furrowed brow hurrying to finish homework as the evening light paled away. In the fireplace, yellow fingers of flame licked up along the smoke-blackened cast-iron kettle. Simmering contentedly it sat over the flames exhaling little puffs of steamy breath. The blaze, chattering as it burned, chased the waning daylight sending ghostly shadows leaping and dancing along the whitewashed walls.

Suddenly the peace was shattered. My father whipped the glasses off his nose, dropped the newspaper to his lap with a noisy rustle, and sat bolt upright.

'What's that I heard', he barked, every nerve alert, his ear cocked at the space behind the kitchen bed.

'I don't know,' my mother replied, 'I didn't hear anything.'

I could hear it then, a barely distinguishable, gentle chirping sound.

'Well swear t'Jasus, if it isn't a bloody cricket,' he howled.

Jumping to his feet he reached for the kettle.

'What's wrong with ye, can't ye leave the poor thing alone. What harm is it doing to you?' my mother protested.

'They're a bloody curse about any house,' my father swore as he poked the coals savagely and waited impatiently for the kettle to come to a full boil.

Like a terrier searching for a rat he poked and peered into cracks high up and low down trying to determine exactly where the sound was coming from. The cricket, seeming to sense the danger, ceased calling. But it was too late. The kettle boiled and, pulling back the bedclothes, my father aimed the steaming spout at the crack between the headboard and wall, a likely hiding place.

The domestic tranquillity well and truly shattered now, my mother dropped her knitting and jumped up to come to a more militant defence of the little creature. Her voice rising, she approached him angrily.

'It's not right for you, they're a lucky thing to have about the house — ye'll have no luck for what ye're at!'

But it was no use, bad luck or good luck could come later; right now it was all the same to my father as he persevered with the scalding hot water despite my mother's fierce opposition. After a while the chirping was heard no more and crickets, not surprisingly, never ventured near our house ever again.

In later years I was told of other more genteel ways of sorting out the intruder, apparently unknown to Petie Mc Gowan. An old lady recalled a similar visit to her house by exploring crickets many years before. Her husband, a born diplomat, had the ideal answer. His remedy was to bang the tongs three times on the hob and say:

'If ye came for good luck — stay, but if ye came for bad luck — go.'

Two days later, she told me, they were all gone.

The speed with which the many beliefs surrounding crickets were established in Ireland is quite remarkable considering their relatively recent arrival here. *Acheta domestica*, to give it its Latin name, is a creature of warm climes and not, as many believe, a native of Ireland. Some accounts say it was accidentally introduced into Ireland from the semi-tropical Mediterranean in the 17th century. The little fugitives, in search of the warmth of their native land, found comfort here only around the warm hearth and lime-washed chimney corners.

Others claim they arrived here much earlier, in the 13th century, brought here from the 'Holy Land' by returning Crusaders. Rarely seen in the daytime, these latter day crusaders came to life at night, moving out from their secret hiding places by the fire to forage. In many houses food was left out for them at 'set times', Halloween, Christmas and so on. Americans might ring the exterminator if crickets were heard in their home on Christmas Day but in Ireland, in a tradition of augury going back to the time of the Druids, it was said:

> Tuar maith don athblían
> Na píobairí teallaigh a chloisteál Lá Nodhlaig
> (It is a good omen for the coming year
> to hear crickets on Christmas Day.)

That crickets would be a good omen is hinted at by the Irish word for cricket, *'píobaire an teallaigh,'* which literally means 'the piper of the fireplace.' Another word for cricket is *'píobaire gríosí'* which translates to 'the piper of the hot ashes'. It is, therefore, understandable to believe that it is good luck to have a band of insect pipers around your hearth celebrating the birth of the Saviour.

This musical serenade, produced by the male in an effort to attract a mate, is made by rubbing a grooved ridge on one wing against the front edge of the other, a kind of built in fiddle. In ancient China these little musicians were so highly prized that ladies of the Imperial Court kept them in gold cages close to their beds to be lulled asleep by the sound.

'Good Heavens' exclaimed the 19th century English novelist, Charles Reade, on hearing the sound, 'how it chirped. Its shrill, sharp, piercing voice resounded through the house, and seemed to twinkle in the outer darkness like a star. There was an indescribable little trill and tremble in it, at its loudest, which suggested its being carried off its legs and made to leap again by its own intense enthusiasm.'

'A chattering wise and sweet' is how W.B. Yeats described it.

Although primarily house-dwellers, crickets were open to exploring new frontiers and often took up residence in outhouses used for boiling potatoes for the pigs. 'You could hear them singing every night,' Marty Nicholson told me. 'In the house they used to sing to each other; when one would start, the other would stop.' This could be good news for some — bad for others. Many didn't like to hear them singing at all, as the saying went: 'they sang for joy or for sorrow'.

The unique melody could be heard in almost every country home in Ireland until the rapid modernisation of housing, which began in the early 1960's, destroyed its habitat. Wellspring of imagination for adults it is most unusual nowadays to find an open hearth with a blazing fire where children too can gather around imagining castles and palaces in the dancing flames. That is why we hear the cricket's song no more, for he loved to make his home where the flames leap. The replacement of flag-stone floors with concrete; sod lined, thatched roofs with slate, and lime walls with inhospitable cement left no comfort or a place for the little creatures to hide.

At the turn of the 21st century there were only two hearths left within a fifty-mile radius of my village where their chirping song was still heard. Now there are none. Long ago people held that their departure from a home foretold a death, and indeed much has died since those nimble creatures departed the chimney side. In these rushed times it is a rare and pleasant thing indeed to hear their song.

Jimmy Flynn has passed on to his heavenly reward, but cherished memories of the pleasant evenings I spent in his company, he on one side of the fire and I on the other, remain. His had been a life of hard manual labour: tending a small farm; carting and drawing stones for Leitrim County Council; cutting meadows for neighbouring farmers. Working early and late his wages were small and on retirement his pension a modest one. However his needs were few and his pleasures simple and many; he was one of the most contented people I have ever known.

Sadly, Jimmy's time, and that of the crickets, had come. His musical charges have found no new advocate. Deprived of his affection and the warmth of the hearth fire, the demise of his much-loved creatures was inevitable.

As we chatted time stood still. It seemed then, that at least in Jimmy's home, nothing would ever change:

'There was a buck of a fella down here one evening,' he scolded, 'he'd be wan of the McGurrins, he scalded a couple of the crickets there with boiling water — he didn't like them. He had a good blue suit on him that night but if he did, it wasn't for long, because when he went home the crickets got at it and he couldn't put it on in the morning with holes — and that was in his own house!

Y'know,' he explained to me, 'if you came here in the morning when I'd be putting down the fire there'd be lots of them — and they're there as long as I mind. They have as much right to be here as I have. They have their ways with them, but there's one thing you have to remember: they won't bother you if you don't bother them.'

Jimmy was right. Although my father wasn't intimidated by the prospect, it was generally considered very unlucky to kill a cricket. Retribution was inevitable. The very least you could expect in the matter of reprisal was to have holes cut in your socks! The man with the blue suit was unlucky, and unwise. 'Maybe they went a bit too far with him,' Jimmy laughed, 'but y'know, it was good enough for him, one lesson bought is as good as two taught!'

Patrick O'Sullivan in his book, *Irish Legends of Animals and Birds*, illustrating the lore that if the killing were unintentional no harm would come to the perpetrator, tells us that: 'Crickets, like their human overlords, were very partial to wakes and funerals. When one of their number died they came together and had a grand wake, and it was surely at these wakes that it was determined whether the passing of the dearly departed had been the result of natural causes or murderous intent on the part of some ill-bred human.'

In Brittany, France, crickets in a house meant prosperity for the family. Believing that the cricket's song foretold happiness and richness a little rhyme was recited to invite them in:

Guersillon
Viens dans ma maison
Chante ta petite chanson
Et répands ta bénédiction;

(Cricket
Come to my house
Sing your little song
And shed your benediction).

They had a reputation as prognosticators as well: In *Ille et Vilaine*, Brittany, our Celtic cousins believed it was a bad omen if the cricket fell silent: it foretold a death. If a person died the cricket would not sing until the remains left the house. In *Côtes du nord* if the master of the house died, the cricket kept a silent vigil for six months.

Mickey Mc Groarty of Selacis in Co.Donegal believed 'there was something unnatural about them. Me father and mother used to feed them in the house but I didn't like them. Every time I'd get a chance of them coming out about the corner I'd hit one with my cap and kill it. In the finish-up anyway I discovered they were getting the better of me — every morning I'd rise there was nine or ten holes in my stockings. The oul' people at the time told me what was the cause of it.'

'Back in 1922 me father was in the hospital in Donegal Town,' he continued, 'it was diabetes he had, an' they had no cure for it that time. My mother an' everyone in the house remarked that for a week before he died ye could see the crickets jumping about the house, going out the door an' jumping across the street an' going into the stone ditch. From that day to this I never found a cricket in the house!'[16]

Some cats had a strange liking for a meal of crickets — but cats that ate them never thrived: 'they never amounted to more than skin and bones'. One man who remembered them in his own home spoke to me about a neighbour who had a houseful of them:

'There was crickets here when I came here first, but they left. They were here in swarms. A fella came here to see them. He was doing a bit of writing. He heard there was crickets here. The house was full of them. Honest to God he sat there till five o'clock in the morning an' he never seen a cricket, not so much as one. I often heard that if you went into a house to see crickets that ye wouldn't see them.

There was another house beside us at home, Hargadons, a man that was living on his own, an' there was often twenty of them fly-ing about the house at the one time at night. He used to have a job to keep them out of the tay when he was eating, they were that plentiful. He had two cats and they used to be eating them. They were sitting one each side of the fire an' every big cricket'd come up they'd grab him an' ye could find them crunching them between their teeth. Their two sides was agin other. Cats that ate crickets never thrived!'

'He's like a cat'd be eatin' crickets' was once a derogatory coun-try expression regarding a person who looked sickly or skinny. The saying, like so many of the time, would not be understood now.

While many people looked fondly on crickets no one wanted that other insect, once common in homes, the cockroach. Simi-lar in some ways, but larger, they were universally loathed. Every-one had them, but no one liked to admit it as they were deemed a sign of poor housekeeping. Often confused with crickets these

---

[16] Bees too empathized with humans. They liked to be told if their master passed away. Wise keepers did so and placed a mourning band on the hive, following which they would cease humming for six months. If no one bothered to tell them they would find out and die — of sorrow it was believed. It is also said that when a hive was shared between two men, and a quarrel developed, the bees often flew away in search of a happier home.

ugly, hump-backed, armour plated, shiny-black, scurrying creatures, lurked out of sight in dark corners in their menacing multitudes. They looked quite unlike the equally detestable, smaller
brown cockroach experienced for the first time by many an Irish
emigrant in the dingy tenements of New York. The only habit
the Irish variety had in common with their American cousins was
that they emerged from their hiding places after lights out
spreading across the floors as they scavenged for food.

The crunchy sound and squishy feel when they were trodden
underfoot was nauseating and at its stomach-churning worst
when experienced in bare feet. Especially spooky was the
scratching noise they made in old houses when they crawled between the lime plaster and the wallpaper. They were after a meal
of the flour and water paste commonly used as an adhesive then.
In the dead of night many a ghost was born of the sound!

All attempts to exterminate cockroaches were doomed to failure. One of the best-known and more successful methods was
based on their fondness for Guinness. When a small drop was
left in a bottle they climbed in after it, drank their fill, but then
couldn't climb out.

The end came quickly, and finally, for them with the advent of
the insecticide, D.D.T. It proved a more lethal and less humane
coup de grace than expiring at the bottom of a porter bottle in a
drunken and, we may suppose, a happy stupor!

'And cockroaches existed, are they in Grange yet, I wonder?'

Hugh Pat G—— was a retired farmer in his late eighties. We
had been chatting late into the night and he looked at me in-
quisitively now: 'It used to be an awful village with them, a terror,
M——'s public house was alive with them. They used to come
out at night. They were mad after the track of porther. The
floor'd be walking with them an' soon as ye shone the light they
were gone. D.D.T killed them off, but maybe concrete floors and
cement plaster had a lot to do with it too.' 'Crickets was different,' he went on. 'There was a lot of superstition attached to

them.'

Hugh Pat was not a superstitious man and, although a mine of information on all aspects of country lore, could not be drawn on poltergeists, haunted houses or those other populous creatures of the dark: fairies, ghosts and banshees. Nevertheless he gave in, albeit reluctantly, that superstitions regarding crickets were popularly held beliefs about which he had some doubts.

'Our house at home was full of crickets,' he recalled. 'I remember when me father died. I was nine years old. A couple of days before he died the crickets left. There was no crickets in the house for years after that, not for years and years, then they came back, until my aunt died and then they left again!

I often heard about that since, and I saw it then, but I don't believe it. It happened! I don't believe it, it's just superstition — but I saw it happen in me own house just the same!'

For good, or bad, it's too late now to save the humble cricket, that's even if anyone wanted to. There are no European grants, selected hearths or nature preserves set aside for them. No more will they come to our houses, sing their song and spread their benediction.

8

THE GENTLEMAN THAT PAID THE RENT

Daintiness and good living won't make a man of ye!

Patrick Doherty

The well-stocked chimney corner sported a string of salt herring, especially in seaside homes, but pride of all, happy was the home that had a flitch of bacon hung from a rafter. It defined the affluent family, fed them in the cold and hungry winter days. Perverse winds that sometimes blew guaranteed billows of turf-smoke from a cantankerous chimney that cured and sweetened the meat.

The well-known maxim of the pig as 'the gentleman that pays the rent' speaks volumes regarding the importance of the humble pig to small farmers in Ireland at one time. Having its origins in south-east Asia it was probably one of the first farm animals to be brought to Ireland and comprises almost one third of all animal bones found at Early Christian sites.

Said to have conferred the monks tonsure on St. Patrick, St. Martin of Tours, born in AD 316, was a convert to Christianity and the son of an officer in the Roman army. In honour of the conferral our patron saint is said to have initiated the custom of presenting a pig for sacrifice to every monk and nun on the eve of Martin's feast.

A ninth century Irish text, the *Críth Gablach*, describes the death of a fat pig as one of the 'three deaths which are better than life' illustrating the importance of the pig to early Irish farming. Its significance became even more critical in later times when having a pig to sell in order to pay the rent meant the difference between eviction to the roadside or survival for another year.

The 'pig in the parlour' was once a well-known stereotype of Ireland. Mr. and Mrs. Hall visited here between 1841 and 1852 and wrote several books on their travels. 'Why shouldn't the pig come into the parlour?' they noted. 'Sure who has a better right to it than the gentleman that pays the rent? The peasant rarely saves — or has the power to save — money for the landlord. The pig is sold at the proper season, and the rent is paid.'

Pigs were easy to feed and therefore a popular choice for smallholders with little land. They were not fussy eaters and could be reared on leftovers, scraps and waste potatoes. In addition it was a good forager, fond of hunting expeditions and 'hoking' in the ground for roots and other edibles. Up to late medieval times, when the land was still heavily wooded, they fattened on the fruit of the beech, oak, chestnut and whitethorn, known as mast. According to Bríd Mahon in *Land of Milk and Honey* it gave the meat a delicious flavour and was so enjoyed by pigs that, 'they would travel great distances did they get but the scent'. Pigs have such a keen sense of smell that in Europe they have been used for centuries to help find mature truffles.

Some farmers fed oats to the pig for some weeks prior to the killing in the belief that 'it firmed up the meat'. Not everyone agreed. Others believed rye grain or even barley was superior. Far ahead of his time in 'lateral thinking' Hugh Pat G——'s logic was irrefutable:

'You know yourself there's always rats in the stooks when you're taking the corn in out of the field at the end of the year. Well! Did you ever notice that ye'll not have a lot of trouble catching and killin' the rat comes out of the rye or barley stack. The best greyhound in the town wouldn't catch the rat comes out of the oats!'

The Congested Districts Board was set up in 1891 to improve the condition of the people of the west of Ireland and to encourage better methods of fishing, farming, etc. A survey of living conditions carried out by them in 1895 in Baltimore, Co. Cork recommended the introduction of Yorkshire boars to improve the stock. In South Conemara Major Gaskell found the breeding sows to be of, 'a nondescript, long nosed, lank-sided sort'. Major Ruttledge-Fair found only, 'great bony, long legged beasts, and very difficult to fatten,' in Clifden, Co. Galway. The introduction of Yorkshire boars was recommended in all cases.

The Sligo surveyor, F.G. Townsend Gahan, gave favourable mention to the quality of pigs in that district. They were 'the staple stock of the smaller farmers and on their good or bad sale largely depends their profit or loss each year,' he reported. Each farmer had two or three pigs and, 'unlike the farmers of county Donegal', they sold two lots each year. He advocated the acquisition of two or three boars by the board. These were to be made available at two or three centres in the district as, 'at present sows have to be taken two or three miles for service.

One of these 'service centres' was at Mc Clures in Tawley, Co. Leitrim. There are still some who can recall sows being brought there on foot, from as far away as Kinlough, a distance of three to four miles. George Siggins of Co. Sligo, who also kept a boar in the 1940s, charged fifteen shillings to service a sow. The bulls service, by comparison cost only five shillings. The higher charge for the boar was because the yield was greater from a sow, which bore several young, as opposed to a cow that had only one calf. One piglet recovered the cost of service. The pig also had a shorter gestation of sixteen weeks compared to nine months for a cow. Subsidies of ten shillings were provided by the County Committee of Agriculture, which reduced the cost to the farmer to five shillings.

Because of the sow's weight it was difficult to transport her by cart to the prospective groom. Even if an owner could get the bulky animal on to the vehicle they preferred to drive them, as horses have an intrinsic fear and dislike of pigs. They will shy away or even bolt if they meet them on the road; the smell of a pig, or of the blood at the place where they are slaughtered, will panic a horse and make it uncontrollable.

Driving the pig to fair or boar was no easy matter. It was an independent creature with very definite ideas of behaviour that befitted its dignity. Contrary to other farm animals it refused to either lead or follow if a rope was placed around its neck. They consented to be driven only when the cord was attached to their hind foot:

> "You may push me,
> You may shuv
> But I'm hanged
> If I'll be druv!"

After the first trip to the boar, the sow needed no more convincing: 'The funny thing about a pig, when the sow would come in heat and ye brought her once, after that she'd nearly go over herself.'

Most animals, even cows, can swim, even if they have never been near water in their life. Embedded in myth and folklore and supported by Samuel Taylor Coleridge's *The Devil's Thoughts* is the belief that pigs 'cut their throat when they swim':

> "Down the river did glide, with wind and with tide,
> A pig with vast celerity;
> And the Devil looked wise as he saw how the while
> It cut its own throat. "There!" quoth he with a smile,
> "Goes England's commercial prosperity."

Happily for the pigs of the world there are many recorded events where pigs did actually swim, none more famously than a pig named 'Tirpitz' that was left behind when the *Dresden* was torpedoed off the coast of South America in March 1915. 'Tirpitz' made his way above deck to swim clear of the sinking ship where he was spotted an hour later by a petty officer aboard HMS *Glasgow* and rescued. The ship's company awarded 'Tirpitz' the Iron

Cross for sticking to his ship and he became a great pet on board. His end, as with most pigs of the world, was not a happy one: he lived on for some years until he was auctioned for charity — as pork — raising £1,785 for the Red Cross. His head smiles down today from a wall of the Imperial War Museum in London with a forgiving and, given the circumstances of his demise, a surprisingly benevolent expression.

'Bacon is the only animal food they eat,' the Congested Districts Board report tells us, 'and that seldom, fish occasionally, and, perhaps once or twice a year a fowl or two. Eggs are more eaten in the summer, as in the winter they are a more marketable commodity. Oatbread is sometimes eaten, but not largely. For dinner, cabbage and dripping is a favourite dish. Breakfast is generally taken at eight o'clock and consists of tea and bread, sometimes porridge. Dinner about 1 p.m., consisting of potatoes mainly which they eat with buttermilk, and cabbage and dripping sometimes. When the potatoes are finished, bread and tea, and sometimes porridge are taken.'

Those who lived on our offshore islands had a prized alternative to pork: seals! A barrel of seal meat was the equivalent of a barrel of pork. Tomás Ó Crohan of the Blaskets recalled that, in the olden days, seals were a great resource for the people, 'both the skin and the meat, and you could get a pack of meal for one of them. And anywhere you liked to take a lump of seals flesh you could get the same weight of pork for it.'

When seal meat went out of favour during his lifetime it continued to be hunted for its oil that was used as fuel for the island lamps. Seal oil is still in use today and is highly regarded by athletes for application as a rub for muscle disorders and sprains. It is also used in the treatment of similar ailments in horses and is held to be very effective as an emollient for burns.

Seals, that provided a rich food source for Blasket islanders, were not hunted on Inishmurray island off the Sligo coast. The residents believed they were souls from Purgatory doing penance on earth. 'If you caught a young seal and took it with you,' Michael Heraughty of Inishmurray said, 'the old mother seal would follow you. They'd try to take the young one off you and they'll cry like a human.' Tory islanders too didn't like to kill seals as they thought they were a kind of people. When they were struck 'they cried like a woman.'

Martin Heraughty of Inishmurray once broke with island tradition, shot a seal and left the body on a rock by the shore. When he went to collect it some time after he found that someone had skinned it and taken the pelt. Martin swore he would leave no stone unturned till he found the culprit. His son, Paddy, was a child in the womb then.

Some time afterwards Mrs. Heraughty went to the back of the house in the early morning to throw out waste water. In the dawn's half-light she was startled to see an unusual shape at this familiar place. It was the sealskin. Hastening inside she told her mother of the fright she just had. 'Quick! Touch yourself where it won't be seen,' was the surprising response Lifting her skirt she touched her finger to the inside calf of her leg. It seems the old woman was familiar with the belief that if a pregnant woman got a fright, the baby would have a birthmark.

Dr. Paddy Heraughty was that child. He was in his nineties when he told me of the incident and revealed that he was indeed born with a birthmark on the inside calf of his leg!!

On the Beara peninsula in Co. Cork *báirneachs* (limpets) were known as 'bacon of the sea'. It was a custom to pick them on St. Patrick's Day and put one at each corner of the house, and in the loft. This brought good luck to the fishing for the rest of the year. In famine times, and for long after, limpets, periwinkles and other such seaside foods kept many a person alive who, without them, would have died of hunger. Today obesity is the latest health threat to a new affluent generation who can have anything they want whenever they want it.

It is interesting to note that a recent article in *New Scientist* mag-

azine states that the best thing to do to extend lifespan is to eat
very little of anything. The life span of mice, rats and other lab-
oratory animals have been significantly extended by giving them
a restricted diet that cuts calories while still providing all the nutrients needed for a healthy life. Animals on reduced diets lived
20 to 30 percent longer than those on a normal diet. There have
been similar results with tests on humans.

Reflecting on changing fashions in diet during his lifetime,
Tomás Ó Crohan remarked that people had lost the knowledge
of what was best for them to eat, 'for men that ate that kind of
food were twice as good as the men of today. The poor people of
the countryside were accustomed to say that they fancied they
would live as long as the eagle if they but had the food of the Dingle people. But the fact is that the eaters of good meat are in the
grave this long time, while those who lived on starvation diet are
still alive and kicking.'

Far away from the Blaskets people who never heard of Tomás,
would agree wholeheartedly with his logic. Science now also
bears testimony to his wisdom. Patrick Doherty of Glenade, Co.
Leitrim told me of remarkable men in his locality who were
'brought up in dire poverty. They're the strongest men going
now,' he said, 'Daintiness and good living won't make a man of
ye!'

9

THE SLAUGHTER

*The blood of dawn was being poured over the hills, and of that other
blood we only thought of how much black pudding it would make.*

Patrick Kavanagh *The Green Fool*

Although the pig's importance to the welfare of the farm was
vital, its end was brutal. In towns and villages up and down the
country, October, or Martinmas in early November, was the
favourite month for the kill. A job as important as this could not
be undertaken lightly. It was overlaid with centuries of experience and custom. Some would undertake the task only in a
month in which the letter R featured. Others believed that if the
killing took place with a waning moon the bacon would 'shrink in
the boil'. Better to do it with a waxing moon when the bacon
would 'swell in the boil.' The moon governed and foretold many
things; its quiet but inexorable force affects all: the weather,
when to plant potatoes, the butchering of pigs, the tides, even the
birth of a child; madness too rises with a full moon.

Up to the middle of the 20th century, when man lived in harmony with nature, every village and townland had its resident
experts who were called upon when the day of butchering arrived. Brian Barry, Denis 'Mick' Gilmartin or Andrew Murtagh
travelled the townlands of North Sligo with the tools of their
trade — heavy hammers and a selection of sharp knives and
scrapers.

On Inishmurray island Jack Donlon and Frank Herrity did the
job. Paddy Rooney killed pigs in Kinlough and in every townland as far as Grange ten miles away. In 1936 the charge for
killing and preparing the animal was two shillings and sixpence.
'Davey Patterson from Mountcharles used to kill the pigs for us,'
Mickey Mc Groarty, of Selacis in Co. Donegal, told me. 'He might

have six or seven pigs to kill in the townland — he got a drop of tay and a shilling for killing the pig and cleaning it and leaving it ready.'

Joe Kane of Ederney, Co. Fermanagh, who had participated at many such events, remembered it clearly: The animal selected for the slaughter was fasted from the night before and word sent to the local 'butcher' that his services were required. These travelling executioners usually made sure there were several killings in an area before they took to the road.

Many country butchers would slaughter a pig or a calf as a matter of course, but not a kid goat. They didn't like to kill it as the sound it made when expiring was like a child crying. In some instances when a goat was killed it was not done in the usual way, but smothered. The anus was stuffed and the mouth and nostrils kept closed with both hands until the animal died of asphyxiation.[17] Could this be a surviving remnant of what was once a symbolic ritual sacrifice? Or could the piteous cry be the real reason why it was suffocated? We will probably never know.

On the appointed morning of execution the gate was opened and the starving pig came galloping out, tail a-curl, eyes aglow, expecting to be welcomed and fed as usual. But, on this morning, its last, there was no food and no friends to meet him. Instead, one man with a sledgehammer and another with a 'cleek', a length of iron rod with a handle at one end and a sharp hook at the other, stood in his path.

When the pig charged out the 'cleek' was shoved into its mouth. A sharp twist and a pull sent the hook out through the pig's jaw, 'then ye pulled the pig on out an' it was roaring an' pullin' agin ye. The other man got round behind it with the sixteen-pound sledge and put a foot on each side of it; you'd still be pulling the pig as hard as ye could out from him with the cleek.

The man with the sledge brought it down on the skull with a mighty blow; then the pig started to tremble and it fell down and you jumped on it as quick as ye could, turned it over and pulled

17 Irish Folklore Collection, Ms. 462, p328.

its feet up and back. The man doing the butchering had a big long blade of a knife. He drove that down into the heart and the blood spewed up all 'round. Later when ye opened the pig ye'd see where the big rip was in the heart.

Well, anyway, the blood spewed up an' ye wouldn't want to be aisy scarred (scared) by watching blood. It'd be roaring for all it was worth; every time it squealed it sent out a big splash of blood an' if that came be yer face ye had to still houl' on until it was bled out. They'd be done bleeding in about ten minutes. Sometimes they'd be cut in the throat instead of the heart. Ye had this sharp knife and ye would drive it down and split his throat from the neck to the bottom of the throat — then the blood would come all out in a gush. Every time it roared there went a big splash of blood out through this cut an' when it quit roaring the blood quit coming then.'

Certainly a grim end for 'the gentleman that paid the rent'!

The pig was sometimes strapped to an ass or horse cart before it was 'stuck in the neck'. The cart was then heeled up, so as to hang the pig to capture the blood in a vessel suspended underneath. This was made into blood pudding. 'Black' and 'white' blood puddings are, even yet, popular items at an Irish breakfast.

Different men had their own favourite system of killing. One of the less successful methods was to flip the pig over on its back and hold it down while another cut the throat and main arteries. The pig was then released and allowed to run about until it fell from loss of blood. This method of slaughter came to an abrupt end in at least one village when the pig escaped through a hole in the fence and took off down the road. Screaming as it went, it trailed a crimson path before collapsing half a mile away.

In Miltown Malbay, Co. Clare, J.J. Malone of Miltown Malbay explained how the killing was done with the crank of a bicycle.

'You'd come along with a big hammer,' he explained, 'and drive it into the pigs forehead. If he didn't die with the first shot you might have to have another go at him. The poor divil of a pig'd be kicking an' tearing around for awhile till he died. Put him up on the table then to draw the blood and scald the skin when you'd get him quietened down. You'd drive the knife right into the heart. The blood had to be drawn quick before he was right dead. You'd stick him right away while he'd be giving the last kicks. Blood thickens awful quick you know. Once he dies the blood starts to thicken right away.

There was another yoke for killing like a hatchet on one side and a big spike on the other. Ye'd draw down on the pig's forehead and sink the spike into his skull but you'd want to have a great shot. You might be going to draw and the pig'd pull away. It was easy to miss.'

The man holding the pig had to hold it firmly in position — and have great trust in the accuracy of the man with the sledge. One such helper noticed that the fellow about to deliver the blow was cross-eyed. Becoming increasingly worried, as he couldn't be certain whether the man was looking at the pig or at him, exclaimed:

'D'you hit where ye look?'

Letting go of the pig he retreated to a safer corner!

Tommy Kelly of Moygowna, Co. Mayo didn't use a cleek: 'You had a short piece of rope, called a 'booteen' that you put in on his foremost feet, one on one foot and one on the other, about six inches between them. You'd have two, or maybe three men there to help. You'd pull on the ropes then sideways to trip him and put him on his back. You put the long rope you had on the back feet up through the booteen on the front feet and tighten it all up to pull the four feet together and put a knot on it. Ye had the pig in a ball then. You got a two cwt heavy jute sack then, that you'd get manure or Clarendo in, and pull it in over the pig's head. He'd be squealing like hell. The man that was going to kill him then knelt down, one knee on each side of the pigs head to hold him steady. He wouldn't be squealing so much then.

You got a basin of water then and a cloth and you washed him where you were going to stick him five or six inches from the head near the foremost legs. You'd make three inches of a cut then with the pig knife. Then you turned the edge of the knife back for the foremost feet. You had a man or a woman there with a basin or small vessel for taking the blood. Ye drove the knife in then with the edge facing the foremost feet, right in for the heart. The blood gushed out and in two minutes the pig was dead. Oatmeal was mixed through the blood immediately to keep it from clotting.'

Some pig butchers tied only three legs. One was left free for the pig to struggle, the better to pump out all the blood.

There are some who can still recall going to school when the killing was in progress. Hating the screams that echoed through the village on that day they held her hands over their ears and went the long way around through the fields to escape the sound. In *The Farm by Lough Gur* Mary Fogarty recalled that her father arranged for the killing to take place when she was in class. Living on a farm one learnt early that death is a part of life, she said. Some animals are great screamers, her father considered, and this could not be taken as a measure of pain.

John Montague the poet remembered the annual sacrifice in verse. 'The walls of the farmyard still hold that scream, are built around it,' he wrote.

But how could it be otherwise? Death was not sanitized. It left blood on your hands. The whole community witnessed the price of a pound of flesh. From birth to death sustenance was interwoven. The humane killer and other sophisticated methods of slaughter are modern concepts. It extends from pigs to men on death row, and washes away spilled blood.

Many readers will recoil in shock from the descriptions of the killing. The Bard of Inishkeen, Patrick Kavanagh took part in the ritual and saw beauty in it. A memorable morning he called it: 'The blood of dawn was being poured over the hills, and of that other blood we only thought of how much black pudding it would make. Our talk had the romantic beauty of reality. We were as close to life and death as we could be.'

Following the slaying came the preparation of the pig for table. It was dipped, one end at a time, in a big tub of boiling water before shaving and cleaning:

'When he'd be near dead ye'd have to help lift one end of it into the boiling water,' Mickey Mc Groarty told me. 'The man doing the butchering'd get a sharp scraper and keep scraping and shaving till he'd have most of the hair and skin off it. Then ye pulled that end of the pig out and ye put in the other end. The pig'd be three and a half to four cwt. so it was an awkward load and ye had to watch and not burn yerself as the water was scalding hot.

When ye had the second end of it done ye lifted it out onto a kitchen table, four feet in the air and him on his back. Ye'd put a wee prop of wood on each side of him and have a pot of boiling water beside you. Everyone took a lick then. Ye'd have two fellas with good sharp knives and a wee tin cup. Ye'd lift the boiling water with the cup out of the pot and ye'd put the hot water on the pig an' shave away the same as ye were shavin' your own face — ye'd turn him over then and finish the job on the other side. It had to be done in a hurry while the pig was still warm.'

Another method of cleaning the carcase was to put down a cartful of straw, place the pig on it and set it alight. In this way scorching rather than scraping removed the hairs.[18] When cleaning was completed the pig was hung from a beam or collar tie for dismembering.

'Nothing was wasted but the squeal', said Mickey when he described for me the cutting up of the pig. Then laughing he added: 'some say that wasn't wasted either, it was turned into rock music!'

'Ye'd rip him, ye'd open him on the back and get out the wee gut and rowl it around in your hand and keep pulling away and cleaning it as you went — it could be anything up to twenty or thirty yards long — it would nearly make a marking line for a

---

[18] Country women used a similar system on killing a hen or turkey. When the feathers were plucked they lit newspapers and held the fowl over the flames as a final cleansing.

field. That was the intestine; ye cleaned that out and put the hot water through it, and if there was a butcher about ye'd take it in and give it to him to use for jackets for the sausages.'

Little of the animal was wasted: Bacon and hams were hung in the chimney for smoking. Neighbours delighted in gifts of ribs, liver and offal. Mary Deery remembered getting one such package in the 1950's from Loughlins in Cliffoney, Co. Sligo: 'It was like getting a Christmas present,' she recalled. The head was a delicacy and quartered before boiling. Fat was rendered into lard for the breakfast or dinner fry. Even the feet were boiled for the tasty picking that could be had from them.

These trotters or 'crubeens' may not have been everyone's fancy but they had, and still have, their own gourmet following.

Some housewives filled the intestine with a mixture of the blood, milk, lard, oatmeal, onions and spices to season. Boiled for thirty minutes this 'black pudding' was unrivalled by any factory or butcher for richness, flavour and taste.

Mary Fogarty's mother supervised the curing and smoking of the bacon: 'From pig's heads she made brawn or collared head, and from the cheeks came what we called French hams which, cured and smoked were good to eat with chicken... We made collared head by boiling part of the head almost to a jelly, then chopped the meat very small and spiced it with pepper, allspice and finely ground nutmeg. After that we put it in a mould that opened on a hinge and was kept shut with a skewer. When it was set and turned out of the shape it made a dish fit for a king!'

Author, John McGahern, certainly wouldn't agree! In his book *Memoir* he recalls his father's fondness for pig's head as just another example of the old man's mean nature. Perhaps John was too harsh in his many criticisms of a man who had lived through harder times than he, who was beyond the grave and unable to speak in his own defense!

'The lights (lungs) wasn't used, that was thrown away,' Mickey went on.

He could see it all now in his mind's eye as if it was yesterday. His face was alive with boyish delight and his heart happy to have a listener with whom he could re-live those rich and exciting days again. He recalled every detail:

'The heart was kept, but ye had to cut a wee piece off near the tail of it that was supposed to be bad for ye. The liver was big and it was delicious to eat. The bladder was tough, it was blown up like a balloon and given to the children for a football. The legs were cut off then at the first joint and used for soup. When the pig was going to the market for sale, the farmer kept the giblets, heart, liver, and so on. I often used to get it for my dinner and I wish I could get it from that day to this — it was lovely, ye couldn't get the bate of it. I wish I could get it every day. There's nothing going today like it anyway, bacon an' all, I'll tell ye that.'

The poisonous piece, mentioned by Mickey, was known elsewhere too. 'A piece near the heart, the gall, the "bigall" they used to call it, was not used,' J.J. Malone explained. 'If it was busted the mate could go bad. If you touched it with the knife t'would spread all over and you could never save that bit of the bacon. Yellow stuff that was inside in it. It was the same thing if you were cleaning out a hen or a chicken. You had to be careful of that. It's close to the liver. It's awful poisonous.'

The 'bigall' was the gallbladder. The yellow matter was bile. Today's butchers too must be careful not to rupture this organ as it permanently stains the meat if not washed off immediately.

Although as children we were kept well away from the harrowing scene, the pig's bladder was a prized possession when all was over. Inflated to hardness while still fresh and dried in the chimney corner it served as a very fine football.

The bladder had other uses: When John Millington Synge visited Kerry in 1905 a local man told him of the French trawlers that fished close to the shore there in April and May who sometimes came ashore to drink and barter goods. 'If you give them a few eggs, or maybe nine or ten little cabbage plants,' the local said, 'they'll give you as much of it [hay-tobacco] as would fill your hat. Then we get a pound of our own tobacco,' he explained, 'and mix the two of them together, and put them away in a pigs blad-der — it's the way we keep our tobacco — and we have enough with that lot for the whole winter.'

After cleaning, the pig was hung from a beam over wooden vats. It was taken down after twelve hours or so, quartered and sorted into various cuts before salting. Coarse salt that came in oblong blocks was broken into granules and the meat rolled in it. Sometimes the salt was put over the hearth fire in an oven 'to redden', and a pinch of nitre mixed in. Sugar was used to sweeten the meat and saltpetre rubbed into the bones. The salt was rubbed in by hand. Some used a flagstone to exert extra pres-sure. The pork was then placed in a barrel or wooden tea chest, the bottom given a coating of salt and each successive layer treated with salt in the same way until the barrel or chest was full.

Brine was made by adding salt to a bucket of water in which a potato was placed. The salinity was just right when the potato floated. Brine and meat was then covered over and left to pickle for nine days, sometimes longer, following which the meat was taken out and hung by 'cleeks' from a beam or rafter, or in the chimney to be cured by the turf smoke. From there it was taken to the table as needed. Some left the remainder in the brine or pickle for up to twelve months.

According to George Sheridan of Blacklion, Co. Cavan, it was sometimes hung unsalted in the chimney to let the smoke do the preserving. As a young man George worked for Terry Tammy Threa Cathal of Glangevlin, an old man who lived alone. At din-nertime he remembered Terry taking down a side of bacon from the chimney that had, 'an inch deep of soot on it'. He scraped some of it off, cut a few slices and fried them on the pan: 'That was the nicest bacon I ever ate,' George recalled. 'Neither the ap-pearance of it, or for that matter the cook, looked appetising, but it tasted well and that's all I wanted.'

'The meat was lovely when it was fresh,' J.J. Malone remembered. 'It was a custom to give it out to the neighbours. I remember one time you'd have up to twenty houses to go to with pork. If ye weren't careful you'd hardly have a bit for yourself. But then you'd get it all back from them when they killed their own pig.

As time went on there was more and more getting out of killing pigs because of all the new regulations and you'd hardly get a piece of meat from anyone. When I was a young fella we'd be fighting to get to the houses for the few coppers they'd give you when you came.'

Insulated today from reality, we now dine with clear conscience on pounds of approved and packaged flesh, never valuing the spent life, never witnessing the slaughter. Adulterated with life threatening dioxins the insipid taste is the price we pay now for antibiotic saturated, saline impregnated, profit-motivated, mass production.

The pig is no more the centre of the hearth or the economy. Intensive farming is in, but is the end result a better product? Pigs live now on factory farms in overcrowded indoor conditions. The majority of breeding sows spend repeated pregnancies in close confinement, either in narrow stalls or tethered. The piglets, which are reared for meat, are usually kept in barren concrete pens. The scale and concentration of pig rearing creates serious environmental problems. Intensive pig farming with its attendant slurry disposal problems has caused some of the most serious pollution for which Irish agriculture has been responsible.

Packed into small and smaller spaces, pumped with antibiotics when they are alive, and with brine when they are slaughtered, the result is an insipid imitation of the pork and bacon of former times. The cry is for organic pig rearing. All small farms were organic farms well into the 20th century — only the term hadn't been invented then. Perhaps the answer lies in the experience of the past; look back and see the future. Isn't it interesting now to witness foreigners with broken English teaching young Irish people how to farm organically. All the more so when we realise that all they have to do is go to the old farmers of the locality who, with their local knowledge, could teach without charge more than these 'experts' will ever know. How much we have lost in one generation!

There's no doubt about it, the gentleman that paid the rent has fallen on hard times. But are things about to change? Are pigs, so long a benefactor to the human species, about to come to our rescue again? Arthur Young reported in 1778 that: 'Hogs are kept in such numbers that the little towns and villages of Ireland swarm with them; pigs and children bask and roll about, and often resemble one another so much, that it is necessary to look twice before the *human face divine* is confessed. I believe there are more pigs in Mitchellstown than human beings…'

Mr. Young's observation may be fanciful, but, conversely, scientists today know that the pig heart is very similar to the human's in anatomy, size and function. Its ready availability in most parts of the world, along with its similarities to the human heart, make porcine hearts a real possibility for transplanting into humans. At present someone needing a heart transplant must wait until a donor dies. With today's technology it is only a matter of time before pig heart transplants are made possible through animal cloning. No one has to die, and the terminally ill receive a heart.

Perhaps the unassuming pig will yet be rehabilitated and restored again to the pride of place he formerly held on Irish farms and in Irish hearts!

10

CAVEAT EMPTOR

*Always remember, a cat looks down on man, a dog looks up to man, but a
pig will look man right in the eye and see his equal.*

Winston Churchill

Twice a year the industrious farmer had a pig or two ready to sell.
Farmers who kept a sow reared the young for two months after
they were farrowed. Then they were ready for market and
brought there in canvas-covered carts for sale to the small farmers of the countryside. These 'banbhs' or 'cart pigs', as they were
called, were bought and sold on special fair days all over the
country:

'About May day ye'd be buying the young ones for 'round about
two pound each.' Mickey Mc Groarty told me. 'There'd come in
a lorry into Donegal Town from 'way through Barnes Gap, and
ass and horse carts with young pigs in them from all over. Ye'd
hear the squeals of that poor wee crathur when ye'd catch it by
the tail and pull it out — it'd go to the heart in ye, ye know. After
ye made the bargain ye'd put them in a bag with a hole in the side
of it to let their heads out for air, throw them on the cart and take
them home.'

There's a story, I don't know how true it is, about a man from
Mountcharles who brought his four pigs to the Donegal market.
When he sold one he went home for the next one. When he sold
that one he returned for the other, and so on. Observing this
strange behaviour, a neighbour asked him why he didn't bring all
the pigs in together.

'You're wasting your time' he said.

'Arrah, what's the matter with you' was the farmer's response.
'Sure what's time to a pig!'

'Matchmaking Fair' on 29th of June in Grange, Co. Sligo was a favourite time to sell. The better off farmers bought as many as four or five young pigs, sold the pick of the crop for the Christmas market and kept the 'rawneen' or runt. This little fellow was let out through the fields to improve and then killed and salted for the family.

The Brehon law of *Cáin Lánamna* decreed that the task of rearing the runt was the responsibility of the farmer's wife. These early laws, which evidently thought of every eventuality, provided for the wife to get two thirds of the meat in the event of a divorce! These rawneens often became pets and, as pets often do, became an annoyance when they got older. The main law text on farming, *Bretha Comaithchesa* refers specifically to the trespasses of a pet pig. Also, 'pet pigs which follow everybody' were recognised as a nuisance and the behaviour classified as a specific offence.

Maggie McGowan often went to the Matchmaking Fair in Grange. 'It was a holyday of obligation and it was known as Ladies Day as well,' she said. 'The women'd all go to Mass, and then go out in their style up one side of the street and down the other and many a match was settled at it! The father'd be there an' maybe the son wanted a wife. There'd be some neighbour's daughter going up the street and maybe her father and his father might agree that she was a fine girl and maybe they could do worse than get together. They might discuss if she had money and how much land the son was coming into.

We used to enjoy ourselves an' dress up for the 29th June. It was a great day! Me father never missed it, he used to buy four or five *banbhs* (piglets) there and fatten them up till Christmas. He'd sell them then and hold on to the rawneen to keep us in bacon for the rest of the year.'

Ladies Day sounds old-fashioned and quaint, doesn't it? Until you realize that, while the simple fair of the country village is no more, the ladies still parade on Ladies Day at the Galway Races in Ireland or at Ascot in England! There the women display in their finest hats, latest fashions and peacock best to be gazed upon by the admiring throng — and we may be sure that many a 'match' is made there too!

That scholar of homespun philosophy, Hugh Pat G——, put matchmaking, and the dowries that went with them, firmly into today's context: 'Matches are being made yet,' he said. 'You'll see people and they'll put their family into a certain social circle, or send them to such and such a college so they'll meet the right match. You'll see a fella with a big job and he gets a lassie with a big job — it's on a bigger scale today only they don't call it a match or a dowry. Long ago they'd settle for ten or twenty quid or a hundred, it's an awful lot more than that now but just a cuter way of doing things. *I can see no difference!*'

Perhaps Hugh Pat, if he was still with us, might comment in his unique way on one important difference: 'Matches' and marriages today do not seem to last as long as they did in the 'bad' old days!

Buying and selling, whether pigs or any other commodity is hardly ever a simple affair. *Caveat emptor*, let the buyer beware, was good advice then and still is. Countrymen had to be ever vigilant against 'tanglers' and unscrupulous dealers. Tales of duplicitous dealings and outright fraud were commonplace. A fool and his money were soon parted:

'There was these fellas used to come into this country, name of Murphys, an' they were always buying a few cattle or pigs or anything at all. This family, Kellys we'll call them, lived down the road from me, six of them in the house and them all over six feet, big harmless people, if they had anything to sell it was the Murphy's that would buy it."

The story is a true one, the parties involved have living relations so the storyteller must remain anonymous. The names of the principals too have been changed:

'The Murphy's had this young sow that they couldn't get in *banbhs*, a "cunyeen" they call them, a pet pig. This pet pig'd lie at the fire an' ramble 'round the house. On a good day she had a habit of going out and tumbling in the ash pit where they kept the ashes — because it was warm I suppose. Into the house then an' they couldn't keep her out from under the kitchen bed.

Anyway these two Murphys were doing their rounds one day. John, the man of the house went to the door. After chatting awhile he said to the 'tangler':

"Mr. Murphy," he says, "I think we'll sell her."

They made the bargain, a pound or two, and the Murphy's brought away the little sow.

"Mr. Murphy," John says, as they were leaving, "Would there be any chance, in your travels, you might get another one for me?"

The Murphy's was fit for anything and they saw a chance. They brought the pig home anyway, washed her an' shaved her and cleaned her up grand. After a week or so they came back to the house and brought the pig with them. The Kellys, all six of them, came out round the cart when they saw the lovely little pig:

"Ah, begod she's grand." they agreed.

Paid him for the pig. As soon as they left, where did she make for except into the house an' in under the bed!

Says Jack to Paddy, "D'ye know," he says, "She has the same oul' tricks as the last one. Let her out till we see what she does. Sure enough the minute she got outside the door she made straight for the ash pit!"

That happened! Them Murphy's over there in C—— were noted tanglers. Ye couldn't be up to them. Buyin' an' sellin', and it wasn't always straight.'

When the *banbhs* were brought home from the fair they were fed with spuds and Indian meal mixed with cabbage and buttermilk or skim milk from the creamery, 'the best feeding ever a pig got'. This 'cart pig' then was fattened and ready for market in about four months.

Sales were held once a month at which live as well as butchered pigs were sold. Prices in the late 1930's ranged from four pounds ten shillings to five pounds for dead weight Grade 2 meat (pigs under 2 cwt.). Five or six pounds each was paid for Grade 1 (over 2 cwt).

In North Sligo horse and ass carts left the villages of Cliffoney, Mullaghmore and Grange before six in the morning to reach the monthly Ballyshannon market, a distance of about twelve miles, before nine in the morning. Horse or ass had to be well shod for such a long journey. On the main roads animals would have had to negotiate unfamiliar tarmacadam surfaces.

In the early years of the 20th century roads were rough and stony. When word went out in the 1930s that the highways were going to be 'tarred' there was uproar. This madness had to be stopped. 'Call this progress?' men exclaimed. How were asses and horses, with their iron shod feet, going to negotiate these new smooth surfaces? Going up or down hills was going to be impossible. Committees were formed, pickets manned, objections lodged and blows struck. Protesters went out at night with picks and shovels to lift the paving that had been laid by Council workmen the previous day.

Cars? What cars? Roads everywhere teemed with ass and horse carts then. Cars were few and far between. The row went on until the Co. Councils backed down. Tarring was delayed for years and when it eventually arrived a band of only eight feet in the centre was covered. A strip either side was left for horse and ass drawn traffic. On the rare occasions when two cars met, one or the other had to get off the tarred strip in the middle to allow the other to pass. In the wintertime 'frost nails' were developed that when driven into the iron shoes gave draught animals a grip on the new, smooth, and sometimes icy surfaces.

Most pigs brought to market were slaughtered, washed, shaved and cleaned prior to sale. 'Donegal market was on a Friday or Saturday once a month or so,' Mickey Mc Groarty told me. 'Ye'd see whole lines of carts going out there. Ye'd put nice clean straw on the bed of the cart and a couple of "Clarendo" bags under it. Ye'd put two pigs, if ye had them, on their backs on top of this with their feet up in the air. That was some weight, nine cwt.or so, across *Alty Dubh* on the way to Donegal Town. There was no room to sit on the cart unless ye sat on the cross head and of course ye wouldn't do that only where the going was easy.

The pigs were hung up at the square, ye know the Diamond there in the middle of town, the night before. Ye'd split the hind leg, put a rope through it, drive a steel pin or a pin of a harrow or something like that into a bush and get two or three fellows to help you hang him up with a 'cleek' onto the bush. Ye cut two sticks then about ten inches long and drove one in on each side of the pig. That was to open it up and let the air in.

The next morning when the buyers came, it was a sight with these pigs all lined up, and the whole side of the street lined with carts. Some sold their pigs live, and some of the carts might have two or three pigs in them. The butcher shops used to buy them, there was not many butchers killing cattle at that time. It was mostly bacon the country people ate. It's all changed now! Ye had to buy two or three pound at a time; there were no slices then. In my young days, when we hadn't our own bacon, my grandfather used to buy bacon for sixpence a pound. Ye had to cut that down with a sharp knife. Ye could cut a big thick slice and it would stand up before ye like a scone o' bread. The stuff that's going now is more like the sides of wellingtons than a slice of bacon!'

At horse, cattle or pig fair, buying and selling centred around that passionate and entertaining street theatre called 'makin' the bargain'. Theatre it might be but it had a very serious purpose. On the successful outcome of this battle of the gladiators depended the financial success or failure of the farmer's year. For those of us who stood with livestock at village fairs and markets it would be more accurate to compare the encounter to the unequal struggle between the lions and the Christians — the 'lions' being the streetwise dealers who attended every fair all year long up and down the country while the inexperienced 'Christians' had only one or two outings a year.

The setting for the play was a congested, dung-covered street in the middle of the village or town thronged with hundreds of shouting, hurrying people, frightened, skittering animals, braying asses, bawling cows, grunting, squealing pigs. Cant men (stall-holders) displayed their wares near the bottom of the town selling second-hand clothes, cabbage plants, pig troughs, baskets, creels, *cruitches* (ass saddles for panniers) corn-cures and hosts of other commodities for the farming community. Island men spread old sailcloths on the ground and spilled stacks of sun-baked, salt-cured fish on to the canvas for inspection by eager buyers. Above the cacophonous multitude, surreal and sweet, might come the voice of Moll Ruaisg singing the *Rose of Mooncoin* or some other popular ballad of the day:

> '...*How sweet 'tis to roam by the sunny Suir stream*
> *And hear the doves coo 'neath the morning's sunbeam*
> *Where the thrush and the robin their sweet notes entwine*
> *On the banks of the Suir that flows down by Mooncoin...*'

As she sang she offered the ballad papers to the passing curious at a penny each.

The seething mass shoved and jostled; stout sticks of pliable ash poked and beat cattle, pigs or asses into orderly, adjacent bunches at doors, windows and sidewalls of shops and houses. Occasionally a crazed beast ran amok to crash through a plate glass window or in one instance through a hall and halfway up the stairs before it capsized back onto the street.

Often the first act of the play commenced a few days before the fair day itself. It boded well for a brisk fair and good demand when the cattle jobbers, in our case Francie Joe Mc Gowan or Tim Gonigle, showed up in their pony and trap prior to the fair day. They walked the fields these shrewd dealers or 'stick men', slapping their wellingtons authoritatively with mean ash plants as they strode with purposeful strides across the farmers' lands. Stopping to poke and prod stirk, calf or pig, they evaluated their worth with narrowed eyes and artful glances before making a bid — which the seller promptly refused, no matter how good he thought it was.

It augured well when they stalked the fair-bound farmers a mile or two out the road on a fair morning, making tentative offers. Plucking the early apple perhaps, but it was much too early in the day to accept, no matter how good the offer, everyone knew that the buyer would give more than his first offer and the seller take less than his first demand. Still, the farmer never knew where lay the middle ground and money could be made or lost in a bad deal. If a bargain could be struck in the field or road it would save a walk of maybe ten or more miles to the fair. More often than not the farmer, having had his confidence raised by this early show of interest, would take his chances at the fair where there might be more buyers and better prices. These were uncertain times and it was not unusual for a farmer to stand all day at the fair, often in pouring rain with not enough in his pocket to buy a dinner, not reach the offer that was made in the field or on the road, and be forced to walk his product the weary, disappointing miles back home again. There would be gloom in the house when he got there; the bill in the shop would remain unpaid and the shopkeepers wait for a better day

Born in 1916, Charlie Ferris of Omagh in Co. Tyrone had stood at many a fair and knew all about the unwritten protocols pertaining to a successful deal:

'There was wild fights in them fairs y'know. If a man'd go in buying no one else'd dare come in. If ye were seen even signing to the man that was selling the buyer'd turn the ash plant in his hand, and a big head on it like yer fist. That was enough. No one wanted trouble. The daler (dealer) didn't want another man bidding against him. It was counted a terrible crime to come in on another man's dale. They carried this big ash plant an' it was root grown, it'd knock yer brains out. Once they turned the stick they'd lay it on one another ye know. Then ye'd have to get them stopped.

The jobber's was them runnin' men, they had nothing, they were only jobbers, they scouted out the good deals. The dalin' man, he was the man with the money. Horse dalers never wore a collar and tie, they wore a wee light scarf around the neck. It was done with a loop with the ends pushed in under the waistcoat. That's how they knew each other: the horse dalers knot.

Cattle, horses or pigs, when the bargain was made they'd start then to argue over the 'luck's penny'. The buyer'd be claiming five bob maybe for luck penny. That was the money given so the buyer'd have luck with the purchase. If that wasn't agreed it would break the deal. The seller'd say: 'I'll not be bound!'

Some kept this money safe until the animal was sold again. Anyway, they'd argue and argue and get near the price an' then maybe a third party'd come in to seal the dale. He'd get the two men's hands together:

'It'll be this way, no other way', an' he'd hold his hand up in the air like that:

'Are ye satisfied?'

The seller would say "I'm not" and there'd have to be another bit of a preamble again. The third man would then make the price:

'Ye'll not break my word' and slap the hands together. (Charlie demonstrates the third man holding the other two men's hands together and bringing his own hand down on top, sometimes spitting on it)

The third man'd say then:

'Lave it to himself, he's a dacent man.'

He'd have to bring them in then an' go through the hand slapping again. Often times then when the dale was done the two or three men, no matter how heated the argument, they'd go away and drink the luck penny. Sometimes they'd argue more over the price of the luck penny than the price of the baste. It was a rare sight too! They always spat on the luck penny. They'd spit on the dale too. From once the two hands was put together, the dale made and the third hand came down, the dale was made, the bargain was sealed.

Sheep, cattle and pig dalers were only an infant class compared to the horse dalers! The horse dalers were the biggest rascals ever. They were different altogether. Things they would have done! Tyrone men would go to Ballinasloe Horse Fair or to Mullingar to buy horses. The dalers then would come up on the train and leave a man to take the horses up home. He'd ride on one horse and have maybe eight others in a file behind him tied together with a rope. He'd have to ride that horse all the way from Ballinasloe to Tyrone, y'know and that'd be seventy or eighty miles on bad roads.

There was this man near us, George Russell, a horse daler. This neighbour man bought a mare off him, he'd be a nifty customer too y'know, he didn't like to part with money. He kept the horse a week an' y'know, probably got work out of him for that week. He was thinking then that he maybe paid too much. He thought and thought about it and didn't he come down to Russell early this morning to see if he could get his money back and take the horse back.

He came to the door an' he says to the woman that answered it: 'Is the boss in?'

That time women were never called the boss.

She says, 'Naw'.

The dealer that time, if there was no fairs he wouldn't rise till dinnertime, y'see. George lived in a thatched house that was a storey and a half an' he put his head out the upper window an' he says:

'What's wrong, Paddy?'

'The horse is no good to me George, ye have to take him back and give me back me money!'

George says, 'Ye'll not get yer money back 'cause I haven't it. It's spent. And my guarantee is the length of the 'helker' (halter).'

In other words there was no guarantee once the horse was released from the dealers rope to the buyers. When he sold that was that. Paddy thought he'd get one over on George and he was ready for this scenario. He had taken a cutthroat razor in a scabbard with him. He pulled out the razor an' he says:

'If ye don't take back the horse, George, an give me back me money I'll cut me throat here on yer doorstep!'

George, who knew he hadn't a damn bit notion of cutting his throat, says back to him:

'Ye'll cut none o' yer throat there on my steps an' make a mess. Go on over to the dunghill an' cut yer throat!'

And that was the end of that!

THE NINEPENNY PIG

My father an' mother were Irish,
An' I am Irish too:
They bought a wee pig for ninepence,
An' it was Irish too;
But it wouldn't grow a big pig,
An' Da took it away
Tae Lisnalinchey Market
All on a Market Day

An' whin he took the crathur
Away from us I sighed,
It knowed, itself, 'twas goin',
For, oh, it squealed an' cried,
But every time I'd coax Da
Tae keep it, he'd say: "No!
The Fairy folk hae charmed it,
An' it'll niver grow."

It strunted an' it grunted,
But Da driv it away,
Tae Lisnalinchy Market
All on a Market day.
An' up there comes a show-man —
Who'd come for the May fair —
An' says he, tae Da, says he: "Sir,
What is it ye hae there?"

An' Da says tae the show-man:
"I'm selling this wee pig,
For, though I've stuffed an' fed it,
The crowl'll nae grow big."
They bargained an' they haggled,
They argued up an' down,
An' then at last Da sould it —
All for a silver crown.

The show-man took that pigeen
An' larnt it tricks, for weeks;
He dressed it in a waistcoat,
An' swallow-tailed, an breeks;
He larnt it for to stand up,
An' walk, an' sit, an' kneel,
An' rowl aboot , an' tumble,
An' dance an Irish reel.

An' now, folk say, that show-man
Has goold and goold galore;
And that he does nae travel
On fair days ony more;
He's marrit tae some ladie
O' great an' high degree,
All through the pig he bought from
My foolish Da an' me.

Padraig Gregory

11

THE BLACK PIG'S DYKE

...And I said to the angel who spoke with me, "What are these, Lord?"
and the angel answered, "These are the four winds from heaven".

Zacharias (Old Testament)

The pig has earned a place for himself, not just in the affections of man, but a respectable niche in literature, mythology and history as well. The American writer, Nathaniel Hawthorne, was fascinated by the swinish world: observing once a pig family of four immersed in straw, he saw in them, 'the very symbols of slothful ease and sensuous comfort'.

Captivated by their almost human traits he watched them as they, 'made careful examination of everything within their sphere, grunting all the time with infinite variety of expression. Their language is the most copious of any quadruped, and, indeed there is something deeply and indefinably interesting in the swinish race. They appear the more a mystery the more one gazes at them. It seems as if there were an important meaning to them, if one could but find it out.

One interesting trait in them,' he concluded, 'is their perfect independence of character. They care not for man, and will not adapt themselves to his notions, as other beasts do; but are true to themselves, and act out their hoggish nature.'

Country people were very familiar with their wise and prescient 'hoggish' nature. Reputed to have the ability to see the wind they became restless and started running about when there was a storm on the way. Ordinary mortals too could acquire the gift: all they had to do was to drink the milk of a sow.

Old Mather in *Myles na gCopaleen's*, 'The Third Policeman', was in no doubt at all that the winds could be observed. Proclaiming that the belief is found in the literature of all ancient peoples, he believed they were not only visible but coloured as well: 'The wind from the east,' he said, 'is a deep purple, from the south a fine white shining silver; the north wind is a hard black, and the west is amber. People in the old days had the power of perceiving these colours and could spend the whole day sitting quietly on a hillside watching the beauty of the winds, their fall and rise and changing hues, and their magic when they interweaved like ribbons at a wedding.'

The phenomenon was well known to the ancient Irish and recorded in the law tracts of the *Senchus Mór* as well as in the epic poem, *Saltair na Rann* (The Versified Psalter). The *Saltair*, 150 cantos on biblical themes, acquired its inspiration from the Bible as, even in Old Testament times, Zacharias described how he 'turned and beheld four chariots coming out from the midst of two mountains. In the first chariot were red horses, in the second black, in the third white and in the fourth chariot were steeds of many colours. And I said to the angel who spoke with me, "What are these, Lord?" and the angel answered, "These are the four winds from heaven".

Is it only pigs now that have the good fortune to retain this ability to see the swirling colours of the firmament, a gift that humankind has lost?

Predating the birth of Christ by two hundred years, and thought to be an ancient frontier defence and boundary of Ulster against raiding parties from the south, one of the oldest, best known and mysterious of fortifications in Ireland is the Black Pig's Dyke. Running from Co. Down all the way through Armagh, Monaghan, and Cavan right through to Co. Leitrim it has acquired a special place in Irish folklore and is, even yet, a source of marvel and speculation. Viewing it, the great 19th century scholar and antiquarian, John O'Donovan, wondered at the 'terrible tusks of the huge boar that rooted the Valley of the Black Pig.'

How did this mighty earthwork get its name? What kind of

beast was this fantastical 'Black Pig'? How did the legend come about?

Some say the dyke had nothing at all to do with frontier defences but was the result of a magic spell that could not be reversed. A man, living near Dundalk in Co. Louth, remarked to his son one day that he was greatly failed. The son replied that the schoolmaster was to blame. Each day, he said, the master used his magical powers to turn the pupils into different creatures. The child claimed he was turned into a hare, and the other children into hounds who then chased him for his life. He said that the master took his power from a book of spells in his possession. In the evening, through the power of the book, they were all restored to their natural forms.

Next day the concerned parent went to the school, confronted the teacher and demanded to know if the story was true. Could he change people into animals? He admitted that he could on which the boy's father dared him to prove it. The man immediately turned himself into a giant boar. The boy's father, seizing the opportunity, took the magical book and following a struggle with the master, now turned pig, threw it into the fire. The schoolmaster, realising he could never again regain his humanity, went berserk. Dashing out the door he ran across the country tearing up the land with his tusks as he went. Upon reaching Tullaghan in the County Leitrim the demented teacher plunged into the sea and was drowned.[19]

Pigs had magical healing powers too. On May morning they were brought into the dwelling house to bring good luck. One of the most effective cures for mumps and whooping cough was to lead the sufferer three times around a pig-sty by a halter or asses winkers! Those making the cure knelt at the door and prayed as well. In Co. Meath, Dr. Pat Logan heard of a woman who came to visit a child with mumps. Following the visit she went to the pigsty and was overheard saying to the pig:

[19] There is a precedent in Greek mythology for this transformation: Proteus, Poseidon's servant, was a shape-shifter who could instantly turn himself into a serpent, panther, boar, tree, or even a torrent of water.

A mhuic, a mhuic, chugat an leicneach seo.
(Pig, pig, here, take the mumps)

Given that the pig is such a friend to man it is surprising to learn that in some parts of England and Scotland, as well as Ireland, the pig was deemed unlucky among fishermen. A mention of foxes or pigs at sea brought bad luck. In East Anglia, England, pigs were never referred to by their proper name but only by nickname. To have them on board or to see them before setting out to sea brought bad luck. A Lowestoft skipper would not allow even a joint of pork or a pound of rashers on his boat.

The belief is not at all unusual and is held in seaside communities as far apart as Killybegs, Co. Donegal and Batu Muang Malaysia.

As with the cure for mumps, in Cheshire, England, the frog was the agent of cure in a similar manner for aphtha or thrush. The head of the frog was held for a few moments inside the mouth of the sufferer. The frog would then be infected thereby relieving the child. 'I assure you,' said an old woman who had often helped with the cure, "we used to hear the poor frog whooping and coughing, mortal bad, for days after; it would have made your heart ache to hear the poor creature coughing as it did about the garden.' There are many other examples of cures being brought about in a similar way.

Such treatments are a remnant of pagan beliefs in which disease can be transferred to other persons or creatures. Cures can be effected simply by simulating the problem, treating it, and transferring the desired result by a process of cause and effect to the diseased body. In the Gospel of Matthew (8:28-34) we find an interesting and somewhat amusing biblical precedent for this:

"Jesus arrived at the other side in the region of the Gadarenes. Two demon-possessed men coming from the tombs met Him. They were so violent that no one could pass that way.

"What do you want with us, Son of God?" they shouted. "Have

you come here to torture us before the appointed time?"

Some distance from them a large herd of pigs was feeding. The demons begged Jesus, "If you drive us out, send us into the herd of pigs."

He said to them, "Go!"

So they came out and went into the pigs, and the whole herd rushed down the steep bank into the lake and died in the water. Those tending the pigs ran off, went into the town and reported all this, including what had happened to the demon-possessed men. Then the whole town went out to meet Jesus."

The residents' response was not one of gratitude however. Fearful of the consequences of any more such exorcisms to the local farming economy they 'pleaded with Him to leave their region.'

12

MUD CABINS AND PETTY PRINCES

It is also in the interests of a tyrant to keep his people poor, so that they may not be able to afford the cost of protecting themselves by arms and be so occupied with their daily tasks that they have no time for rebellion.

Aristotle in Politics

In the 18th century, living conditions of the peasantry in Ireland was wretched indeed. Following centuries of warfare nine-tenths of the native population had been dispossessed and their lands confiscated by Cromwellian soldiers and adventurers of English or Scotch extraction.

Foreign travellers in Ireland were appalled at the resulting poverty. They noted with interest the number of pigs in the Irish countryside. English traveller, John Barrow, noted in 1835 that Carrickfergus had, 'nothing about the place to remind one of its being an Irish town, except, indeed the great number of pigs grunting in the street, some of which I observed had the complete run of the houses, apparently on the most friendly and familiar terms with the respective inmates.'

These scenes must indeed have seemed quaint to the class of person so privileged in those years to have the means to travel in luxury about Ireland.

Richard Twiss, an English visitor who came here in 1775 was scathing in his observations of Irish housing and general conditions: 'I then proceeded to Dunleer; the country produces potatoes, flax and oats, the enclosures are mostly of loose stones piled on each other; over the door or chimney (the same opening serving for both) of many of the cabins I observed a board with the words *good dry lodgings*; however as I was sure that hogs could not read, I avoid mistaking them for styes…

Being obliged to seek shelter during a violent shower of rain, I retreated into a cabin where the cocks and hens familiarly perched on my knees to be fed; they were so tame that I suppose they would have roosted in the same position, and I afterwards found the ducks, geese and other poultry equally familiar throughout the whole country.'

Of the landlords he remarked that, 'most of those whose fortunes enable them to choose their residence, unaccountably prefer residing in England, or anywhere else, to living upon their own estates, where sadly, they would be respected as petty princes; whereas by squandering away their fortunes among strangers, they not only impoverish their own country, but live unbeloved, and die unlamented.'

Although he spoke well of Ballyshannon, Co. Donegal, and admired the 'salmon leap' and waterfall he gave the neighbouring Co. Sligo a miss. 'Neither did I go into that quarter of Ireland called Connaught,' he wrote, 'which comprehends the counties of Mayo, Sligo, Leitrim, Roscommon and Galway, as I was affured that they were inhabited (efpecially along the coaft) by a kind of favages, and that there were neither roads for carriages, nor inns.'

Residents of these counties should not feel abused at the slight. Mr. Twiss's opinion of the Irish in general was poor. He quotes another traveller in 1619, William Lithgow, who was contemptuous of the other provinces as well:

'The barbarian Moor,' he wrote, 'the moorifh Spaniard, the Turke, and the Irifman, are the least induftrious, and moft flug-gifh livers under the funne, for the vulgar Irifh I proteft, live more miferably in their brutifh fafhion than the undaunted or un-tamed Arabian, the devilifh-idolatrous Turcuman, or the moon-worfhipping Caramines; fhewing thereby a greater neceffity they have to live, than any pleafure they have, or can have in their living.'

The 17th century Irish scholar, Geoffrey Keating took a poor view of English writers such as Twiss and Giraldus Cambrensus. In his History of Ireland he wrote that 'it is almost according to the beetle they act, when writing concerning the Irish. For it is the fashion of the beetle, when it lifts its head in the summertime, to go about fluttering, and not to stoop towards any delicate flower that be in the field, or any blossom in the garden... but it keeps bustling about until it meets with dung of horse or cow, and then proceeds to roll itself therein.'

The ladies of Ireland were much outraged when Twiss turned his sarcasm on them:

'The other most goodly sight I saw, was women travelling the way or toiling at home, carry their infants about their necks, and laying the dugges [breasts] over their shoulders would give suck to the babes behind their backs without taking them in their arms: such kind of breasts, me thinketh, were very fit, to be made money bags for East or West Indian merchants, being more than half a yard long, and as well wrought as any tanner in the like charge, could ever produce such leather.'

He would never get away with that kind of guff these days!

In 1835, a decade before the Great Famine, Lieutenant P. Taylor, was employed as a researcher with the Ordnance Survey[20]. His field report can be relied upon to give an accurate indication of the condition of the people at that time and of the importance of the pig:

'Great are the evils and much to be deplored the baneful effects of landlord absenteeism... A glance at the wretched hovels, scantily covered with straw, surrounded and almost entombed in mire, which everywhere present themselves, sufficiently testify that the total absence of all activity in industry is one source of the wretchedness and misery which almost overwhelms the land.

Potatoes are the staple article of provisions of the peasantry; every other article of produce is bought up for the English market. Considerable quantities of oats are ground into meal by the mills of the district and forwarded to the same country. Butter varies from five pence to seven pence

[20] Cartographic exercise carried out between 1825 and 1841. Additional information was gathered on antiquities, place names, social conditions etc.

per pound and almost the whole of this produce also is transferred to England.

In no kingdom in the universe does so general an appearance of poverty and destitution prevail as in the persons and domiciles of this intelligent, lively community... Potatoes and thin buttermilk constitute their chief and almost only source of subsistence. Butcher meat or butter form no part of their daily meals, and their well-fed pigs nowhere suspend in massive fletches from their dingy rafters, for the purpose of kitchen to their vegetable diet. All are transported to make up the landlords rent, and nothing remains but the light, gay and cheerful spirits of the emaciated frames of a half starved population...'

From a 21st century perspective the condition of the people then is indeed difficult to imagine. Noting their misery and, once again, the critical role of the pig, Gustave de Beaumont, a Frenchman who visited Ireland in the 1830's, described the typical cabin of an Irish Catholic farmer or agricultural labourer:

'Imagine four walls of dried mud, (which the rain as it falls, easily restored to its primitive condition) having for its roof a little straw or some sods, for its chimney a hole cut in the roof, or very frequently the door through which alone the smoke finds an issue. One single apartment contains father, mother, children, and sometimes a grandfather or grandmother; there is no furniture in the wretched hovel; a single bed of straw serves the entire family. Five or six half naked children may be seen crouched near a miserable fire, the ashes of which cover a few potatoes, the sole nourishment of the family.

In the midst of all this lies a dirty pig, the only thriving inhabitant of the place, for he lives in filth. The presence of the pig in an Irish hovel may at first seem an indication of

Jimmy Flynn, Laghey Barr, Kiltyclogher, Co. Leitrim sharpening the blade in preparation for a days mowing c 1985.

Jimmy Flynn mowing the meadow with his Bamford one horse machine c 1985.

Bernie Kelly, Mullaghmore, Co. Sligo drawing handshakings in preparation for making a trampcock c 1986.

Harvest home: Kelly and Rice families stooking rye c 1986.

Jimmy Boylan, Latoon, Co. Fermanagh 'splitting' seed potatoes in preparation for planting c 1990.

Jarlath Watters cutting turf at Uragh, Co. Leitrim 2006.

Benny Moen and son Enda operating their McCormack Deering reaper at Clontribet, Co. Monaghan c 2005 .

Benny Moen, Clontibret, moul'ing potato stalks with Gray manufactured drill plough and horse team c 2005.

Farmers in Limerick deliver their milk by cart to the creamery lorry c.1950.

Farmers delivering milk to Ballymote creamery c.1900. Photo: Courtesy EBS, Sligo

Market Day at the Diamond, Donegal Town c.1950.

A 'cart pig': Jimmy Whelan and John Devine 'bringing home the bacon' Swanlinbar, Co. Cavan, 1951. Photo Elsie Howden -Abbott

Butchering a pig in Kinvara, Co. Galway c.1948. Photo: Courtesy Ann Niland, Kinvara, Co. Galway

Tom Couley, pig killer, Co. Antrim, 1895. An ignominious end for the 'gentleman that paid the rent'. Photo: Courtesy Ulster Folk and Transport Museum

Blacksmith Mick Brennan at work c 1990.

L to R: Paddy Clancy, blacksmith, Sean Swiney, Ignatius Maguire and Jimmy Boylan 'shoeing' a cart wheel at Latoon, Co. Fermanagh. Iron tyre is heated to cherry red in fire upon which it expands and is fitted onto wheel. Arrows show two wheels waiting to be shod c 1993.

misery; on the contrary, it is a sign of comparative comfort. Poverty is still more extreme in the hovel where no pig is to be found…'

Given the conditions mentioned above it is not difficult to understand how the failure of the potato crops in the mid 1800s brought utter devastation, and to Ireland its own Holocaust! Improved housing conditions followed slowly and painfully in the wake of agitation for reform by the Land League in the 1880's. A series of reforms commencing with Gladstone's Land Act of 1870 and culminating in the Wyndham Land Act of 1903 provided a measure of freedom that eased the miserable condition of small landowners. Following the War of Independence and the birth trauma of the Civil War, the passing of the Irish Free State Land Act of 1923 broke the stranglehold of the landlord system forever. Security of tenure and outright ownership brought fresh confidence to a new nation and a will to improve to former tenants.

For many, the recovery was long and arduous; wretched housing conditions persisted into living memory. Maggie Mc Gowan saw it all in the early 1900's:

'A lot of my neighbours lived in huts,' she remembered, 'a room and a kitchen built with mud, there was any amount of them in my time. They had a wee low door and a wooden bed they made for themselves one side of the fire in the kitchen, the best place for it! They had a good feather tick and pillows. A big hobstone each side of the fire and a hole in the hob for the pipes.

They had daub floors but I seen that in our own house before the flagstones came in. It was a red clay that was dug out of the ground. Ye spread it on the floor, the same as mortar now, and rolled a tar barrel or something on top to level it. Ye couldn't wash it but it was easier to keep than the cement floors that came later.

They used to make a rug mat for beside the bed; that was a sack with bits of cloth sewed into it. Every row across had different colours on it. There was another one in front of the fire too for when they'd be sitting down at night.'

Around the turn of the 19th century flagstone floors replaced the daub that Maggie mentions. Quarried laboriously along the shore or in a neighbour's field, and laid by the man of the house, they were a big improvement. Householders then had to have many skills: stone mason, thatcher, tiler, carpenter, weaver, tiller of the soil. Plumbing or electrical skills weren't needed as there was neither plumbing nor electricity.

Up to the middle of the 20th century it was not unusual to see sows, when they were ready to farrow, brought into the kitchen and placed on a bed of straw. They were kept there for a week or so until the piglets became strong. Calves too were brought inside. Assisting with the birth was one of my earliest duties. Sometimes this necessitated an all night vigil, my father anxiously walking in and out and up and down all evening: 'like a clockin' hen' my mother said laughing.

When I got old enough the night shift was left to me.

Prancing about all night the cow, tied to a stake, became more and more restless. No sooner would she lie down than she was up again. Up and down, up and down. Her anxiety increased until finally she lay pressing and bawling in the pangs of calf birth. After a while when the water bag emerged the calf's feet could be seen moving on the inside. When the water broke, or was punctured manually, much strenuous pulling, sometimes with a rope attached to the feet, was required as the head and forelegs were coaxed and pulled into the world. Eventually the whole calf slid out on to the floor upon which we carried it, upside down with its dangly head tucked between very slippery forelegs, from the byre to the kitchen and placed it on a bed of hay.

My mother danced attendance too. Now that I look back she probably understood the procedure a lot better than the men, understood from experience the agony of birth. After the birth she would mix a poultice of oatmeal and place it in the hollows near the 'calf bones' on the cow's back and feed the exhausted creature a mixture of bran and sliced turnips.

The birth of a calf was a critical event in the farming year. On it depended the success or failure of the family's finances. It's impossible to imagine today the shock and distress caused to the smallholder by the death of a cow, calf or pig. It was akin to a death in the family.

On a successful outcome, what a proud moment it was following a successful calving, especially if it was a more marketable black bull calf. Satisfaction showed on my fathers face as he rubbed down the struggling, spindly animal thoroughly with hay. The calf stayed in the kitchen for a week or two until it became strong and healthy upon which it was placed in the byre with the other cattle. A bucket of water, strong washing soda and diligent application of a strong scrubbing brush left the kitchen flagstones gleaming white as before.

On daub and flagstone floors hens too had the run of the house. Bright-eyed, red combs at a jaunty angle, heads angled expectantly, when they ventured on to our kitchen floor they were welcome visitors. Never mind the mess. My mother was a pragmatist.

'Shittin' luck is the best o' luck,' she said.

If the pig was 'the gentleman that paid the rent' then surely the hen was the lady that bought the groceries. My father didn't like the mess and shooed them out:

'Bloody hens', he'd yell.

But he knew where his crust came from and tolerated it when my mother threw a fistful of 'Injun' meal on the floor for them. They ate it hungrily and as gratefully as a hen can be, left their calling card, and departed as they had come. No harm was done. There were no carpets. Once again lashings of hot water and a sturdy scrubbing brush washed away dirt and calling cards and left the flagstones clean and bright. There was no point in arguing with the woman anyway; in sickness and in health, hens, turkeys and farmyard stock were her whole life, and safe under her protection.

Some houses had half doors. Providing light and air, they kept the children in and the fowl and farm animals out. In an interesting way they could be used as a measure of a family's progress too. Charlie Ferris of Omagh Co. Tyrone recalled the reply of a neighbouring woman when she was asked how the family was doing:
'The two boys are getting' on fine,' she said. 'They can piss over the half door now. Their wee sister is mad because she can't!'

The fireside was a haven for my mother's sickly chicks and turkeys in the springtime. She nursed them and the heat restored them. Sometimes they took the 'pip'. Choking and gasping like asthmatic drunks on the worms that clogged their windpipes it seemed there was no hope for them. But this resourceful woman knew what to do. Taking them in a firm grip on her lap she held their beaks and gently pulled the tongue out to reveal the windpipe. Braiding a horsehair into a mini plait she pushed and eased it expertly down. When she withdrew it, trapped in the weave of the horsehair were the squirming white worms that caused the debility. Her patients almost always recovered.

As I left Ireland for America in the sixties those that could afford it were getting rid of their half doors, uprooting their ancient flagstones and replacing stone with cement and thatch with slate. That was progress. Soon would come 'rural electrification'. Fashions change. On my arrival in the U.S. it was something of a shock to see that a flagstone or slated entry hall was the covering of choice and the height of elegance — for those who could afford it.

The wheel has come full circle and the values and lifestyle that I saw in sixties U.S.A are now current in Ireland. Up is down and down is up. Stone and slate is fashionable again for flooring. Previously only those who could not afford slated roofs lived in thatched houses. To replace our thatched roof with slate was a dream far beyond my father's wildest imaginings.

Now only the very wealthy can afford a thatched house.

13

VAE VICTIS WOE TO THE CONQUERED

...Hidden away among rocks on the bleak mountain sides, or soaking in the slime and ooze of the boglands, or beside the Atlantic shore where the grass is blasted yellow by the salt west wind, you find the dispossessed people of the old Gaelic race in their miserable cabins.

Constance Markievicz

The lifestyle depicted in the previous chapters, set in the first half of the 20th century, had its roots in centuries of colonization, strife, rebellion and warfare. It was a time when all over Ireland the trappings of Empire, although declining, were still visible. Inside the demesne walls the shape of British Ireland still retained some of its old elegance. Classiebawn Castle in Co. Sligo, holiday home of absentee landlord and twice Prime Minister of England, Lord Palmerston, sat on a hilltop commanding a view of mountain, land and sea. Built during the hungry years of want and famine it had a 'Pine Walk' that ran three miles through needle-carpeted pinewoods to the next village. Exotic trees and shrubs acquired on foreign voyages lined its verges. A separate tree-lined avenue — the banks on either side graced by tall plumes of elegant pampas grass in late summer, daffodils and snowdrops in spring — wound in graceful curves for two miles to its majestic entrance.

Like ants we were on small farms underneath, or worker bees, and just as susceptible to the whims of wind and weather as we shook out the hay on warm summer days, or feverishly made 'lappings' if rain was on the way. Most of the time it was. Above us, Classiebawn, that impressive Gothic hulk of Mountcharles sandstone, looked impassively down. Vying for attention with Benbulben and Maeve's Knocknarea, those majestic natural landmarks, it failed — but only just.

When the current owner, Lord Louis Mountbatten, Admiral of the Fleet and 1st Earl of Burma, came on holidays he flew his house flag from the castle walls realising that to show the Union Jack would be provocative. Too busy then with concerns of crops, cattle and survival in the hungry '50s, we knew nothing of the castle's history, and cared less. Palmerston's coffin ships, famine evictions, they had all receded into a collective amnesia. Too horrible to remember, they were long sanitized from memory.

Bachelor Watty Bracken, his brother Jules, his wife Felicity and daughter Yvonne lived in a spacious two storey stone-built house on the estate. Prior to Mountbatten's time, Lord Ashley, successor to Palmerston, employed the Brackens as gamekeepers and managers of Classiebawn, its grounds, cattle, rabbits, pheasants and peasants. They protected the teeming rabbit warrens, hatched and raised flocks of pheasants that shrieked and primped on tree branches and hid in the long grass. The two brothers managed the woods and grazing, poisoned predators, controlled and trapped the rabbit warrens. Raising and releasing the pheasants in season they also conducted the hunting parties that shot them.

Wearing tweed knickerbockers, jackets and hats, the Bracken's manner of dress alone, apart from religion, pointed them out as different to everyone else in the village. Their relationship with the villagers was a Jekyll and Hyde one. On pitch-black winter nights they patrolled the Classiebawn demesne with shotguns and flashlights, protecting Lord Ashley's rabbit warrens. The poachers with their carbide lamps and hounds played cat and mouse with them. There was nothing personal in their encounters. The Brackens had law on their side; the hunters felt they had a moral right. Laws were made for the rich the rabbiters claimed; they had a God-given right to the lands of their ancestors. Sometimes the poachers won and carried off a haul of rabbits; sometimes the Brackens succeeded and the miscreants were forced to plead their case before a hard-faced D.J. in Grange District Court.

When morning came it was business as usual. Poacher and gamekeeper exchanged civilities and engaged in the commerce of a small village as if nothing at all had happened. Men who skirmished with the gamekeepers and stole the landlord's rabbits the night before now went to the Brackens for permission to cut a load of firewood in the Classiebawn woods. A cartload of timber cost five shillings. It was all very civilized, a game almost, and no one thought it odd. It was as if nothing at all had happened the night before. If the firewood could be removed as easily as the rabbits there would be no question of paying.

The Brackens kept a dairy too. When our cows ran dry we bought milk, and delicious salty homemade butter, from those people who were so different from us, but still in a detached sort of way, were yet a part of our community. Old ghosts live there now, but I remember the Bracken family for the efficient and homely dairy they kept, for well scrubbed flagstone floors, for the smell of fresh buttermilk, for the men's strange tweed hats and baggy plus-four trousers, for Mrs. Brackens kindness to a small boy, for the fresh milk we bought when our cows ran dry, for the rich, salty taste of their delicious home made butter. Sights and sounds so commonplace long ago, exotic now, but etched forever in a child's mind.

Acknowledging local sensitivities and politics, these agents of a foreign landlord knew when to look the other way. There were invisible lines that were respected. Republicans were billeted in Classiebawn during the War of Independence. Hostages were taken once and held there to secure the release of condemned IRA prisoners, Johnson, O'Shea and MacBride. The castle was mined with dynamite: any attempt at rescue and it would be blown sky high! If the Brackens noticed anything unusual in their patrols, and they must have, they said nothing. 'Less said is easiest mended' was an old country saying. They were on Lord Ashley's payroll, and then Mountbatten's, but the people who lived in the small community at Mullaghmore were their friends and neighbours.

During the Civil War, soldiers of the new Freestate were stationed there. Many years later, the war a fading memory, Jules Bracken often stopped at our house. Leaning across the stone ditch my father and he talked for hours. About the concerns of small farmers I suppose: cattle prices, weather, will the turf be saved at all this year? Don't mention the poachers — or the war!

Hordes of shooters with tweed knickerbockers and marbley accents came at appointed times of the year to shoot pheasant and wild duck frighted towards them by 'beaters', lines of local men employed for the day to flail the grass and bushes: their job the shame of a beaten class; their pay the crumbs from the master's table. They halloed and scoured, flushing concealed birds to an artillery of shot, and hoots of victory. The victor's prize the crumpled feathers and obedient peasants.

When the Right Hon. Evelyn Ashley brought his new bride to Classiebawn Castle, Mullaghmore in July 1891 he had good reason to be highly pleased with their nuptial trip to the village. The Sligo Champion reported that they were 'accorded a right royal welcome.' A section of the tenantry had erected flags and banners all along the avenue up to the castle. At the gatehouse, while he was introducing Lady Ashley to the admiring and the curious gathered around the carriage, 'the horses were unyoked and dispensed with for the remainder of the journey. The carriage, drawn by a number of stalwart men, went at a very rapid pace until they arrived at the Castle, when Mr. Ashley again thanked them on his own and on Lady Ashley's behalf.'

Tom Barry's judgement of such servility was harsh: 'The sycophants and lickspittles,' he wrote in *Guerilla Days in Ireland*, 'happy in their master's benevolence, never sought to question how he had acquired his thousands of acres, his castle and his wealth or thought of themselves as the descendants of the rightful owners of those robbed lands.' Even the English treated such sub-servience with contempt: 'They are on their knees still before English fashion — these simple wild people: and indeed it is hard not to grin at some of their naive exhibitions' wrote W.M. Thackeray in August 1846.

Over the entire country, 'big houses' cast their shadow of oppression, the tenantry humbly acknowledging their servitude towards it. Not only to the master did they bend in slavish humility, but even to the hirelings of the Establishment prudence told them it was wise to have as friends.

Asenath Nicholson, an American Protestant missionary and philanthropist, visited Ireland in 1844. Of the labouring classes and the cottiers she met on her visit she wrote that they 'were ever praising their master. Just as in America, although the slaves may be often under the lash or in the stocks, yet to a stranger they durst not speak out, lest some "bird of the air should tell the matter"; so the peasantry of Ireland are in such suffering, that lest they should lose the sixpence or eightpence they occasionally get while employed, they will make an imperious landlord an angel to a stranger.'

What then of the people behind the high stone walls and barred gates who owned the rabbits and rabbit warrens so desired by the hunters? Throughout Ireland, even yet, may be seen these definitive barriers that separated the 'haves' from the 'have nots'. Inside the walls, separated from the rest of the population, not just physically but psychologically as well, the 'haves' lived in the 'Big House' or castle. Outside of the wall lived the 'have nots', the wretched and dispossessed who maintained the 'haves' in the lap of luxury.

Some of the privileged were conscious of the divide. Very few were honest enough to articulate it. Sir Horace Plunkett, recognising the existence of that other invisible barrier wrote in the early 1900s that: 'Those who are familiar with the story of Ireland know how it came about that between two sections of the

Irish people stands a great dividing wall, the foundations of which are racial, the stones political and the cement religious.'

Cricket and rugby were their sports, not the Irish games of the Celtic Revival such as Gaelic football and hurling. William Bulfin observing a group of the ascendancy attending a regatta observed once: 'Most of them showed breeding both in feature and carriage. Yet they saddened me. They impressed me as being hopelessly aloof from their country and their time. There was nothing about them to show that they regarded themselves as Irish people. In dress, accent, social conventions and amenities they had fashioned themselves by English models... Standish O'Grady, one of themselves, and one of the best of them, told them the truth when he said that they were going, going — "rotting from the land without one brave deed, without one brave word."[21]

Liam de Paor in *The Peoples of Ireland* relates that while, 'some members of the Irish ascendancy were vigorous and enterprising, too many were content with the slothful exploitation of their privilege and lived dissolute and useless, if colourful lives in the style picturesquely described by Jonah Barrington... The penal laws, coming after centuries of warfare, had done their work of erecting a formidable barrier between the privileged colonials and the excluded natives.... The thousand petty humiliations of a resentful subservience could be met only with the glib deference and the placating comicality that masked hatred. This hatred was directed against the ascendancy, so many of whose members were at the time proclaiming their devotion to Irish liberty...'

In 'Children of the Dead End' the writer Patrick MacGill tells us that the train was crowded when he left home as a boy of twelve to go to the hiring fair. Noticing that the first class carriage had only one passenger he asked his friend for an explanation.

'Shure, ye know nothin', he answered. 'That man's a gintleman.'

[21] Bulfin, William, *Rambles in Eirinn*, p57

'I would like to be a gintleman,' Patrick answered.

'You a gintleman!' roared the other boy… 'D'ye know who that gintleman is'? he asked.

'I don't know at all' replied Patrick.

'That's the landlord who owns yer father's land and many a broad acre forbye.'

'Then I knew what a gentleman really was,' reflected Patrick. 'He was the monster who grabbed the money from the people, who drove them out to the roadside, who took six ears of every seven ears of corn produced by the peasantry; the man who was hated by all men, yet saluted on the highways by most of the people when they met him…'

'I suppose – a landlord is – a sort of louse', Daisy McEwen of Fleuchary in the Scottish Highland's reflected.

Various Land Acts had freed the small farmer from penury and given him ownership of the land he worked, but, in the early years of the 20th century, Ireland still had its huge estates. In Sligo, the Gore-Booths, the Wynnes, the Ashleys, and many others, still held their thousands of acres. The houses of these Protestant landed gentry, descendants of Cromwellian soldiers, were built and sustained from the millions collected in rent from their tenants; their walls mortared by the blood and tears of the poor.

Behind these sturdy fences was lived a world apart and idyllic indeed. Around the 'gentry' their many labourers, grooms, gardeners, bootboys, butlers, ladies-in-waiting, 1st, 2nd and 3rd footmen, nursemaids, groom valets, and countless other minions tended their every need. Tunnels and sunken roads were built to the servant's quarters so the common help didn't offend the eyes of the lords and ladies as they looked out to admire their vast estates. The Duke of Bedford recalled once how his grandfather had never allowed workmen to be seen in his presence: 'If my grandfather appeared in the distance they all [the servants] dived into a cupboard until he had gone past.'[22]

For the privileged classes there was shooting, hunting and cockfighting, debutantes' balls in London, and safaris to darkest Africa to while away the time. Sir Henry Gore-Booth of Lissadell, Co. Sligo voyaged to the Arctic in search of whales and seals in his fifty-ton yacht, the 'Kara' while at home the tenants whose rents provided his wealth lived from hand to mouth.

Dinner for those in the Big House started at five or six in the evening and lasted till midnight as they quaffed bottle after bottle of wine. There was no indoor plumbing so the chamber pot was kept handy behind the curtains. When nature called the gentlemen beckoned to the maid and the chamber pot was brought to them. Over the table they sipped their wine and smoked cigars; under the tablecloth they relieved themselves and passed the pot on to the next gentleman until it reached the end of the table. The ladies, who sipped their refreshments in the drawing room, had a similar facility, slipper shaped to take account of milady's contours.

Vae victis, woe to the conquered! If they had the finest things in life and those outside their walls didn't, why then, it was God who ordered it that way. To the victor the spoils. No pangs of conscience ever disturbed them:

> 'The rich man in his castle,
> The poor man at his gate
> God made them high or lowly
> And order'd their estate...'

they sang at service on Sundays.

We looked upon our tenants as animals that lived in hovels around the bogs,' George Moore of Moore Hall, Co. Mayo wrote, 'whence they came twice a year with their rents.'

The length of the avenue leading up to the 'big house' was a matter of great pride to the owners. The longer it was the greater the prestige among their peers. Sir Robert Gore-Booths' of Liss-

---

[22] Chambers, Anne, *At Arms Length*, p71

striding up and down the street. Buyer and seller struck up a friendship immediately so when Pat told him that he was looking for a replacement the jobber promised he'd keep an eye out for him. If he found what Pat was looking for he'd let him know. Their companionship deepened and the deal was closed over a few drinks of black 'porther' in Lang's Pub. Pat was very satisfied.

It wasn't long after until the jobber returned to Pat with an ass in tow. He had good news for him. He had found an ass that might be to his liking. It was a fine healthy animal with a black shiny coat and a lively step. In fact the beast's strength and agility was so great that the jobber had difficulty keeping him in check. He pranced and flung and could be held only with some considerable difficulty. Bucephalos, the mighty steed of Alexander the Great, was all set to replace Rosinante.

Pat pretended he wasn't impressed — but he was. That was all part of the game:

'He who despises me horse buys me horse,' was an apt country adage.

It wouldn't do to seem too interested. The bargaining began and after some ritual hand-slapping and tough negotiating they agreed on a price. The deal was sealed, 'luck's penny' decided upon, and the steed changed hands.

Pat felt he had done well. Experience had taught him, and many a man before him, that honest jobbers were hard to find so he was doubly delighted with his newfound friend. Feeling a pleasant glow that sprung, not just from pints of stout consumed at Lang's Pub, but from the banter and camaraderie of the day too, Pat walked his ass the seven miles home to Mullaghmore well pleased with his days work.

When he came to the fork in the road near his home he didn't think it strange when the ass took the turn for the little house in the woods without any bidding. A coincidence perhaps. His brother Owen came out to meet him. Taking off his hat he scratched his head and, looking at the two of them, exclaimed, 'Good God, Pat surely you didn't buy that ass!'

'Troth I bought him surely,' Pat bristled, unsure what his brother meant by the remark.

Wasn't that why he went to the fair: to buy an ass? The warm glow within him began to diminish. That was the trouble with families. A man never got any appreciation no matter how hard he worked.

'I'm afraid its th'oul' ass you have back with you,' Owen said doubtfully. 'Take the winkers off and see if he tumbles in the spot the other one used to tumble in.'

The donkey was released and sure enough headed straight away for the old spot where he tumbled joyfully and brayed a great bray of delight. It was great to be home! For Pat, the sinking feeling in his stomach told him he had been fooled.

Through time the story came to light that the jobber took the ass, which he had just bought from Pat, to a spot on the outskirts of the village. Here he got a complete makeover: hooves cut and polished, a pair of new shoes installed, his hair trimmed and dyed. For the final touch the conman put a ginger stick up the ass's behind. It was an old trick. The irritating ginger made him kick and dance and fart like a young animal. The trap was laid and Pat's deception ensured.

That's a peculiarity of the equine family that's worth noting: they have the ability to pass wind at will. Indeed they seemed to recognise this expression as a rude protest and often used it as a means of asserting defiance or contempt. One of my jobs as a youth was to catch and harness our ass for the day's work. Eying my approach with rope in hand she instinctively knew there was a hard day's work ahead. She immediately turned and, heading in the opposite direction, kickd up her heels, galloped, and blew wind in a most unladylike path to the furthest end of the field. Ears back, head down and tucked into the corner like a back to front prizefighter she would lash out with her hind feet when I

got close. This manoeuvre however seemed to be more play-act-
ing than real as she never landed any blows. The displays were
more like a ritual, a demonstration of her will to be free, a declaration that her spirit, like that of her wild ancestors who roamed
the prairie free, was still intact.

You could never be certain however, and so kept a respectable
distance from the flailing hind feet — just in case. The outcome
of our encounters was always the same. She must have known
she couldn't win. She knew her limits, how long to hold out and
when to give in. Capture was inevitable and retribution swift if
the game went on too long.

The rehabilitation of the ass is now complete and their days as
beast of burden over: 'Donkeys need the dentist too' went the
heading of a recent newspaper article:

'Up to 21 donkeys got to visit the dentist over the May Bank
Holiday weekend at the Sathya Sai Sanctuary in Castlebaldwin.
Equine dentist Lisa Molloy from Drumshambo and her colleague
Sally Kingsley from Yorkshire in UK corrected the teeth of 21
donkeys in the sanctuary.'

When we pause to look at how things have changed in our lifetime, we might be forgiven for thinking we have gone through
the looking glass with Alice. Not so long ago people couldn't afford a dentist, let alone the family ass. Toothpaste was a luxury.
Soot or baking soda did the job, and most houses didn't have a
toothbrush. When the miseries of toothache came a heated,
sweaty sock — it had to be old and stiff with sweat — held to the
affected jaw in what was often an all-night vigil, cured the pain.
A clove held to the cavity sometimes did the trick. If that didn't
work and you lived near Ballinamore in Co. Leitrim a round of
the stations in the local graveyard at midnight was sure to work.
When the pain became unbearable people in Ballintrillick, Co.
Sligo went to a stone image at the entrance to Keeloges ceme-
tery. All you had to do for relief was go there at midnight, kiss the
stone three times and ask to be cured.

There was no money for doctors either; so traditional cures were as numerous in the countryside as were ailments. A black cat with one white ear cured 'the Rose' (erysipelas). All you had to do was rub the affected spot with a hair out of the cats tail. In Donegal 'a cure for a stob [prick] on the hand is something that ye get on the road: when a star falls on the road it makes a sort of jelly. You can tell what it is because even in the summertime it's very cold. Take this and wrap it onto the stob as a poultice.'

A cure common all over Ireland was 'the cure of the burn'. Burns, whether by fire or scalding water, were treated by people who had acquired the remedy from licking the belly of the 'man-keeper' (newt) three times while saying certain prayers. Application of elm bark extract was an effective treatment too.

Every district had its believers and its own particular antidotes.

15

HARD DAYS AND 'COWLD' NIGHTS

Thanks be to God, times have mended
Cakes and tea for supper
When stirabout was intended

Charlie Ferris

By the third decade of the 20th century, it's new freedom purchased in blood, Ireland had a measure of independence. Newly emergent it was still an infant and impoverished nation on the brink of starvation. No one died of hunger but, spectral and persistent, want was never far from the door. Housing was basic. There was no dole, no social services. People had to fend for themselves. Make do or starve.

Maggie Mc Gowan had seen it all:

'A kitchen and a room an' only wan door on them, no chimneys or anything. McLeans house near where I grew up was built out of mud. There was several of them around Ballinfull, the Feeneys and the Mc Gloins, all wee, wee, wee houses. The Gore-Booths in Lissadell evicted them all an' they built these wee houses on a bit of ground that someone gave them out of pity. They had no land of their own, no nothing. They had to labour. I saw them meself, picking spuds all day for pennies and the Gore-Booths livin' off the fat of the land with their thousands of acres.'

Hard to believe then that, bad as they were, the early years of the 20th century were a vast improvement on earlier times! In the previous century poverty, destitution and disease were pandemic. Housing was poor with, 'the brute and human beings inhabiting the same huts, the walls of the poor cabins are made of sods, roofed with some rubbish of sticks and thatched with some rubbish of straw and rushes.'

Newspapers accused the landlords of plundering and impoverishing the people and, 'keeping them on the brink of starvation while they revel in all the luxuries of life regardless of all the heart-breaking wretchedness around them.' Arthur Young who visited Ireland in the late 18th century was appalled at the treatment of tenants and castigated the 'lazy, trifling, inattentive, negligent, slobbering profligate' landlords.

'A Landlord in Ireland can scarcely invent an order which a servant, labourer or cottier dares refuse to obey' he noted in his Journal. 'Disrespect, or sauciness he may punish with his cane or his horsewhip with the most perfect security; a poor man would have his bones broken if he offered to lift his hands in his own defence. It must strike the most careless traveller to see whole strings of carts whipped into a ditch by a gentleman's footman to make way for his carriage.

Landlords of consequence have assured me that many of their cottiers would think themselves honoured by having their wives and daughters sent for to the bed of their master.'

Young doubted the claim and deduced that the practice was 'more a mark of slavery that proves the oppression under which such people must live. If a poor man lodges a complaint against a gentleman,' he observed, 'or any animal that chooses to call itself a gentleman, it is considered an affront and will infallibly be punished. With such a conspiracy against law, to whom are the oppressed people to have recourse.'

Gustave de Beaumont wrote his *Ireland: Social, Political and Religious* in 1839 following a visit there some time before. In it he revealed the brutality, indifference and intolerance of those holding the reins in Ireland:

'I have seen the Indian in his forests, and the negro in his chains, and thought, as I contemplated their pitiable condition, that I saw the very extreme of human wretchedness; but I did not then know the condition of unfortunate Ireland... Like the Indian, the Irishman is poor and naked; but he lives in the midst of a society where luxury is eagerly sought, and where wealth is honoured. He is dying of hunger, and restrained by law; a sad condition, which unites all the vices of civilization to all those of savage life.

I will not undertake to describe all the circumstances and all the phases of Irish misery; from the condition of the small farmer, who starves himself that his children may have something to eat, down to the labourer, who, less miserable but more degraded, has recourse to mendicancy - from resigned indigence, which is silent in the midst of its sufferings, and sacrifices to that which revolts, and in its violence proceeds to crime.

Irish poverty has a special and exceptional character, which renders its definition difficult, because it can be compared with no other indigence. Irish misery forms a type by itself, of which neither the model nor the imitation can be found anywhere else. In all countries, more or less, paupers may be discovered; but an entire nation of paupers is what was never seen until it was shown in Ireland. To explain the social condition of such a country, it would be only necessary to recount its miseries and its sufferings; the history of the poor is the history of Ireland.'

The new Irish nation did its best to redeem the misery and the sufferings. It almost went under during the 'Economic War' of the '30s when the Irish government under DeValera refused to continue paying land annuities[25] to England. For someone on their own without family support, especially women, it was almost impossible to survive. John Joe Leydon, in the frank and forthright speech of the Irish countryman, a richness of language now fast dying out in the vernacular of the countryside, told me about his neighbour, a woman we'll call Winnie:

'She farmed on her own till 'she wasn't fit to carry a bucket, she was dragging them after her and her not fit to do it!'

She milked three cows and sent the produce to the creamery. When she was younger the family had a pony. 'The father and mother passed away and when the pony died she didn't have the money to replace it and then she had neither pony or ass.'

[25] Repayments to the British Government for loans made to Irish tenant farmers to purchase their land under the Land Acts of 1891.

A dull light struggled through the cracked, cobweb-covered window as John Joe stood with me on the stone-flagged kitchen floor of Winnie's old home. It lit a room adorned with a few meagre sticks of furniture, dust-covered and riddled with woodworm. Epitomising her zest for life it still retained the simple flourishes of a poor but house-proud woman, a person who struggled to keep up appearances, a self-respecting lady who never lost her dignity or her pride. Ponjers that hung on the wall were covered in bright tinfoil saved from cigarette packets, concealing the rust and holes underneath. The 'brace' and fire surround was painted in bright-coloured square and diamond patterns. 'She covered the ponjers to make them nice looking,' John Joe said. 'The designs on the brace she made up herself. It was like a circus wagon!'

There were six or seven neighbours going to the creamery who took turns bringing her milk-can with them. She kept two cows till she was seventy years old:

'By Jasus she seen some hard days and cowld nights!' John Joe declared in admiration.

The neighbours used to get together and put the hay she saved into store cocks for her at the end of the year. 'The young ones that's going today wouldn't give a neighbour as much help anyway. If ye can't do it yerself now, forget about it! They'd only be laughing at ye: "Ye're only a fucken eejit, what are ye at? That's what they'd tell ye!'

Most farmers and smallholders were hardworking and thrifty. They had to be. But there were shiftless men too, who were 'natural born lazy'. Martin was one of these. His wife Sis did the best she could. When she tripped on stone steps while bringing water from *Pollyarry* spring well she broke her leg and was taken to hospital. Care of the home was now left to her idle husband. The Sisters of Mercy nuns, who had a convent in the village and occasionally distributed some small charities to destitute families, were concerned:

'About three weeks later,' Brian K—— said, 'Mother A—— and another nun came up from the convent and wanted to send the children into a home. John, the oldest boy, he was about eight at the time, kicked and battered the shins off them and ran away. He wouldn't go with them but the three sisters were taken.

The mother was in for nearly a month and when she came out and found the children gone she was heartbroken. She walked the sixteen miles into Sligo the next day to try and get them back. They wouldn't be given to her as they were signed into care. If Martin had paid one lousy shillin' a month for their keep she could have got them.

When she came home she came up to my mother telling her the whole story. She was in an awful way about it, nearly off her head, an' could ye blame her? She took to sitting on the steps looking out at the sea and combin' her hair. This went on week after week 'til one day meself an' me mother went down to the house to her. Women that time wore their hair in a bun but she had her hair combed down on to her shoulders this day.

"Kate,' she says, 'I'm in an awful way, there's an awful noise from the sea. What'll we do at all? Can ye hear it?"

> 'Queer are the ways of a woman I know:
> She comes and stands
> In a careworn craze,
> And looks at the sands
> And the seaward haze
> With moveless hands
> And face and gaze,
> Then turns to go...
> And what does she see when she gazes so?' [26]

'That evening she was taken to the mental hospital. She was only a month there when she died. Died of a broken heart, an' her only a young woman in her 40s.

[26] The Phantom Horsewoman', Thomas Hardy (paraphrased)

Martin was left with young John to look after an' sure he was in our house most of the time for a bite to eat. He used to be out back of the hills all day with nothing to eat an' he'd come into our house in the evening cryin' with hunger. It wasn't too long before Martin got sick an' died laving young John on his own. When he got old enough he went away and joined the army. One of the girls did domestic work in the hotel for awhile an' to this day I don't know what became of the others, if they're dead or alive.

Them oul' bitches o' nuns was good for nothing anyway. I always blamed them for interfering. They used to be comin' to the Gonigles too with soup an' food. There was three brothers in it, Pat, Francis and Martin an' they used to spend their time puttin' up searods; Martin was blind and Francis was deaf. They were uncles of Jim G——'s wife. Word was sent to them about the nuns an' the visits so they came down, brought Pat into Sligo and got the place signed over to the family.

That was the finish of the nuns and the soup. Weren't they the right oul' hypocrites? Sisters of Mercy! They had no mercy — they were all for themselves.'

16

RICH IS THE SEASHORE

You must teach your children that the ground beneath their
feet is the ashes of our grandfathers. So that they will
respect the land, tell your childen that the land is rich
with the lives of our kin. Teach your children what we have
taught our children, that the earth is our mother.

Chief Seathl's Testament

Following the failure of the potato crop during the great famine
of 1847, desperate people trekked to the seashore looking for
something to eat. Thomas Boyle, an old man of Mullaghmore,
Sligo once recalled that, in famine times people travelled in con-
voys, with ass and creels, from the mountain districts to the
seashore. Gathering all the shellfish they could find they lit fires
along the road to cook them. Eating their fill they carried the remainder home. They ate so many *báirneachs (bairnigh)* and 'winkles' that their skin and eyes took on the colour of the food of
their salvation.

So why did people with access to this resource die during the
famine years? The question arises again and again. For coastal
dwellers the answer is self-evident. In normal times seaweeds
and shellfish gathered along the shore can supplement meals
now and again. When there was nothing else to eat the
seashore's finite supply could not support the hordes that de-
scended on it. Fish could only be caught when they were in season and not during the long winter months. Even in season luck
played a big part in a successful outing. Fish were not there for
the taking any old day. Herring boats were badly equipped and
often weather-bound in the harbour. Some sold their nets and
lines in the bad times to keep starvation at bay for another few
days.

Until recent times most breadwinners supplemented the potatoes and vegetables they grew on their plots and small farms by trying their luck at the shore. Potatoes were stored in the 'upper room', Mickey McGroarty of Selacis, Co. Donegal told me. 'That's because it was at the back of the fire — it kept them warm and dry for the whole year round. There's not a potato grown now in the whole parish of Inver. It's sad now and odd too because you wouldn't see a ridge of potatoes at all now if ye were to travel between here and Killybegs.'

Pollack, mackerel, glassin and ballan wrasse were caught with hand-lines at rocky outcroppings along the coast: *Leac na Meala, Poll Ui Dhuirmuide, Leac Cam* and so on. Each rock and inlet of the wild seashore gardens had a name that was intimately known to everyone in the community. It was as important to other generations to know these names as it is now for shoppers to know the streets and addresses of favourite shops in our towns and cities. The younger generation acquired the lore as they grew up and worked alongside the older people. While spoken Irish has died out generally, most country people retain the old knowledge and still refer to seaside places by these Irish names.

A perfect understanding of the sea and its secret places was essential for a successful outing. Good fishing spots and marks were handed down from one generation to another, a lore that is being lost in our time. If it is finally lost — and it seems inevitable that it will — it is knowledge that will have to be painstakingly re-learned by decades, or even generations, of trial and error.

Rich is this shoreline, a natural larder stocked with high energy, high protein foods. Although not as healthy or as wholesome, food on supermarket shelves, pre-packaged and ready to go, is much more suited to modern lifestyles. Even though these seaside plants are wholly organic and packed with nutrients, a new generation is growing up that never heard of them and wouldn't know where to find them. Organic foods are appreciated — if they can be picked up labelled and pre-packaged from a supermarket shelf

Crannach and *sleabhac*, *báirnigh* and periwinkles were, and still are, available in abundance along the coast, and carageen moss at spring tides. Carageen was bleached and dried on a grassy bank by the shore and then stored for winter use. Boiled and strained, the extract was a panacea to prevent or cure all ills, particularly chest infections, colds or flu. Mixed with milk, simmered and allowed to set, it made a choice dessert. Fed to cattle it fattened them, produced a glossy coat and put a satisfied smile on my father's face when he made a few extra pounds from a well turned out beast at a fair in Grange.

Sleabhac is a peculiar grass-like substance that appears mysteriously on bare rock along the foreshore during the winter months. Reminiscent of the biblical manna that inexplicably appeared to feed the Israelites, this hardy plant springs forth only during the winter months. It flourishes still, when little else will, during the short, cold wet days of winter. Perversely, it shrivels and disappears with the lengthening, warmer days of spring when everything else bursts into growth, leaving only bare inhospitable rock. When you find it, simmer it slowly over a low flame for an hour. Add an onion, a pound of bacon, boil some potatoes and know what it is to feast like a king — or a chieftain!

Each spring I pluck the dark brown weed and think of my parents and the old people who knew when and where to look for this food. They crowded the seashore until not a pick was left, a people who lived by their wits and their intimate knowledge of Nature. They knelt in the same places that I do and gathered this manna of the sea that re-generates miraculously year after year. I think too of the hungry, emaciated creatures that scoured the seashore in famine times. When the pig and grain crop went to pay the landlord[27] they scoured the fields again for an overlooked turnip or a potato. Failure to pay meant the 'crowbar

[27] Over three million live animals were shipped out of Ireland in the famine years of 1846-50 — three times the number of people who died of starvation in the same period. *'There's enough food to support the population until a new harvest but the landlords must get their rent, so to meet their demands the grain must be sold. The grain will be sent out of Ireland to feed English horses…':* Sligo Champion, August 1847

brigade' would be sent to tear down the roof and put young and old to the side of the road. A small bag of *sleabhac*, mixed perhaps with *báirneachs* and winkles, would keep them alive for another day. As I work, somehow, I feel their spirits close by.

The roar of the ocean beside me is timeless and reassuring. Alone with my thoughts, I gather and reflect as I take heed of the old people's warning to 'never turn your back to the sea'. I am grateful to be here in this beautiful place at the edge of the Atlantic, and grateful for the knowledge the previous generation has passed on to me. Oblivious to the secrets of nature hidden in the landscape, sleek cars and power-walkers whiz by on the cliff road above. They stare, and perhaps wonder, at the unusual sight of a lone hunter-gatherer crouched by the waves.

Sleabhac grows only in special places and is best plucked after a spell of frost. Every section of shore had, and still has, its own designation and a reputation for good fishing or good seaweed.: *Leac na Mealdha*, the honeyed rock, named for the variety of edible seaweeds that grow there; *Oilean Mór* the best place for carageen at a spring tide or for a good take of ballan; *Cul a Chait* for a plentiful supply of *crannach*; *Poll na Weegoge*, *Ros Caoireach* or *Poll Eamonn* the best place to go for winkles. *Cruc an Gabhair* for the iron in the spa well that was an essential spring tonic and an efficient wormer; *Poll a Ghearraidh* for the *tor's* of wrack that washed up in abundance on its stony shore. Every coastal town held its own knowledge. These names are not found on maps; they were never noted by any cartographer but passed on by word of mouth.

Báirneachs (limpets) and periwinkles could not be eaten in any month with an 'r' in it, we were told. Infinite patience was needed to prepare and pry the winkle from its shell. The leathery *báirneachs* remained tough even after a lengthy boiling and simmering. Nevertheless when cooked along with *crannach* and a lump of salty bacon it was healthy and tasty fare. Cockles, mussels and sea-urchins added to the variety of foods that still grow, although not so plentifully now, along the seashore.

'Cuckoo' storms, so called because they often coincided with the first call of the cuckoo, seldom disappointed and arrived every year driving the weed on to the shore at *Poll a Ghearraidh*, *Poll a Churraigh* or *Claddagh Dubh* in perfect time for the planting season. Just as predictable was the 'May wrack' that washed ashore with the inevitable 'May storm'.

When autumn arrived there was an added urgency to stock up for the winter. Mackerel were caught, salted, pickled and laid out on the roof to dry. 'Rusty' mackerel they were called from the reddish hue rendered by the process. Hung from the rafters or in the chimney corner they were picked as needed for the dinner table.

'Bulgoges'(smelts) are no longer sought after but were very popular years ago. They came in great shoals in the harvest time and were caught in abundance with nets: 'We used to heel cartloads of them up on the strand, take the heads off them, gut them, wash them in the salt water and take them home and salt them for the winter,' Willie Devins of Aughaged told me. 'One fella used to have them hanging from the roof to cure. He'd carry them in his pocket and eat them like sweets. Anything extra we had we used to sell for thruppence a can.'

Fished from the rocks, ballan wrasse, known also as baiyan, bavin or morran, was a favourite for salting. At their best in the autumn, they were fished all year beginning when 'the flaggers (wild iris) are in bloom'. Fishermen travelled in small sailing boats from the Sligo coast to Bomore rock, near Inishmurray island, ten miles away, to fish with hand-lines for ballan. It was not unusual to return with as much as 'twelve score fish' per boat.

'Ye know the rock between Seadain and Bomore rock they call the Porthauners? There used to be savages of ballan there, they'd ate ye in it!,' Johnny Mc Gowan of Ardtrasna, Co. Sligo told me. Pocket nets were used to catch them too. Baited with crushed crab they were set to do their work while the crew fished hand lines.

Ballan grazed inshore on shelly bottoms in deep water in the springtime. As summer arrived they moved out to the open sloping flag and the fishermen followed. Lugworm was the most popular bait but mussels or *portáins* (a small green crab) or the larger brown crabs were also effective. The hard-shelled brown crabs were dragged unceremoniously, with a hooked steel rod, from rocky crevices along the shore at low tide. The body was used for bait and the claws brought home for the table. Ballan was fished almost exclusively with handlines or with a short stout pole.

With a coming tide there is nothing more exciting than a good 'take' from these voracious feeders. When the catch of ballan was brought home it was gutted and a cut made along the bone to allow the salt to penetrate. Layers of salt and fish were then packed into a waterproof container. The fish was soaked in the resulting pickle for nine days after which it was dried in the sun and then hung from the rafters or in the chimney corner to cure.

Glassan was formerly a very important and popular part of people's fish diet. In addition to their food value the Rathlin islanders extracted their oil for use as fuel in crusie lamps. Ballan, as with coalfish or glassan, sometimes called 'blackjacks', are now disdained as table fare.

Crannach and carrageen moss was gathered for sale as well as for the family table. Bleached and dried in the sun it was brought into market in Sligo town:

'Ye'd go to the rocks at a spring tide an' ye'd pull the crannach an' dry it on the flags, d'ye see, an' when it was dry then ye went to Sligo with it,' a veteran of the seashore explained to me. 'It was grand when ye'd boil it with a half pound of bacon — ye couldn't get yer fill of it man! It was sold by the score, 20 lbs, sometimes ye'd get half a crown for it. I seen it goin' up to a pound for a score once.

They'd sicken yer arsh now about getting' up early in the

mornin'. They don't know the first thing about early! We'd have the ass harnessed and be on the road for Sligo by two in the morning with a load of *crannach*, sometimes we'd be away by one o'clock.

We were the first round these parts to get sale for *crannach*. Me father and mother warned us again tellin' anyone. "Keep yer mouth shut an' don't be tellin' yer business", is what they said. Someone found out anyway and the next that was at it was Martin B—— down there below. After that the Rourkes and James Mc Cannon, Lord a' mercy on him, started it, an' then it was a drove of bucks from Inismorra. That buggered it altogether an' put the price down t'hell!

It was all fish was a-eatin' that time and praties. In the time I'm talkin' about, the '30s and 40s, there was six or seven carts going out of Mullagh selling fish all over the countryside. Ye'd get dried fish too. At the fair in Grange ye'd see heaps of pollock an' ballan as high as yer waist; an oul' sail or a canvas under them. Every one of them'd be soul' and the people glad to get them.

For drying they used to split the fish along the back, wash them in the salt water an' spread them out on the flags. Of course there was weather in it that time what there's not now! When they were dried and well soaked they'd dip them again and again in the pool: that was the sort of saltin' they got. It was very natural. If ye go along *Carraig Fhada* or *Leac na Meala* ye'll still see salt in the pools where the tide goes in and out the self an' same as what ye get in the shop.'

The lifestyle of the past generations was so different to ours, yet our physical make-up, needs and requirements, are the same. We are organic beings, dependant on the soil, and part of it. Living in harmony with the earth, a bond dependent on respect, man was in tune with the natural rhythms. There was a balance. We were not dependant on artificial energy. We relied on our own strength, developing the power and skill to work in harmony with the earth and reap its rewards. They had all the skills necessary for survival in a natural environment; we have all the skills necessary to live in an artificial environment. Will it always be enough?

The greater the distance between earth and man, the more artificial life becomes. In the resulting struggle the earth is bled and man goes soft. Gone the harmony: in its place exploitation and ruin. Moving from country village to global village we have moved away from ancient knowledge and exchanged *Leac na Mealdha* and *Leac Fion Ruaidh* for *blather@braveneworld.com*, an unreal cyber earth.

We are boldly, perhaps even foolishly, going 'where no man has gone before'. Despite warnings of global warming, melting polar icecaps and impending Armageddon, it seems that go we must.

17

SING A SONG OF SIXPENCE

Sing a song of sixpence, a pocketful of rye, four and twenty blackbirds baked into a pie…

A benevolent Gulf Stream washing Ireland's shores keeps arctic weather at bay that, given our northerly latitude, we might expect. Weeks on end of frost, ice and snow, that in former times curtailed the food supply of wild birds, seldom occur now with the advancement of 'global warming'.

A mountainous coastline and moisture laden Atlantic winds ensure that the only thing constant about weather on the western seaboard is constant change. Prior to the advent of the Met Service, the signs, for shrewd, weather conscious farmers were written in the landscape. Scanning sunsets, cloud formations and animal behaviour, they viewed the cold, dry, northeasterly winds with apprehension. Noting the frost-hardening ground: 'It's drying up for snow,' they might say, and they were hardly ever wrong. Willie-wagtails gathered closer to the rick at hay-pulling time and grew bolder. Sensing the snow, they wagged and bobbed and worried, picking up hayseeds as they went.

Sure enough the wagtails were right. Like flower petals the delicate flakes came floating down, uncertainly at first. Playfully they waltzed, searched, rambled and settled on the ground. Swirling eddies danced exuberantly down, hesitated, soared again, teased, pirouetted in graceful arcs and drifted lightly to earth. An unremitting invasion of whirling white followed. Thronging the air it painted the ragged hedges, the sodden fields, the stately trees. Resolute, persistent, all day and into the fading light it blotted out the rain-washed, wind-battered, winter world. Transfiguring the winter landscape, dreary shades of waterlogged, winter grey were changed to hushed and pristine white.

Morning broke to a renaissance of creation. Resplendent in newly acquired gowns of flowing white, the mountains were transformed. Benbulben was sublime, a bride, virginal. Bedecked in wedding white, serene, the surrounding hills were bridesmaids in attendance.

Departing snowstorms cleared the way for tranquil days of bright sunshine and azure skies. Sun-bright, fleece-white clouds floating serenely over newborn earth came to see what God had wrought. An eerie stillness, unusual and strange, spread over the sea that had lately spent its rage on the shore; now it murmured news of foreign lands on the stony shore.

Worried about the prospect of diminished rations in a strange new world, sparrows bunched in the hedges chattering excitedly. Short aerial sorties triggered clatters of cacophonous discourse in the branches. What happened? There was nothing to eat! What will we do?

Hens made exploratory forays around the farmyard. Disoriented by the strange white-blanketed earth they picked their steps carefully, suspiciously. Pausing on one leg, the better to contemplate it seemed, they puzzled at the strange landscape; the other leg pulled up into a warm glove of downy breast feathers, they angled an inquisitive eye at the snow covered ground, and then expectantly at the open kitchen door.

Water sparkled and dripped from icicles hanging from thatched eaves: extruded crystals they seemed, fairy spears for a De Danann king. Soft drips from the thatched eaves made brown craters in the white carpet beneath. Three-cornered tracks left by hares tell-taled across the fields. Fox paws followed. Safe in brush and bank, hedgehogs slept their winter sleep. Thrushes and fieldfares that normally foraged in the meadows gathered closer to the farmyard, hunger overcoming their fear of humans. There was no food for them in the usual places, no water. Now unwary birds were at greatest risk from man.

Freeze-ups lasted long enough to increase the winter population. Men all, they were made of snow and stood silently, sto-ically, day and night in gardens and along roadsides. I don't know why, but we never had snow women! Friends to children every-where, when the inevitable thaw came, these men with coal black eyes and carrot noses toppled drunkenly, disconsolately, into oblivion. We hated to see them go when with drooping heads and hats askew, they grew smaller and smaller and vanished into the ground.

Nature slept beneath this cloak of white. Plants, grasses, flow-ers, all that delighted our summer eyes rested unseen — but rebel daffodil, iris, snowdrops stirred below. Responding to Nature's call they were first to awake to spring's renewal.

Long frosty nights installed a thick layer of ice on the lakes — strong enough to walk on, or ride a bicycle. Jack Frost called when we were asleep and left sculpted, surrealistic ice fern shapes, bejewelled, on the windowpane. If it was freezing outside then it was freezing inside too! Now, central heating has taken away his canvas, put an end to his artistry. Temperature con-trolled bedrooms provide no studio for his skills, no welcome for his art.

Early spring was judged the best time of year for new births on the farm. Cows were heavy with calf in January and February. The fields and muddy lane they traversed were often frozen hard. Before the freeze-up, their great weight left holes every-where they trod in rain-softened meadow and lane. Filled with water and glazed with ice they crackled underfoot. No point in taking a chance they might slip on the ice and break a leg or 'slip calf'. Best to keep them indoors now.

Bucketful by weary bucketful two gallon tinker-made tin cans and galvanised buckets of spring water were carried miles to be instantly sucked into cavernous and, it seemed, bottomless bel-lies. Back and forth we went to *TobairLeice*, the spring well, and back and forth with limb-dragging effort. A week or two of this and my arms wouldn't have looked out of place on an orang-utan!

The hayricks shrunk rapidly. 'Benches' were made at one end, hay stripped off and carried in huge armfuls to restless cows. Straining at ropes and chains they looked back wild eyed, impatient, hungry. They were precious animals that had to be well cared. In them resided the wealth and welfare of the family. 'A man without a cow has no need of a scythe and a man without a dog has to do his own barking' went the old proverb!

Even the posts that restrained the cattle were chosen with care. Not any old stick would do. They could be made from any wood except holly. 'If a holly trunk was used as a stake the cow was always restless at it, it never settled down'. Neither would a farmer ever strike an animal with a holly or 'boothree' (elder) branch. Nan Gilmartin of Drumfad heard from her father that 'twas branches of boothree and holly that was used to beat Jesus when he was being crucified' and so it was unlucky to use them to goad any creature ever again.

Winter: cheerless, hungry winter. Rats gnawed the potatoes in the barn and scuttled under the daub floor with their prize. Robins begged for crumbs. Blackbirds scratched and tore chunks out of the thatch. Could the poet Patrick Kavanagh's industrious shoemaker father have been so careless as to allow the cheeky birds to poke a hole through the roof of his house? That is just what Patrick claims in the first paragraph of his book *The Green Fool*.

Patrick was two years old at the time and lying in the onion box that his father had converted into a cradle. It was the first time he had ever noticed the black oak-timbered roof common to all country houses then. 'If I did not see stars it was my child observation that was at fault,' he wrote, 'for the blackbirds had pecked holes in the thatch… The blackbird was a great enemy of old thatch and in its search for the little red worms in the decayed straw would stop at nothing.'

Not surprising then, that blackbirds were treated as an infernal nuisance. Insects flourished in the thatch, particularly in houses where rushes were used as a covering. The blackbirds, following their instincts, eagerly pursued this tasty food so attractively packaged and freshly preserved in the straw! 'When there came snow and ice,' Hugh Pat G—— of Ballintrillick said, 'the blackbird got hungry and he dug the thatch looking for grubs and worms.'

Before net wire there was no effective protection from these scavengers. They had free access. The feathered raiders were early risers. At first light they were busy at work digging for the worms that made a good blackbird breakfast. The homeowner was the unwitting victim as everywhere they dug a hole the water got in and rotted the straw. If the thatch was thin the first sun into the room beamed, not through the window, but through the roof! One man declared, 'There was nearly a credit for catching a blackbird because he had the thatch destroyed with hoking!'

'Sing a song of sixpence, a pocketful of rye, four and twenty blackbirds baked into a pie...', meant more than just a nursery rhyme not so long ago — it was a celebration of fact! Today it seems strange to us, even barbaric, but back then this annoying habit spurred frustrated homeowners, and young people looking for sport, to catch blackbirds and other small birds by means of home made cages and snares. They were trapped, killed and eaten without compunction.

Contraptions inappropriately named 'bird cradles' were commonly used. Almost every house had one. Capture by this method was common all over Ireland and a favourite pastime, especially for young boys. Sometimes they ate their catch but often they were caught just for sport and released. Robins, finches and other small birds were always freed.

'The bird cradle was an art', Brian K—— chatted as we made one together. 'Ye made it from four pieces of sally and young boothree (elder). The boothree was boast in the centre and light, it was important to make them as light as possible so they were easy to prop. Ye bored a hole in two of the sticks to make the cradle twelve inches by twelve inches square and ye put a sally rod through the holes. Ye put another sally around that in a hoop to keep the other rods from falling out and tied them above at the top, doubled. Ye started to build the rods then pushing them around and around between these other two sticks and building them up into a pyramid shape with a wee space between them until ye had something looked like a crib.

Ye set this up in the frost and snow when the birds were hungry with a few crumbs scattered inside. How ye set it was, ye tilted it up on one end and ye put a light sally rod from one of the corners resting on the ground and brought it around in a loop to the other one. Ye got a wee fork stick then to keep the trap tilted an' left it on what we used to call the pan; when the bird hopped up on this pan made from a sally rod, he knocked the trap down on top of himself. Ye'd get more robins than thrushes but we let the robins go.'

Nooses made of single or doubled horsehair were used for trapping as well. They were attached at intervals to a string suspended between two pegs driven in the ground, or to a bent sally rod: 'ye'd get three strands of horse hair sixteen inches or a foot long, twist it and make *duils* (snares) out of them.' The *duils* were set at intervals by the side of a drain that was free of snow. 'Ye put a twine across and hang the *duil* down about three inches from the ground; ye could get two or three blackbirds in it. We used to get snipe and woodcock the same way, thrushes too.'

According to those who sampled the wild birds they were delicious to eat: 'Ye pluck the blackbird and clean out the inside; he was fresh, tasty and clean and ye put him on the tongs on a coal in front of the fire. They call it a barbecue now, the same thing we used to do with the tongs! They tasted lovely but *there wasn't much on them more than roasted bones!*'

One old proverb claimed that the three most wholesome foods for a drover were the back of a herring, the belly of a salmon or the head of a thrush!

Maurice O'Sullivan in *Twenty Years a-Growing* described small groups of two and three going out to catch thrushes on the Great Blasket at Hallowe'en in the early 1900's. When they came back from their hunting trip the catch was, 'all thrown out on the table, and when everyone had added his share there were a hundred. "Let all begin plucking now", said Shamus O'Donlevy.
We began plucking the feathers, all except my sisters, Maura and Eileen, Kate O'Shea and Kate Peg, who were busy roasting and washing plates.'

On the sea cliffs of Rathlin island and other offshore islands seabirds congregated in great numbers. Catching them was big business, particularly during the war years. Exported to England, birds and eggs were in great demand there to alleviate food shortages. July was the favoured month for trapping; whatever couldn't be eaten or sold was salted for winter use.

In the 19th century it was not at all unusual to find songbirds on the menu in London clubs and eating-houses. A letter to the English 'Field' in 1858 described a correspondent's experiences of shooting small birds in 1847, a winter of deep snow. The writer told of clearing a space ten yards by four feet on his lawn that he baited with oats and cabbage leaves. 'The larks pitched there eagerly', he wrote, 'and it was as much as I could do to fire and load, pick up and change places fast enough to receive them as they came.' In two days he shot 552 larks, 13 fieldfares and 35 redwings, which he ate and shared with his friends.

In 1912, Maurice Headlam, Treasury Remembrancer at Dublin Castle went on a bird shoot at Clonmel in Co. Tipperary. 'We were attended each by a small boy carrying a sack,' he wrote, 'and my recollection is that we got far more than the traditional "four and twenty", and that an excellent pie was the result.'

Across the channel even the corncrake wasn't immune! Now a much cherished bird high on the endangered species list, it once featured as a delicacy on dinner menus. Mrs. Beeton's cookbook published in 1861 has a recipe for roast landrail, as the corncrake was also known, and relates that 'the bird is seen in large numbers in the island of Anglesea. On its first arrival in England it is so lean as scarcely to weigh above five or six ounces; before its departure, however, it has been known to exceed eight ounces and is then delicious eating.'

'Conservation' and 'environmental awareness' are modern discoveries of an era of plenty. The diet of modern man has certainly lost some unique dishes. Where now can you find a good corncrake drumstick? Or a dog steak for all that! Yes, dog. It was a favourite food in medieval times. Recent analysis of bones recovered during excavations at Carrickfergus, Co Antrim reveal that even puppies of five months old went to the table.[27] Similar discoveries have come from sites in Scotland and from Yorkshire in England.

After fish, hides came next in importance as an export during the late medieval period. Documentary evidence from 1560 points to a trade in Irish dog skins from the town of Youghal in Cork to Bridgewater in England. Anyone looking for dog steak today must travel to countries like China or Korea where its flesh is considered a delicacy with important medicinal properties.

Different cultures, different tastes!

[28] Archaeology Ireland, Volume 14, Issue No. 51, Spring 2000, p24.

18

THE CRY OF THE PILIBÍN

'It was a grand starry night by this time an' away under Classiebawn
there, ye could hear the pilibíns rising an' crying — there was a lot of
them in it that time. That was one of the ways that the gamekeepers
could know when there was fellas out huntin' — when they heard the
pilibíns being disturbed.'

Bernie Kelly

A privileged spectator on a small farm atop *Mullagh Mór* (Big Hill)
in the county of Sligo, I look out on a great amphitheatre of sea,
mountain and sky as impoverished February tightens its grip.
Majestic banks of winter clouds tower and threaten, surge and
swell along Benbulben and Knock-na-Rea. Descending in furious haste they unleash their wrath in wind-driven, drenching rain
or white-skirted fusillades of hail. Black curtains of wind and
rain sweep across the moiling sea from Inishmurray island; en-
veloping the mountains they drench again, and yet again the rain-
soaked fields and cast their 'thunder on the stones for all that
Maeve can say'.

Winters jagged edge is everywhere apparent; yet, there is a
stark and sombre elegance in the land prostrated below: in the
gaunt and elegant outline of naked trees, bare hedges, grey stone
ditches resolutely hunched to wind and rain. Nature unfolds.
Gods of wind and light command the ultimate stage, first dousing the sodden land, then, unexpectedly, a burst of radiance:
above the western horizon a crimson sun breaks through, paints
a multi-coloured blaze on a palette of surging clouds. The flam-
ing orange ball descends slowly, exquisitely, rolling down the
slope of Nephin in far Mayo, blushing the Ox Mountains and

Benbulben's noble head.

Short dark days left little time to get the multitude of tasks accomplished let alone to stand and stare in appreciation of the landscape's changing moods. Yet, unbidden, appreciation of its beauty left an indelible imprint, touched a resonant chord somewhere deep within my soul that still abides. The countryside here has changed little; on short winter evenings the sun still burns a fiery vermilion path down Nephin's slopes, blazons its glory on winter clouds.

Cows were kept inside. Housed in warm byres they were fed with hay that had been harvested painstakingly under a summer sun. Fistful by laborious fistful it was now pulled out of a huge rick built in the hay garden and carried in armfuls to the waiting stock. Fires were piled high, doors shut tight.

Every season had its duties and its pleasures: hunting and snaring rabbits was one of the pleasures, a winter occupation that began in harvest and continued to the end of February. It was a way of life for a countryside populous with young men. The hunting, the snaring, the trapping, the chase: it was sport, but it had a serious purpose too. Rabbits were a cheap source of food. They made a tasty, if scant meal. There was not much meat on the bone but boiled they made a very tasty soup. 'Thanks for the rabbits for the soup was grand,' was a popular saying.

The rabbit, although thriving on Irish soil, is not a native. Like the ass, which arrived in the 17th century, it is an import. The Normans carried up to one hundred on each ship to provide fresh meat. Following the 12th century Norman invasion of Ireland some were brought ashore and, well, they bred like rabbits! From the time of their introduction 'rabbit warrens' became a valued possession on estates. They provided hunting for sport, food for the table, and pelts for clothing. Many old estate maps and deeds carry details of these warrens, thus illustrating their importance.

The carcase was sold for food and the pelt converted to fur

coats. During the war years (1939 - 45) poachers went from house to house selling rabbits at five shillings (€0.32) a pair. Buyers such as Johnny Mc Garrigle purchased the skins for half a crown per dozen. By today's standards these seem like trifling amounts but back then it was very good money indeed.

Those who went out hunting had to have proper equipment: a carbide lamp to blind the rabbits and a good hound to chase and catch them. The carbide lamp was a poacher's lamp for salmon as well as rabbits. It gave a piercing beam of bright light produced by burning carbide gas in a chamber behind a magnifying glass. The carbide vapour was produced from two compartments attached to the bottom of the lamp. The upper compartment contained water that dripped into a lower unit containing carbide. The mixture of water and carbide formed a gas that expanded through a nozzle. When a match was touched to the gas it produced an intense, incandescent flame that blinded and rendered helpless the prey.

Carbide provided great sport for young people too. We strapped the empty cylindrical tin boxes that the carbide came in, to a look-alike wooden gun. When a small amount of powder was placed inside, and water added, gas was produced just as in the lamp. A match applied to a tiny hole in the base exploded the mixture blowing the lid off with a convincingly loud bang. This homemade gun was used to good effect in games of 'Cowboys and Indians', popular at the time. As with so much else of the period, carbide lamps are to be found now only in antique shops, and carbide not at all.[29]

With infinite patience the men fed and groomed their dogs and waited. They checked and polished their carbide lamps, pa-

---

[29] The 'Irish Calcium Carbide Co.' commenced the manufacture of carbide in Collooney, Co. Sligo, in 1898. Following a decline in the demand for carbide after the First World War the mill closed. When carbide again came into demand at the beginning of the Second World War, 'Carbide Co. Ltd' purchased the mill. The new company continued in operation there until 1945 when a decline in demand for the product again brought an end to its manufacture. A chain factory replaced the production of carbide. The present company, Stewarts of Boyle, Co. Roscommon, in addition to drawing power for their own use from the nearby waterfall sells its surplus, a considerable 3,000,000 units annually, to the E.S.B.

tiently biding their time, the right time. Then it came: a sudden blessing of warm air carried on a gentle wind from the south. Wafted on the breeze that soft bouquet, the sweet scent of rain. Bred from generations of experience, they instinctively knew this was when the rabbits were out of their burrows, carefree and vulnerable.

A south wind was best too for 'tramming' trout in the estuary with illegal nets. Inexplicably, creatures on land and within the waters respond to the soft wind, the moisture-laden air above. When this happened my father reached for his fishing rod, made ready line and bait and headed for the shore. At a time when man's connection to the land was intimate and strong it was just something instinctively known. Every fisherman knows that:

> Winds from the North, don't venture forth.
> Winds from the East, fishing is the least.
> Winds from the South, blows the lure in their mouth.
> Winds from the West, fishing is the best.

When darkness fell small bands of intrepid hunters raided the demesne of the local landlord with daring and audacity. The landlord may have thought of it as stealing but no one else did. When a poacher was caught there was no stigma attached. A successful raid, a good haul of rabbits and a safe return home created a great sense of excitement, of victory over the odds.

Poaching was a risky venture, but young men rose to the challenge of bailiffs and gamekeepers. Bernie Kelly, an old man when I knew him, wizened and work roughened, but young and athletic then, sat by the fire and re-lived the thrill of the chase. Change the place names and the names of the characters and you will find a scene here that at one time was enacted and re-enacted in every village in Ireland:

'I was working in Gleniff with Patrick Pat John at the time. When the weather suited I'd be away hunting rabbits all night and away early in the morning off on the bicycle to work. Martin Rourke and Paddy Duffy came here to the house about nine o'clock one evening — they were mad anxious to go hunting that night. We had a hound here and he was that good he'd nearly talk to ye! Once he got sight of a rabbit at all he'd nail him. All you had to do was put him in across the estate wall, he was away like a shot and he'd carry the rabbits out across to ye; everyone wanted to hunt with him.

Paddy used to do work for the gamekeepers, the Brackens, so we sent him up to see the lie of the land — ye know, to see if the gates was shut and if they were closed up and settled down for the night or if it looked like they might be going out watching. Anyways, when Paddy came back:

"Aah, ye're dead safe", he says, "There's not a stir on them, they'll hardly be going out tonight."

Well, at the heel of the hunt, I didn't want to go because me shoes and clothes was still wet from work that day. Anyway me father let me put his shoes on so that mine would be dry for the morning and away with us, Martin Rourke, me brother, Dan, God be good to the two of them, they're dead now, Paddy Duffy an' meself, away for Moffit's Burra.

We didn't rise no rabbits until we got as far as the back of Classiebawn and there we nailed five o' them as quick as a flash. As soon as we put the light on them the dog had them! Things wasn't going so good after that and we had a chat to see what we'd do. I was for going out to *Ros Caoireach* and, looking back on it, if I had to get me way we'd all have been caught [*Ros Caoireach* is a long promontory easily blocked off]. Martin Rourke and meself tried *Poll na Weegoge* and there wasn't a rabbit to be seen. Martin says to me,

"There's no rabbits here, we'll go in and try the Black Rocks under Classiebawn." We were just going out by *Poll na Weegoge* when what did we see but the two lamps coming. 'Twas Wattie and Jules Bracken, they were so sure they had us trapped that they kept their lamps lit — they were certain they had us blocked.

Paddy Duffy and Dan was in the open and they made their escape. Martin and meself had to come in through the big stones and poor Martin, he kept the lamp lit so we'd see where we were goin'. He ran as fast as he could an' when he got as far as the sand banks, poor divil, he nearly burnt the hands off himself when he opened the glass to quench the lamp. The two boys was hot on our heels so we split up. I took the cartway towards *Pollachurry* and down through the *claddagh*. There I lay for half an hour, I still had the rabbits with me, an' the Bracken's with the lamps overhead searching. I could hear them calling to one another. After awhile anyway, all went quiet and I figured the other fellas was surely caught.

I waited another half an hour, took the rabbits with me, climbed up the bank an' who did I see but Jules Bracken going up over the hill near the Salmon Hole with his big lamp. It was getting so you could see a little bit because it was getting very starry and the next thing didn't I spot Watty lying in the cartway down under me, stretched out an' waiting, but he didn't see me.

I decided to go back down an' hide the few rabbits I had in the *claddagh* and try to jook (steal) 'round him. I started to creep past him when didn't I spot our hound circling in the banks searching for us. Watty saw him too and started calling the dog an' coaxing him over to him. When he got close to the dog he took off his scarf and put it round the dog to hold him. I lay there below him for ages shivering with the cold and wet — he had the dog an' he was a great wee dog — I didn't want to go home without him. After a long time anyway I got up and started towards Watty, the two of them was there then an' they put the lamps on me.

"I have ye now" says Jules, "Ye might as well tell me who was with ye."

"There was no-one with me" says I.

I wasn't going to give the game away!

The next thing they wanted to know was where the rabbits was but I told them nothing and after awhile they gave me the dog and when they did, away home with me across the Burra. It was a grand starry night by this time an' away under Classiebawn there, ye could hear the *pilibíns* (plover) rising an' crying — there was a lot of them in it that time. That was one of the ways that the Brackens could know when there was fellas out hunting, when they heard the *pilibíns* being disturbed.

Eventually when I got down as far as Pa Duffy's I lay at the rick there for half an hour waiting for the rest of the fellas, Dan, Martin Rourke and Paddy Duffy but there was no sign of them. I had the dog with me, it was three in the morning an' I didn't know what to do. I chanced it anyway an' knocked on Duffy's door. There they were, the three of them inside! Bee, that was Pa's wife, had a coat over the window so the Brackens wouldn't see the light of the paraffin lamp through the window. She had a big pot of tea made for the boys and a big cake on the table.

"Jasus", says I, "Is it here ye are an' me waiting for ye all night. Were ye caught?"

"No", they said, "We got away alright."

"Ye ran away and left the dog there", says I, "But I had to go back for him or he'd have been shot!"

Well, to finish the story anyway, meself and Dan had to go to Brackens to sign that we wouldn't hunt for rabbits again. It was that or get a summons and go to Court. When we went up to the house, Jules came to the door and he nodded to us to go 'round the back.

"What the help doesn't see won't trouble them," he says.

We had to sign a paper there in the front room and when we were ready to leave, "Will ye tell me now who was with ye last night," he says.

"Well, to tell you the truth," I says to him, "When I didn't tell you first, I won't tell ye now."

He looked at me then: "I'll give ye credit now for that," he says.

Well that was that, but, of course, we went back again, that didn't stop us from hunting. We had a hound here, the best dog any-one ever had; he was that good, he used to go into the pound field and take the rabbits out to us over the ditch. You could hear the rabbits squealing but if the Brackens didn't actually catch ye on their property they couldn't do a bloody hate with ye. Jules was a good runner. He knew everyone was at the rabbits. He could see the hounds at the people's houses, but he had to catch ye to prove it.

Tom Gilmartin of Cloontybawn was buying the rabbits. He sent them into Sligo. Ye'd get fourpence for a pair of rabbits in the 30's. If ye went from house to house ye'd get a shilling or more a pair. Johnny McGarrigle from Ballintrillick, came around later with a horse and spring-cart buying them.'

Bernie was lucky he wasn't born a few decades earlier when the penalty for getting caught with the landlord's rabbits was trans-portation for life to Van Diemen's Land, now known as Tasma-nia, an island off the Australian coast. Very few ever returned from that distant shore. In the 1900s the worst that could hap-pen was a fine when the offender was brought in front of the Dis-trict Court. Oftener, as in Bernie's case, minor offenders were chastised verbally and released with a promise to respect the rights of property in future.

The Brackens were the only family with a wireless (radio) back then so the entire village packed into their kitchen on a winter's night in the '50s to cheer the debut of a local fiddle player of note, Peter Mullaney. He had recently been recorded by Radio Eire-ann and was going out on air this night. It was a big occasion — but not everyone was impressed. A local man, Dan D——, recog-nised the occasion as the perfect opportunity for a raid and laid his plans accordingly.

Next morning, when he was spotted heading away to catch the early bus weighed down with two suitcases, no one thought any-thing of it. Everyone, including the gamekeepers, presumed he was heading overseas for work, as was common at the time, or about some other legitimate business. Later in the day, when the empty traps were discovered, it dawned on them that Dan had had a great night's sport. It didn't take long to figure out that it wasn't clothes he was carrying in the trunks! His audacity on the night of the great rabbit raid is still remembered by veterans of the era with great amusement.

Ferrets were the preferred method by some for catching rabbits. Jimmy Mc Gowan was a common sight in the rabbit warrens with his sleek, creamy coloured predator slung in a wooden box from his shoulder. His technique was to seal off all the rabbit holes in the warren with nets, except one, into which he put the little furry killer. A leather muzzle covered its snout in order to thwart its natural instincts of killing and gorging on his prey. The terrified animals, on scenting the ferret, shot out of their burrows at top speed and straight into the waiting web. All Jimmy had to do was take them out of the net, break their necks and bag them.

There is no such thing as a perfect plan and Jimmy often had to wait hours for his charge to return. Sometimes they never did. Recognising a perfect food supply, and a freer lifestyle, they sometimes surrendered to the call of the wild.

Ferrets had other uses — of a medicinal kind. Owners were often called upon to provide a cure for 'chin-cough' (whooping cough). The remedy was in the milk they drank. When their thirst was quenched they spat into the milk and, thus impregnated, the milk was believed to be a very effective treatment.

Snares of slim, braided copper wire attached to a stake and placed on rabbit 'runs' or paths was another efficient method of trapping and killing rabbits. Experience was essential here too as just any old place wasn't good enough. Rabbits always used the same path to and from the burrow. In addition, they hopped on exactly the same spot every time leaving an indentation on the ground, with a grassy mound in between that was easily recognisable. Everyone had their own special techniques but generally the noose was set four fingers high and placed between the 'hops' on the rabbit runs.

Hares could be snared in this way too but being bigger and stronger they required a sturdier stake. Sometimes the preferred method was to tie the snare to a stone. When the animal was caught in the noose it dragged the stone until it suffocated. Although hares too used paths, the most effective placement of the loop was in front of openings in the stone ditches that they used when travelling from one field to another.

If the stone selected was too light there was a danger it would be dragged across several ditches and fields before the copper wire tightened sufficiently around the hare's neck to choke it. I will never forget the soft downy fur, the hopeless, pleading brown eyes, the sharp 'rabbit punch' to the back of the neck when the hare was caught. This mercy punch quickly put the animal out of its suffering.

Now, in the springtime of the year, I watch these agile animals lope across the fields and meadows and marvel at their grace and lithesome beauty. I remember too and repent my heartless youth and insensitivity of long ago when I also travelled the moonlit fields on winter nights setting the deadly wires.

The introduction of the killer disease, myxomatosis, spelled the death knell of the rabbit industry. Myxomatosis is a viral disease spread by fleas. It was developed in Australia to control the population of the European rabbit that had increased to uncontrollable proportions there. Its introduction to Ireland in the 1950's was a shock. The new and strange sight of disease-stricken rabbits staggering blind along fields and roads with swollen heads and protruding eyes was revolting.

Almost immediately they ceased to have any food value. Country people blamed butchers for introducing the epidemic thereby eliminating a competing source of meat supply. In addition, the eradication of rabbits made more grassland available for grazing cattle. Rabbits never regained the popularity they once had as a food source and is now regarded in the wild only as a pest.

It was the end of a colourful era. No more predatory game-keepers, hounds or carbide lamps. No more midnight hunters or hunted travelling the fields with dog and lamp by starlight tuned in to the thrill of the chase and the cry of the *pilibín*.

I, PETER GILMARTIN, of Carnduff, Creevykeel, in the County of Sligo, hereby admit that I trespassed in pursuit of game on the 8th day of December, 1915 on part of the lands of Creevykeel, in the occupation of Mr Patrick Gilmartin. I hereby express my apology to Mr Wilfred Ashley the owner of the Game on such lands and undertake not to repeat such trespass. I further agree to pay the sum of Ten Shillings as and for the costs incurred by Mr Ashley in this matter.

Signed by the said Peter Gilmartin:
in presence of :-

Peter Gilmartin

Jules Bracken

Received from Mr Peter Gilmartin the sum of Ten shillings costs mentioned in the above Apology.

Apology for trespass on fields of Patrick Gilmartin, tenant of Classiebawn estate, property of Lord Ashley.

19

WITCH HARES AND SILVER BULLETS

'It was all muzzle loaders they had that time, y'know. They got the silver and powder, made up the cartridges, and Brian set out to catch the witch hare...'

Mickey McGroarty

Unlike rabbits, hunters felt there was something dark and sinister about the hare. This may be because it was once a common belief that witches could turn themselves into hares in order to travel about the countryside unnoticed. Preferring not to come across hares at all, huntsmen removed and discarded the distinctive white scut immediately on capture. There is no logical explanation for the practice and hunters could not explain why they did it. Some said that if the animal was brought into the presence of an expectant mother without the scut being removed it would cause the unborn to have a harelip. They couldn't say why, but it was passed-on information and they believed it. Perhaps this fragment of ancient beliefs was once recognised as a means of neutralizing the witch's power.

Stories of women who turned themselves into milk-stealing witch hares were once common. The transformation was rarely seen but some instances are recorded. 'Hare, hare, God send thee care; I am in a hare's likeness now, but I shall be a woman even now; hare, hare, God send thee care,' was one of the incantations used to reverse the conversion'[30].

Journeymen: tailors, carpenters, boat-builders, all once travelled from village to village staying a while here or there wherever they found work. One of these, a tailor, was given lodging in the loft of a farmhouse in Kilfenora, Co. Clare. As the dawn light filtered through the window he was awakened by a bustle of noise in the kitchen. Looking out from his bed he saw the woman of

[30] Visions and Beliefs in the West of Ireland, Lady Gregory, p308

the house filling a tub with water. When it was full she mixed in herbs and a coal from the fire. Throwing her clothes off she stepped into the mixture and was instantly transformed into a hare. The astonished man watched as she sped out the door and off down the field. After an hour or so the hare returned, jumped into the water and was immediately turned back into a woman.

The witch-hare was feared — but there was a defence against it: a silver bullet. Mickey Mc Groarty knew all about such things and often spoke of strange encounters in his native Selacis, Co. Donegal, and how handed-down knowledge saved the day:

'There was this man that lived out there at the Church at Ballindiver, we'll call him Brian — there's a man in there now the name of Willie Ray — but this was before his time. This other man had eight cows in the byre. In the early part of the spring-time he used to have plenty of milk but as time went on he'd go out mornings an' he'd have hardly anything at all!

One night he was rambling an' talkin' to this neighbour man an' tellin' him the story about the cows not doin' so good.

"Take care my good man," says the neighbour back to him, "is it the witch hare that's at it, this oul' woman that lives down by Drumbleigh, maybe she's sucking?"

"Begod," says Brian back to him, "right enough when I went out the other morning there was a hare going across the road an' it went away down the field but I thought it only natural and passed no notice of it."

"Oh," says the other fellow, "that was her away with a bellyfull of milk!"

"What'll I do with her," says Brian.

"Have ye a gun?" the other man replied.

"I have, an' a good one."

"Well go into Donegal Town, go into the shops there an' get all the silver thruppeny bits ye can gather, and a bit of gunpowder, then come to me an' I'll make a few cartridges for ye."

It was all muzzle loaders they had that time, y'know. They got

the silver and powder, made up the cartridges, and Brian set out
to catch the witch hare. He got up early in the mornings and sat
near the byre watchin' for her. On the third morning he was
watchin' as usual an' didn't he see the hare goin' down the lane an'
her swerving with the weight of a big bellyfull of milk!

He put up the gun anyway, pulled the trigger an' missed, but he
broke her hind leg just the same. Away with the hare limping as
best she could, an' away with yer man after her. He followed her
down to the field an' down to the house in Drumbleigh. He went
in after her an' there was no hare but the oul' woman lying on the
floor, all blood, an' her roaring a meela murdher!

She was taken away to the hospital but she lost the leg with
gangrene and was given a wooden leg. That was the end of the
suckin' of the cows anyway an' there was plenty of butter about
the Glebe at Tullyfin after that. That's a true story y'know, they
could do them things!'

It wasn't the only time this happened in Mickey's neighbourhood. There were other strange goings-on that involved hares,
cows and milk stealing. In addition to silver bullets, black
hounds too had the power to kill or injure the hare witch.

Two of Mickey Mc Groarty's neighbours hunted rabbits regularly with a pair of hounds, one black, the other grey. Hunting
was poor one night so they decided to leave Druimagrath near
Mickey's house and go out behind Drumbline to see if they could
do any better. Crossing the ditch they noticed a hare racing
through a field of grass. Unaware it was being observed it made
its way down into a field where there was a herd of cattle. Watching from cover the two men were amazed to see the creature
going from cow to cow. Sitting underneath each cow she seemed
to be sucking the milk from the udders.

One of the men remembered hearing about witch hares and
stolen milk. An old man had once told him that the only dog capable of killing such an enchanted creature was a black hound.
Seizing the opportunity they brought the black dog up and crept

closer and closer. When they unleashed the animal it sped off in pursuit of the hare, which at once bounded away from the cows and off down the meadow. The chase was on and Mickey recalled the creature's cleverness.

'There wasn't a turn or a trick in the book but she knew,' he said

The chase wound and twisted. It went over ditches, across hills, through briars and fields of whins, the hare all the while slowly losing ground. Bit by bit it made its way closer and closer to a house down under Drumbline. Just as the hare cleared the ditch into the field where stood the little house, the black hound got close enough to make a snap at it. Snatching a mouthful of hair and blood it tumbled the hare across the fence.

The two men then lost sight of the chase. Crossing the ditch they went into the house to enquire if anyone had seen which way the animals went. The man that answered the door told them he had seen or heard nothing. As he spoke the men saw drops of blood leading behind a curtain that concealed a kitchen bed. Thinking they had found the hare they walked over and pulled back the drapes. Instead of a wounded animal they were surprised to see an old woman lying there. She was stretched out on the bed tending to an injury on her thigh. Apologising for disturbing the household the men left.

Later, when the men told their story to Mickey and his friends they began to put two and two together. This woman was known to have only one cow but yet 'she could have a "butt" of butter to town with her as good as the man that had seven cows.'

Nothing could be proven but it seemed a strange coincidence that she got her injury at the same time as the hound injured the hare. She wasn't seen for a long time after that but when she recovered she never sent butter to town again. From that day on, according to Mickey, she had 'a wee lame step with her'.

My father once sent me over to our neighbour, Johnny Barry, to help him save his hay. It was a dry, hot day of brilliant sunshine. My father wasn't taken in with this tease of a heat wave on the way.

'Boiling rain!' he said emphatically. 'Never mind yer football, go over and give the man a hand. It'll be pouring outa the heavens tomorrow.'

The sun shone down and the sunny hours went slowly by. Johnny and I chatted all day as I forked the hay to him; we built, shaped and roped trampcock after trampcock. Johnny had been out milking early that morning, he informed me, and found a little stool in the pasture.

'A grand wee stool' he said. It might have been a painter's bench he surmised. Artists often set up their easels out in the fields to paint the landscape.

'Wouldn't it be funny', Johnny said, 'if we were to say that it was a hare dropped it going out the gap!'

We both laughed at that and the talk turned to instances where hares had been found milking cows. Could they really be witches we wondered or were they just ordinary hares that liked a drink of fresh milk — and would the cows let them take the milk anyway?

We didn't know.

Next day the rumour spread like wildfire: Johnny Barry had found a hare milking his cows. He had told a neighbour woman and sure neither of them was ever known to tell a lie. John Terry Billy Gallagher's mother in Carnduff stopped me on the way home from the creamery for a sweet can of skim milk, as was her custom.

She was agog.

'Was there any truth in it?' she wanted to know.

'Oh, aye, sure, didn't I see the stool myself!' said I not wanting to kill a good story.

And so it went.

Eventually when Johnny and I thought the joke had gone far

enough and decided to tell the truth no one would believe us. They thought we were denying it because of all the sensation and publicity.

I have no doubt but there are still some people in North Sligo who remember the incident, and are still convinced that a hare had indeed once been found milking cows in Mullaghmore!

It was once commonly believed that a hare crossing the path of a pregnant woman caused the child, when born, to have a cleft palate or 'hare's lip'. Most women knew what to do and tore their petticoat immediately in order to neutralize the curse. In England the belief was similar: 'Insomuch as some in company with a woman great with childe have upon the crossing of such creatures, cut or torn some of the clothes off that woman with childe, to prevent the ill luck that might befall her.' How strange it is then that, conversely, the worldwide belief that the carrying of a rabbit or hare's foot brings good luck!

Looking back in time we see that even the ancient Romans believed hares had special powers. They used them for divination. Boadicea, Queen of the British Celts may have learned the art from them and used it to advantage over her enemies. Accounts relate an occasion where she 'opened her bosom and let go a hare,' prior to a battle with the Roman enemy in order to foretell the outcome of the fight. 'The frighted animal made such turnings and windings in its course, as, according to the then rules of judging, prognosticated happy success.' Boadicea and her armies, greatly encouraged by the sign, attacked the Roman enemy with confidence and routed them.

The Welsh too used the animal to predict success or misfortune: if they ran before a man it was a sign he would be able to conquer his enemies; if they ran to the right he could anticipate danger; to the left he had enemies in his household. As with Boadicea if they went in a zigzag before him he would have much success — but if they ran back on their path it was an omen of death.

Whatever we may think about such beliefs it has been shown that animals have a sense of the preternatural that humans do not. A dog or a horse can sense or see things that are invisible to human beings. The dog whimpers and trembles, the horse shakes with fear and becomes almost paralysed. In the dark night the hunter's hounds sometimes cowered in situations where they would normally tear a rabbit to pieces on the spot. Jack Jordan of Templeboy, Co. Sligo feared neither ghost, fairy or banshee. He hunted with hounds and lamp at all hours.

On one memorable night his dog started a rabbit near a fairy fort and gave chase. To his astonishment the normally timid creature, instead of running away, suddenly turned towards the dog. The hound fled and 'went between my legs squealing and round about me with the hair standing up straight on his back'. The rabbit, if such it was, raced past him. Despite Jack's urgings the hound wouldn't budge from between his legs. Afterwards, when Jack spoke about the incident he recalled that almost immediately he heard 'great music and great laughing and shouting around the fort'.

Alarmed by the experience he immediately set out for home but went astray in fields well known to him and was unable to find his way home until morning.

Hares were not the only animals into which mortals could be transformed. In England and on the Continent people believed at one time that humans could turn themselves into wolves. There was a similar belief in Ireland but here the transformation was not that of the dreaded werewolf but a peculiar Irish mutation.

Giraldus Cambrensus was first, c1184, to record the phenomenon. His accounts are notoriously unreliable but nevertheless, as little is recorded of Ireland in the 12th century, we have little to pick and choose from. According to his account a priest on his travels was astonished when a wolf came and spoke to him asking that he confer the last rites on his female companion, which he did. It transpired that a clergyman had turned the luckless pair into wolves. The wolf-man explained:

'We are natives of Ossory. From there every seven years, because of the imprecations of a certain saint, namely the Abbot Natalis, two persons, a man and a woman are compelled to go into exile not only from their territory but also from their bodily shape. They put off the form of a man completely and put on the form of a wolf. When the seven years are up, and if they have survived, two others take their place in the same way, and the first pair returns to their former country and nature.'

The priest gave the last rites as requested but balked at giving Holy Communion to an animal. When one of the creatures peeled back her fur to reveal a human body underneath, the priest relented. Some accounts relate that it was St. Patrick who inflicted the curse some centuries earlier, following a refusal by two of the congregation to listen to his sermon. Baying at him like wolves he cursed them and they shortly took on the shape of the animals they imitated!

Witches were another aberration universally feared and hated in medieval and, to a lesser extent, in modern times. The penalty on discovery was death. Given their suspected magical powers the difficulty was to gain enough evidence to prosecute them. A common method of testing the guilt or innocence of a suspected witch was to tie her right thumb to her left toe, her left thumb to her right toe and throw her into a pool of water. If she sank she was innocent. If she floated she was a witch, 'for water, as being the element in baptism, refuses to receive such a sinner in its bosom.'

The Irish did not engage in witch-hunts and were tolerant of people whose mystical powers they did not understand. Hares suspected of stealing milk were chased but there is no record of any woman being victimised by neighbours for such an offence.

Nevertheless a witch burning did take place, that of Petronilla de Midia, Alice Kyteler's maid, in Kilkenny in 1324 by Anglo-Norman colonists who were predominant there.

DeMidia's burning, and the persecution of Alice Kyteler, was at the instigation of Bishop Ledrede, the papal appointee in Ireland dubbed 'an ignorant low-born vagabond from England' by Arnold le Poer, the chief judge and highest official of the court in Ireland at that time.[31] In the hysteria of the age, Pope John XXII, who had a great fear of sorcery and believed his own life in danger from witchcraft, had listed such practitioners as heretics in a papal bull.

One of the most famous witch trials in Ireland was that of Florence Newton of Youghal who was arrested on the 24th March 1661 for bewitching Mary Langdon. When the Mayor sent for a boat to carry out the 'water experiment' she immediately confessed to the lesser offence of 'overlooking'. Was this the first recorded instance in history of 'plea bargaining'?

Eight women were tried and found guilty of witchcraft in 1711 in Carrickfergus. They were sentenced to a year's imprisonment during which time they were forced to stand four times in the pillory where they were pelted with eggs and cabbage stalks. A woman found guilty of witchcraft in Sutherland, Scotland in 1722 was strangled and burnt.

Suspected witches were hanged in the United States as recently as the late 17th century. The story of Goody Glover, executed in Massachusetts in 1688, depicts an unfortunate end to an ill-starred life. Although living in the U.S.A., Goody was not American but an Irish Catholic and a native Irish speaker. Transported to Barbados from Ireland in the aftermath of the Cromwellian confiscations, she was only one among many thousands sent out at that time.

Goody's execution was followed some years later by the notorious Salem witch trials where, in the space of sixteen months, two hundred women were accused of witchcraft. One hundred

[31] History Ireland, Vol. 2, No. 4, Winter 1994, p23. Also Irish Witchcraft and Demonology, St. John D. Seymour

and fifty of these were imprisoned and twenty-five hanged. The Irishwoman Glover's trial and death marked the beginning of a wave of debased self-righteousness and vindictiveness that has ever since characterised American Puritanism and Salem as a by-word for intolerance, cruelty and injustice.

'You have burnt all the witches,' the poet W.B. Yeats accused the Scots. 'In Ireland we have left them alone. To be sure the "loyal minority" knocked out the eye of one with a cabbage-stump on the 31st of March, 1711, in the town of Carrickfergus. But then the "loyal minority" is half Scottish. You have discovered the faeries to be pagan and wicked. You would like to have them all up before the magistrate. In Ireland warlike mortals have gone among them, and helped them in their battles, and they in turn have taught men great skill with herbs, and permitted some few to hear their tunes.' [32]

Such was a healer was Moll Anthony who lived near Red Hills in Kildare in the early 19th century. Crowds came from all over Ireland to benefit from her supernatural powers of divination and healing. Her cures came from a bottle filled with water, 'darkly coloured by a decoction of herbs, gathered with certain incantations near a rath that afforded the necessary *materia medica* of fairy doctors for the cure of a special disease.'

Clarewoman, Biddy Earley, was the most prominent 'witch' in Ireland until her death in 1874. Her fame lived after her. People came to her from far and near to have their ailments cured and to seek advice. Still remembered for her benevolent powers of prophecy and healing, Lady Gregory recorded this incident illustrating her powers as a clairvoyant:

'There was a boy of the Cloonans I knew was at Killinane thatching Heniff's house. And a woman passed by, and she looked up at him, but she never said, "God bless the work." And Cloonans mother was on the road to Gort and the woman met her and said, "Where did your son learn thatching?' And that day he had a great fall and was brought home hurt, and the

[32] W.B. Yeats, Mythologies, 'A Remonstrance with Scotsmen for having Soured the Disposition of their Ghosts and Faeries', Collier Books, p107

mother went to Biddy Earley. And she said, "Didn't a red-haired woman meet you one day going to Gort and ask where did your son learn thatching? And didn't she look up at him as she passed? It was then it was done." And she gave a bottle, and he got well after a while.[33]

[33] Visions and Beliefs in the West of Ireland, p81

20

THE EVIL EYE

'Ye shouldn't begrudge anything you sell, even if you sell it too cheap.'

Bernie Kelly

Customs and traditions long held, proven by experience, and passed down from generation to generation controlled many aspects of farm life. For instance, when the head of a household died, it was customary for the surviving son, daughter or wife to bring the farm livestock for sale to the next fair. If they were sold, some portion of that money, a pound or two or five was kept, depending on what the family could afford. This was put away and kept safely in order to bring luck to the house. Not so long ago this custom was taken very seriously in rural Ireland.

'Selling the cattle on a death continued up till about thirty years ago', Hugh Pat G—— of Ballintrillick, Co. Sligo told me as recently as 1996.

'The reason for it was that when a person died in a house it was well noticed that lots of cattle would die, *which I saw happening*. I saw it happening in houses! I saw it in one house, hens and pigs an' everything around the house died! If a man that died had a horse, he was definitely sold, afraid the horse'd die too. In my young days it was the custom, people used to do it, but people don't do it so much now. Back then ye were talking about small money for a cow — three or four pounds. A person that had five or six cows was a wealthy man!'

'Death never comes empty handed,' Bernie Gallagher of Laghey, Co. Donegal told me. 'If somebody died in a house ye'd lose cattle or ye'd lose a horse. Ye'd have to sell off three or four cattle. Ye wouldn't sell them all together, a few at a time.'

In Co. Mayo it was common practise to sell the family horse immediately following the farmer's death. A Swinford man recalled his father going to buy a horse near Charlestown. When he discovered the horse was being sold because of a death in the family he 'changed his mind' and bought elsewhere.

Luck was a fragile thing and easily unbalanced. As we have seen, one death often brought on several more. The belief that death or bad luck could also be inflicted on animals, or people, by a person's look was universal. In biblical times the faithful were advised: 'Eat thou not the bread of him that hath an evil eye, neither desire thou his dainty meats: for as he thinketh in his heart, so is he' (Proverbs, 23 verses 6-7). In Greece the influence of the terrifying Gorgon daughters of the sea god Phorcys and his wife Ceto were legendary. All avoided them as one glance from them turned the unwary to stone.

The original purpose of the bridal veil was to protect the bride from the harm that could be inflicted on her by jealous or envious eyes. Two thousand years ago Pliny, the Roman writer and scientist pondered on a remedy for people affected by the curse. As an antidote he believed in the effectiveness of spittle. We are not surprised. When Jesus opened the eyes of the blind man wasn't he just practising an old Jewish superstition by mixing clay with spittle?

On receiving 'luck penny' at country fairs in Ireland the purchaser spat on the money before putting it in his pocket. In some places you may still see the buyer and seller spit on their hands before slapping them together to seal the bargain. It's not seen so much anymore but friends who had not met for a long time often passed their hand over their mouth to receive a small spray of spit before heartily shaking hands.

In Ireland the earliest and most terrible example of the 'evil eye' or 'drohuil', is found in Celtic mythology in the person of Balor of the Evil Eye, leader of the Fomorians. During the Ordnance Survey of 1836 O'Donovan in his letters wrote that, 'It is said by the people that he was perfectly skilled in the Magic Art, that he always kept a cover on his eye, which he took off whenever he intended to do an injury by his look.'

Fortunately it was only on the battlefield his fearsome power was unleashed. When the eye was exposed no warrior could stand before it, they were immediately destroyed. Legend has it that he acquired this awesome gift when his eye was involuntarily exposed to a venomous concoction being brewed by his father's Druids.

The Tuatha dé Danaan, under the leadership of King Nuada, defeated the Fomorians in a great battle at Moyturra in Co. Sligo.

> 'The Tuatha dé Danaan
> By force of potent spells and wicked magic,
> And conjurations horrible to bear —
> Could set the ministers of hell at work
> And raise a slaughtered army from the earth —
> And make them live and breathe and fight again...'

Nothing could stand before the fairy people: Balor's fate was to have his eye put out during the battle by the victorious Tuatha de Danaan, 'the blood from which gushed forth to form the lake of Lochán na Súil (Lake of the Eye) near Moyturra in the parish of Kilmactranny in Co. Sligo.'

In recent times a woman from Maugherow, Co. Sligo recalled having a small bag of salt attached to the hem of her skirt or jacket as a protection against such dangers. She often spoke of an incident she had witnessed as a young girl concerning her neighbour John who was reputed to have the evil eye. A neighbour, Pat, had a fine healthy pig about to have *banbhs*. John passed by one day when the beast was out 'hoking' on the side of the road. The animal was fat and heavy and he passed the remark that she'd 'have a good litter of *banbhs*'— without expressing the customary 'good luck to the baste'.

'He wasn't right gone from the place,' she recalled, 'till the sow came into the yard, lay down an' got very sick. The cure was that if ye could get the person with the evil eye to come to the house an' say, "Good luck to the beast", well, the beast would get up. That was one of the cures for it. They found him and brought him back to the house anyway and brought him out to the pigsty but no matter what tricks they used they couldn't get him to say it.

They were puzzled as to what to try next. Then the woman of the house remembered hearing one time that if ye got an article of the man's clothing and burned it under the sick animal's nose, it would be cured. She had a scissors in her hand but couldn't get a chance to get a bit of his clothes. When the man left the house anyway didn't he leave the cap after him an' that was her chance. She took the cap and cut a piece out of it an' went out an' lit it and put it under the sow's nose. The next thing was the animal was up an' around the yard lively as anything an' looking for food. That's as sure now as I'm telling ye!'

Another woman remembered cutting out the letters of the alphabet for her father when she was a young girl. If the person who did the overlooking was unknown the letters of the alphabet were placed in a bucket. In that way the person's name was included among the others, no matter what it was. All was then burned under the cows nose, 'in the name of the three persons of the Blessed Trinity'. Whatever letters were left unburned spelled out the name of the culprit. She saw it happen that way. If the overlooker's name was known, then only the letters of his name were burned.

A Laghey, Co. Donegal, man, had a neighbour who was 'a great man to look at your cows. He'd say nothing only look at them. It was noticed that he had the evil eye. He'd come to your house, you might be milkin' an' he could walk in. Jasus they'd rather see the divil coming. He'd never say "good luck" to them or anything.'

'This fella was peculiar in his ways,' Brian went on. 'He'd be slow to thatch. He'd go out at night when the storm'd be raging.

The rick would be shaking and the roof with the straws flying off it like hell. He used to pray to the Blessed Virgin, he'd pray up to the sky: "If you leave a roof over my head this night it'll be a while till I bother you again." He'd be for thatching then but of course the next good day came he wouldn't thatch again, he'd wait on. He always had a mind to thatch. You could see the stars out through the roof!'

According to Enid Porter in *The Folklore of East Anglia*, belief in the malign effects of the evil eye was alive and well there in the closing years of the 20th century. As recently as 1974 a woman glared out of her window at a group of children playing hopscotch in front of her house. The villagers blamed her when one of the boys fell over and sprained his ankle.

In Norfolk, if a Mrs. Millinger took a dislike to anyone, 'she would look sideways at his pigs, and they invariably sickened and died.' Her gaze could even penetrate a wall for it was said that if she sat at night by her fire and was in a bad temper her neighbour on the other side of the wall could not get his fire to burn. Although living alone and completely housebound she seemed to know all her neighbours affairs and was able to tell her visitors, which were few, of happenings in the village about which they knew nothing.

A Cambridgeshire woman once found her brood of ducklings covered with vermin and dying one by one. She knew immediately what she had to do. Suspecting the use of the evil eye she bought an ounce of new pins and sticking them in one of the dead bodies she threw it on a blazing fire at midnight. Within minutes the overlooker was at the door screaming in pain. Next morning the ducks were healthy and free from lice.

The burning of a piece of thatch from the house of an old woman in Toft, Cambridgeshire, was successful in curing sick pigs which she had overlooked. Drawing blood from an affected animal was another way to break the spell. When the blood was burned the bewitcher suffered the pain of burning too. Hunchbacks too were believed to be able to give protection. The kings and nobility of England and even further afield in France, and in the Hapsburg Empire, employed them as shields against the affliction.

How then was the evil eye obtained? Was it an inherent evil within some people or was it involuntarily acquired?

In the Mediterranean where eyes are normally dark it is people with blue eyes that are suspect; in northern Europe where people generally have light coloured eyes it is the dark eyed person that causes concern. In Ireland 'blinking' has nothing to do with the colour of the eye. A jealous or malicious person could willingly use it, or it could be involuntary. Even Popes weren't immune: Pius IX was said to have the curse so that 'when he blessed people, some would avert their faces and spit to avoid the spell.'

Some people had no control over its ill effect — many were not even aware they possessed any special power for evil. Even so, most 'overlooking' was believed to be malicious. Death, illness, bodily injury or any number of ill effects followed from it.

It was believed that, 'if a mother was breast feeding the baby herself, if she had a lot of work to do some days and couldn't be bothered to breast feed, she might put the baby on a bottle. Well, then, the baby might be happy enough on the bottle, but she'd put the baby back on breast feeding again when she had the time. All this changing back and forth from one to the other is what gives the baby the evil eye.' Similarly, when a nursing mother didn't have enough milk, a 'wet nurse' sometimes took over. It was to such disturbances that the acquisition of the evil eye was attributed.

A woman once informed Lady Gregory that some of her neighbours believed the power was acquired by those who were baptised wrong. She didn't believe it herself but thought instead that, 'when a woman is carrying, some one that meets her says, "So you're in that way," and she says, "The devil a fear of me," as even a married woman might say for sport or not to let on; the devil gets possession of the child at that moment, and when it is born it has the evil eye.'

Country people had to be constantly vigilant. There was no point in pretending these things didn't exist. Better to be prepared, better to know who or what to look out for; it was wise to take precautions, to know the antidotes. There were individuals with whom it was unlucky to do business as the animals acquired from them wouldn't thrive or, worse still, die. My neighbour, Bernie Kelly was emphatic about it: 'Ye shouldn't begrudge anything you sell, even if you sell it too cheap,' he said.

Extravagant praise of a child's beauty or cleverness or good health, or the health or numbers of a farmer's herd should be accompanied by a counteracting expression of goodwill. 'Good luck to the beast' was the customary declaration which averted any ill consequences for animals. Fynes Moryson (1566-1630), an English traveller and historian to Lord Mountjoy, Lord Lieutenant of Ireland, recorded the practice on a visit here in the early 17th century: 'The farming community', he wrote, 'are much offended if a man commend their Cattle, except withal he say God save them, or ells spitt upon them. That some men's eyes bewitch their horses, and if they prove lame or ill, old women are sought to say short prayers and utter many incantations to recover them'.

'Good luck to the animal but always God bless the child,' a Leitrim woman told me. It was not appropriate to call on God's blessing for animals. Likewise, 'Good luck to the child', was inappropriate for youngsters. The two invocations were not interchangeable. W.B. Yeats, pondering why Mary Hynes of Ballylee might have been 'taken' observed that, 'the admired and desired are only safe if one says, "God bless them" when one's eyes are upon them'.

Discussion of an individual's blemish or deformity was, and sometimes still is, accompanied by the invocation, 'God bless the mark.' 'God bless all here but the cat' has been degraded to a humorous greeting in our time but it was not always so; cats were deemed to have associations with satanic forces on which a heavenly blessing was either wasted or unwelcome. It was often that people, when they were moving from one house to another, would not take the cat with them! 'It was indeed unlucky to do it,' Peig Minihan of the Beara peninsula in Co. Cork believed, 'but if it followed you in any way there was nothing against it then.'

The brutal clearances by Sir Robert Gore-Booth of the entire population of the 'Seven Cartrons' on the Lissadell estate in Co. Sligo in 1839 left a deep and painful scar that is still remembered. There is to this day a place near the Lissadell House known as 'Cat's Corner'. It earned its name at the time of the evictions when, it is said, the cats of the area, also homeless, gathered there when the people left. Locals still recall stories of their piteous cries that could be heard for miles around as they sought vainly for something to eat or someone to feed them.

On first hearing of the event I wondered why so many cats were gathered there. And why only cats! Where were the dogs? Perhaps the explanation is that the evicted tenants, even in their distressed and desperate plight, were observing a deeply imbedded belief! Like so much of old knowledge the answer is interred with their bones.

When entering a cow byre at milking time 'God bless the work', (Bail O Dhia air an obair) or 'Good luck to the work', was a familiar greeting. If a visitor left without imparting this or some similar expression of good will it did not go unnoticed and the sinner came in for criticism on their departure. The omission was so important it could not be inadvertent — it must be deliberate.

'God bless you, Polly', we said as, milking finished in the lantern-lit byre, we dipped a thumb into the froth and traced the sign of the cross on the cow's hind quarters or 'elder'. This was to bring a blessing, to ensure continued good luck, and an expression of thanks too. Milk was our wealth. Our precarious existence, balanced on a knife-edge, depended entirely on the bounty of three cows.

The practise of blessing the work is ancient. Workmen, on handing over a finished product, were required by the old Brehon laws to give it their blessing. The craftsman who omitted to do this was subject to a fine, 'equal to a seventh part of the cost of his feeding'. The first person that saw the work after it was finished was also required under law to give it a blessing. It was especially incumbent on women to bless the work of other women.

As we have seen with fishing communities, the farming economy too had a fragile base. Its delicate balance was easily upset. Success and good fortune depended on many imponderables: weather, nature, and entities that, although unseen, were nonetheless potent. Expressions of support and goodwill were reassuring. It hurt no one to deliver such a friendly greeting. It was an expression of kindliness, of solidarity, a lovely old custom we would do well to retain.

Donegal man, Mickey Mc Groarty knew all about these old proprieties. 'In oulden times,' he told me, 'when ye'd go into a house an' the people'd be eating at the table, the first thing ye'd say'd be "God bless the good work here". If they weren't eating, a visitor would declare, "God bless everybody here". In this way ye took nothing away with ye.'

In Sligo, the local curate once went to visit a house near Carney village where a child with a disfigurement had been born. Commiserating with the father he expressed hope that the young person would improve and grow up to be a credit to the family.

'We must accept God's will,' the priest said.

'It had nothing to do with God's will,' the man responded.

'How do you make that out?' the priest said, 'Don't you know that man proposes but God disposes.'

The man was adamant:

'Not in this case,' he said flatly.

'Tell me what you mean then.'

'Well it's like this,' the man started. 'It was springtime and I was up cutting turf on the bog. Mary there came up with a can of tea and a few slices of bread about lunchtime. We sat down on the heather to eat. It was a lovely warm day, the wife there she looked good so I threw me arm around her. One thing led to another and before we knew it nature took its course and...'

'But what has that to do with anything,' the priest interrupted impatiently. He didn't like the direction this story was taking. It might be leading to an infringement of canon law. Perhaps the rest of it was best told in the confession box.

'It has everything to do with it,' the man replied. 'When we were in the middle of it didn't that bugger Jack C—— go by on the bike and he never so much as said, "Good luck to the work". How could ye have luck?'

21

RED-HAIRED WOMEN AND
THE SEACHRÁN SÍDHE

*'To the present day yet, from the time they invaded the island, if we met
a red-haired man or woman first thing in the mornin' going over to
Grange fair we'd bless ourselves an we'd put two straws in front of us on
the road in the shape of a cross an' we'd turn back with the cattle,
to the shore*

Joe Neilan

Although red hair was prevalent among the early Celts, and held
in high regard, it is curious that until recently red-haired women
were regarded throughout the Irish countryside with dread and
suspicion. The belief was strongest among fishermen. They
would turn around and go home if they met one. Farmers too
thought it a bad omen on the way to a fair or market and turned
their cattle for home immediately. There's an antidote for all ills
though and Paddy Watters of Ballinfull, Co. Sligo, saw for himself how the influence of red-haired women, as well as the 'overlook' or evil eye could be neutralised:

'There was a man, Mick M—— lived near here, he's not long
dead, God be good to him. Well, if he met a red-haired woman
on his way to the fair, he'd turn back again even if he was only
about a half mile from Grange. It happened anyway, that he had
a cow that he thought was overlooked an' she died on him. He
went out to the field to dig a hole to bury the cow an', Joe H——
, that was with him that day, is dead too Lord ha' mercy on him.
They dug the hole for the cow anyway an' dropped her into it
"Hold on now," says he to Joe, "till I come back, I won't be a
minute."

This is no yarn now that I'm telling ye; away with Mick down to
the house an', the next thing, didn't he come back with the grand-

est wee *bacóg* of hay with him under his arm that ever ye seen, and a hatchet. Down he goes into the hole alongside the cow an' he puts the *bacóg* of hay under the cow's head.

"Now," he says to the cow, "you were good to me when you were alive, an' now I'll not forget ye."

He took the hatchet then, hacked the legs off the cow an' threw them in alongside of her. He stood up in the hole after that an' shook the hatchet at a house across the field, "Now ye red divil ye," he says, "Ye'll not get her."

I don't know who he was getting at, but that happened not twenty years ago. He must have thought that this red-haired woman overlooked the cow and he figured that this way she wouldn't have the use of her. He was a good level headed farmer, the same man, an' I'm telling ye there was no flies on him any other way!'

Superstitions regarding red-haired women are not confined to Ireland. In Germany they say:

> 'Rotes Haar und Elsenholz
> Wachst auf keinem guten Boden.'
> (Red hair and iron wood
> Out of good earth won't grow.)

The fear is explained as a residual memory of the terror felt by Teutonic soldiers who often had to engage in battle with the Celtic enemy, many of whom had red hair.   Primitive man feared blood, especially the blood of women. Blood was regarded as sacred or taboo. A superstitious fear and regard of the menstrual cycle, associated in the mind with the symbolism of red hair, particularly in women, may have been the world origin of the belief.

Cave drawings in France and Spain were painted entirely in red. Scholars interpret it as an indication of the colour's considerable importance for our ancestors — even in Stone Age times.

A young man belonging to this period found buried in a cave in South Wales was thickly coated with red ochre. Archaeologists theorize that it may have been an attempt to symbolise life-giving blood, or an attempt to bring back the colouring of life to the dead man's flesh.

In Mexico, victims whose flesh and blood was scattered on the seed-corn or on the fields in spring were painted red. In ancient Egypt it was only red-haired men that were sacrificed to the corn spirit, Osiris. In order to fertilise the fields the victim, or some part of him, was burned and his ashes scattered while the people prayed that he would return in the form of vigorous crops the following year. Red-haired men were deemed to be representatives of Typhon, the enemy of Osiris, 'and the killing of them was regarded as an act of vengeance inflicted on the enemy of the god.' Red haired puppies and oxen were sacrificed in Rome for the same reason.[34]

Joe Neilan of Co. Sligo spent many years on Inishmurray Island before eventually marrying an island woman and settling in Sligo town. He believed the superstition was a folk memory of the ruthless savagery of the Danish invaders. Their murderous attacks on Inishmurray and on other monastic settlements, are etched in folk memory:

'They were a red headed people that raided Inishmurray. To the present day yet, from the time they invaded the island, if we met a red-haired man or woman first thing in the mornin' going over to Grange fair we'd bless ourselves an we'd put two straws in front of us on the road in the shape of a cross an' we'd turn back with the cattle, to the shore. We had a dread agin them, we had a superstition against the Lochlainn. Down to the present day we dread to meet a red-haired person, especially a red-haired woman for we wouldn't have any luck.

The buyers at the fair, the cattle jobbers, they'd be waiting for the island cattle, they knew there was always great calves on th'island. They'd be waiting for us and wondering what happened on

[34] For more on this see *Echoes of a Savage Land* p49

the day we'd have to turn back. They'd come out to the shore then, to the strand to buy the cattle, an' mark them an pay for them.

When we'd be paid an' the cattle marked we'd bring them over to the fair then. We had our bargain made then y'know. Nothing bad could happen.'

As we have seen, in Ireland's seaport towns fishermen turned around and went home if they met a red-haired woman. Going to sea after such an encounter invited bad luck. A red haired woman coming into a house where milk was being churned was unwelcome too. The butter wouldn't come. In the northern counties and in Scotland, where 'first footing' was a custom on the arrival of New Year, no one wanted to be first footed by a red-haired man or woman.

We know how farmers and fishermen felt about red-haired women. But how did the women feel about it? Their thoughts are not recorded. Did some stay indoors on fair days or when they might chance to meet a fisherman heading to sea? Did they sometimes take to the road for mischief or to hinder the progress of someone they didn't like? We may never know — the custom is no more, and it's too late to ask!

Other charms have survived from ancient times, their origins and significance lost. Goats grazing with cattle were believed to have many beneficial effects, among them an ability to keep away 'black quarter' and 'redwater' from the cattle. Neither would the poisonous ragwort do the cows any harm. A goat's foot brought good luck to a gambler. It was hung somewhere around the farm too for luck as was a horseshoe or palm blessed at Mass on Palm Sunday. The legs of an animal that died of blackleg were cut off and hung in the byre as an inoculation against further infection.

A man who had a bad run of luck with his stock was advised to hang the shinbone of a goat in the byre as a deterrent. Afterwards he declared it was so effective he 'never looked back, a

baste never died on me since, it warded off something anyway.'
What ancient animal doctor or druid determined in a dim past
that the shinbone of a goat had power? And why the shin bone?

As a further protection against evil, St. Brigid's crosses made
on the eve of her feastday were hung up in the cow's byre.[35] Red
ribbons plaited into or attached to an animal's tail or positioned
over the door of a house had power to avert the overlook. 'Red
cloths were attached to the tails of cows after they calved in Ros
a' Mhíl, Co. Galway, red string was tied on cows' tails in Co. Long-
ford to prevent them being 'overlooked'.'

Numerous beliefs and superstitions, remnants of the old religions, were alive in Ireland until recent times. A few still survive.
In our schooldays we were taught that St. Patrick came to Ireland
in the year 432 A.D. to convert the 'pagan' Irish to the new religion, the one true God. However it doesn't seem to have been
that simple. Closer examination reveals that pagan religions and
practices co-existed comfortably alongside the new faith for over
1,500 years. A great resurgence of these took place during the
term of the Penal Laws as noted by Archdeacon T. O'Rourke in
his *History of Sligo*:

'These barbarous and sinful customs became enormously ag-
gravated about the close of the 16th and the earlier years of the
17th century when the Catholic Church was under the ban of the
Government, its actions paralysed and its priests in banishment.'

According to O'Rourke a Synod was held in a hiding place in
1660 that 'denounced those fearful scandals and concerted meas-
ures for their suppression.' Paul Cullen, Archbishop of Armagh
from 1840 to 1870 banned pilgrimages to holy wells, forbade station Masses in houses and at Mass Rocks and advocated or even
supervised the destruction of some sacred stones.

Denunciations by the Church don't always have the desired effect. Old customs die hard. For instance, 'elf shot' was one of
the maladies that formerly affected cattle. It was believed that
this came about when the fairies at play in the pasture fields ac-

---

[35] St. Brigid's feastday is also the first day of the Celtic quarter festival of Imbolc.

cidentally struck the animal with an elf stone as they frolicked through the pastures playing their favourite game which was throwing elf-stones from one to the other. When the beast was hit it went down and was unable to rise. Adherents to a quasi-pagan faith, many a farmer who went to Mass on Sunday to pray fervently for the recovery of a sick cow treated their 'elf-shot' beast with the magical 'elf-stones' when they went home. The cure was to dip the elf-stones, which had been gathered in the fields and carefully kept over the years, in the water of a three-mearing drain[36] to treat the sick animal. A special ritual was used which I witnessed as recently as 2006.

One can still attend ceremonies at special places like *Tobair na hAingeal* (Well of the Angels) in Co. Donegal where echoes of a pagan faith remain. Here the 'rounds' are done at twelve mid-night on May eve, which is of course, the eve of the Celtic festi-val of Bealtaine. The rounds are performed clockwise or 'with the sun'. Following the blessing at *Tobair na hAingeal* (Well of the Angels), and the taking of holy water, the congregation take, one at a time, seven egg-shaped stones in succession and circle torso, limbs and head three times with these objects. Then: *'bless your-self with each stone and kiss it. Take some water from each well, put it in, wash stone and wash with it...'* Pitted with age the stones were evi-dently sacred to the Old Religion and pre-Christian worship; a remnant surely of a time when people who were converting to the new belief were loath to fully abandon the old!

In a discussion of such practices — which could be used for evil purposes as well as good — it was once explained to me that:

'If ye were having bad luck for a long period, cattle dying and so on, what they used to do was — everyone in them days had lots of hens — they'd take a few rotten eggs and throw them into a neighbours garden, that person would then get the bad luck. The bad luck would go with the eggs.'

She was hesitant to speak about the procedure in case I might think she herself, being familiar with the belief, had practised it.

[36] Water from a drain or well where three townlands or farms meet.

She went on to say that when an animal died people got a grain of salt, wrapped it in a piece of paper and threw it into the hole along with the beast. This was to prevent further losses.

Her son, listening to the conversation, disagreed saying that in his experience it didn't work that way. He had a lot of losses even though he used the salt each time. He got fed up and stopped using it and things actually improved. The mother replied by explaining that was the year her husband died and when you have a death like that, a lot more will follow.

The practise was widespread and varied, even outside of Ireland. David Craig in his book, *On the Crofters Trail*, writes that at Evie in the Orkneys two old women, deprived of grazing for their geese and sheep, were so incensed by the exclusion that they decided to put a curse on the property: 'Part of their ritual consisted in placing eggshells filled with butter on various parts of the common.' As the butter rotted so would the luck of the new owners.

Red haired women, evil eyes, hare witches: they were all part of the warp and weft of country life long ago. Gamekeepers and enchanted hares, mentioned in a previous chapter, were not the only hazards to which rabbit poachers were exposed. Farmers have been known to walk round and round familiar fields for hours without finding their way; others to drive for hours, only to find themselves back where they started. In Italy people are led into confusion by a harbinger of death called 'death fires'. In England the lost traveller is said to have experienced 'led-will', meaning 'led astray'. One way of breaking the spell is to burn an article of clothing.

There are a few wayfarers left who can still tell hair-raising stories of strange apparitions seen at dead of night, or who were 'put astray' by a mischievous act of the fairies, making them lose their sense of direction, and wander lost till morning. Unless... unless, they were wise in country ways...

It happened once to our rabbit poaching friend, Bernie Kelly.

The experience seared his soul so much that he remembered the incident in every detail. It was as if it took place the day before:

'It was during the war years, money was scarce then and five shillings a pair for the rabbits was good money, we were glad to get it. We had a great wee hound here and the Conway's had a wee white dog — he was a nailer! Four of us arranged to go out this night anyway, there was Boyce in it and Thady Conway, meself and the brother Dan. We had carbide lamps with us an' they were that strong they'd cut th' eyes out of yer head. We headed away for the Wee Burra, the rabbits were plentiful and we had six or seven killed in no time. We went out the racecourse — it was staked that time to keep foreign planes from landing during the war. We killed a few more rabbits there and, begod, when we went to come out of the racecourse, we couldn't get out of it! There was water all around us no matter which way we went — the channel was all round us, the sea was below us and the Brook on th' other side.

The four of us went together first an' when that didn't do any good Thady an' me kept one side and Thomas Boyce and Dan took the other side an' still we couldn't get out — water in front of us no matter where we went! Thomas says to me then, "I can tell ye now we're here till morning. This happened to meself and Tommy Fowley one time before and we couldn't make our way out till it broke day."

It didn't look good, but I was lucky, I remembered I heard Paddy Barry telling me father one time that he was put astray one morning coming home from Mac Barry's, his brothers house. I was small at the time but I was listening to them talking and re-membered Paddy saying that he turned his coat inside out an' that's how he got home. If ye turn yer coat or cap it has the power to break the spell.

Thady an' meself said we'd try to get out one more time so out and around we went again, an' still no use. We still couldn't find a way out!

"Do you know what I'll do now," says I to Thady, "I'll turn me coat inside out an' see if it does any good."

I turned the coat inside out, put it back on me and, I'm telling no lie, we didn't walk twenty yards until we were on the race course, the sticks was there and I could see everything before us. We called the other fellas, they were still on the other side of the channel but they came to the sound of our voices and made their way out too.

"Do ye know what we'll do," says Thomas, "Make for the gate-house an' we'll get out on the road an' go home."

That's what we did an' if ye think I'm telling a lie now, Thomas is above there in the house, ye can go up and ask him an' he'll tell you the same thing I'm telling ye. I used to laugh at Paddy Barry when he'd tell us about being put astray, but I was laughing the other side of my face that night, I'll tell ye!'

Bernie had fallen victim to the 'shaughran' or *seachran sidhe* (fairy wandering). It was an enchantment that caused travellers to lose their way on paths and in fields well known to them. Malevolent or mischievous fairies were held responsible.

As with every theory and custom there were the believers and unbelievers, the doubters and the defiant: Pat Dan and Paddy Mc Sharry, two Cliffoney men, took a short cut home across a commonage known as Parkes' farm. They chatted as they walked across fields they had travelled innumerable times before. On this night however things took a different turn. No matter which way they walked, or how far, it was to no avail, they could not find their way home. They tried and retried, they went this way and that, but it was no good. Familiar fields and paths looked unfamiliar to them as if they were in a strange land. Finally it dawned on them that they had somehow, some way, been put astray. Mc Sharry, having heard others describe similar experiences suggested they take their coats off and turn them inside out to break the spell. Pat Dan was having none of it:

'I'll see them in hell before I'd give them the satisfaction!' was his indignant reply as he prepared to sit it out till morning.

Should we scoff at these beliefs? Scorn the storyteller?

'*Oh day and night but this is wondrous strange,*' Horatio said of the apparition of the king of Denmark's ghost in Shakespeares' 'Hamlet'.

'*And therefore as a stranger give it welcome,*' was Hamlet's reply. '*There are more things in heaven and earth, Horatio, than are dreamt of in your philosophy*'.

We must admit that strange and unexplainable things do occur. Credible witnesses tell of inexplicable experiences in every detail. There are times when even the most hardened sceptic must allow that there are occurrences, like the *seachran*, for which we have no rational explanation.

'But how is it these things don't happen today?' I hear you say. 'When is the last time you walked home across the fields from a neighbours house as people did long ago'? I ask. Perhaps we don't disturb the fairies anymore in their nocturnal comings and goings and consequently they don't bother us.

Quite recently a north Sligo man proceeded to level a ringfort on his own land. Working all day and late into the evening he headed for home when night fell. Walking this way and that, re-tracing his steps and trying again, and again, he could not find his way through fields that he knew well and had often travelled by night and day. Afterwards he recalled that, around him all night as he tried and tried to find his way, he heard the sound of horses galloping. When the first streaks of morning light came he found himself on a roadside more than a mile from home.

Did the 'good people' take vengeance on him for disturbing their home? Was it sheer coincidence that he lost his way on that one night of all others? Some say that when he returned to the mechanical digger it was completely dismantled, no two parts of the machine were together.

22

THE STRAY SOD

"What" says I to her, "is it".
"Fairies" she says, "that's no new thing!"
"God knows," says I, "I wouldn't like to meet them!"

James Eddie Costello

The 'stray sod' or '*fóidín mearbhaill*' was another element that
added to the travellers' confusion. During famine times when
people died in great numbers the remains were carried long distances overland to be buried. It is said that the sward where the
coffins were put down to rest became the 'stray sod'. Ever after,
anyone taking a shortcut across fields at night who step on this
piece of ground is liable to be 'put astray'.

It happened to a Co. Sligo family in the famine year of 1848.
There was no food in the sod house where Grace W. lived with
her mother along the D—— river. Begging was futile as the neighbours had nothing to eat either.

Some time previously a man by name of McManus was found
nearby, lying in a drain. The person who found him went to two
or three houses to see if someone would take him in. They refused, being afraid he was infected with typhus fever. Placing
him on straw in a haggard overnight they returned in the morning to find him dead and 'dreadfully mutilated'.

An inquest held on January 12th, and reported in the Sligo
Champion of January 16th 1847, showed that 'both the legs, as far
as the buttocks, appeared to have been eaten off by a pig; I am of
the opinion his death was caused by hunger and cold. There was
not a particle of food found in deceased's stomach or intestines.'
Those who saw the body were of the opinion, from the agonized
expression of Mc Manus's countenance that he was alive when
the pig attacked him!

It was against this terrible background that the old woman died of hunger. Her daughter 'was in a terrible way for she had no money or any means to buy a coffin in which to bury her mother. She thought of a plan. She put the corpse into a creel and carried it on her back to Kilmacshalgan old Churchyard where she buried the remains. On her way to the Churchyard she laid down the creel a few times to rest. To this day it is believed there is a "stray" in the places where she rested the creel. It is said that any place a corpse is rested there is always a stray in that place.'

The *Féar Gortach* or 'hungry grass' was another phenomenon known all over Ireland. It looks no different from any other grass but is believed to grow on the spot where some poor person died on the *Casán na Marbh* or Path of Death during the great famine. The coffins were carried long distances across the fields for burial. Every spot where the coffin was left down to allow the bearers to rest had , from that time forward, the power to afflict anyone stepping on it with the pangs of famine.

In boggy, marshy places, people were often misled by fairy lights. Known in England as Will o' the Wisp, Jack o' Lantern or Jenny Burnt Arses, travellers in places such as East Anglia were in mortal fear of them as they lured many an unwary traveller off the hard road into the boggy morasses where they dwelt. None dared whistle to keep their spirits up, as 'the lantern man will always run to the whistle to come agin you and to kill ye, if so he be able'.

Milton knew of the phenomenon and in 1658 described it in *Paradise Lost*:

> 'A wandering fire
> Compact of unctuous vapour, which the night
> Condenses, and the cold environs round
> Kindled through agitation to a flame,
> Which oft, they say, some evil spirit attends,
> Hovering and blazing with elusive light,

Misleads th' amaz'd night wand'rer from his way
To bogs and mires, and oft through pond and pool
There swallow'd up and lost, from succour far.'

'Fairies! Well there wouldn't be as many soldiers in Finner army camp as fairies in the Muckrim hills,' a Largydonnell, Co. Leitrim woman exclaimed.

The enchanted lights paraded along with her uncle one night when he was coming home from rambling. She herself had often seen as many as twenty flames travelling along the fields in rows after dark. As the fairies walked along they 'heized and lowered' their lights as someone walking with a lantern might do in order to see their way more clearly. The illuminations were frequently seen coming and going in the vicinity of a fairy fort in an area that was rife with strange happenings.

Lawrence Connolly, another uncle, went to a spring well on his land to draw water late on a summer's evening. 'As soon as he dipped the bucket he didn't know where he was', she said. 'Where was he only in a city with lights and people and music all around him? He was there a long time until it all lifted. Anything Lawrence told you was true,' she said earnestly, 'he was a very honest man. Fairies were great around Muckrim.'

James Eddie Costello of Castlegal, Co. Leitrim, was leaving Pat Ned Gallagher's in nearby Tawley around ten o'clock on a winters night. He immediately saw a great array of lanterns travelling along the river. Moving three or four abreast, they started, 'from the steps beyond Kerrigans there, went on round by the river and disappeared at the bridge above Willie John O'Beirnes.

'Pat Ned's wife, Nabby, pulled me back into the house,' he told me as we sat by his fireside one evening:

"C'mon now, let them go their way," she says to me.

Sure I didn't know what it was, but back I went into the house anyway. After awhile:

"What" says I to her, "is it".

"Fairies" she says, "that's no new thing!"

"God knows," says I, "I wouldn't like to meet them!"

Those who have witnessed it say the display appears in the form of brightly coloured wispy flames dancing about in an erratic pattern, or gliding a short distance above the ground, creating the effect of someone carrying a lamp. They alternately ignite and extinguish, one lighting up as another dies out some short way off giving an impression of movement. People who foolishly followed these fires in the past, out of curiosity or mischief, often drowned in the marshy places to which they were led.

Scientists say the phenomenon is caused by methane gas produced by animal and vegetable decomposition in the bogs and swamps. For a long time it was unclear how the methane ignited until a recent discovery showed that the process that produces methane also yields a gas called diphosphane. This ignites spontaneously on contact with air thus, theoretically, solving the mystery of the 'fairy lights'.

There are some things that have no need of explanation and I believe this is one of them. Let the scientists have their pipettes, vacuum jars, sterile labs and theories. There are still those who believe the fairies laugh at their explanations as they continue to carry their lanterns across bog and heather in busy procession, as they have always done.

'Fairy lights', 'Will o' the Wisp', *ignis fautuus*, Jack O' Lantern, *or* 'foolish fire', call them what you will, they were more often seen years ago than now — but that's not surprising: in the years they were populous, neighbours were out and about at night visiting and travelling from place to place on foot or by bicycle. Cocooned in our cars we now hurtle through the darkness seeing nothing but the beams of the headlamps, hearing nothing but the radio or CD player.

In this book we have travelled far in our exploration of man's struggle with the formidable forces of Nature on land and sea.

Despite the fact they were unseen, neither did wise men upset the equally daunting forces of the spirit world that were but dimly understood. Scorn not their beliefs. It carried our forbears through such difficult times, hardship and penury as we can hardly imagine!

> *'The fairies keep their ancient places.*
> *Turn but a stone, and start a wing!*
> *'Tis ye, 'tis your estranged faces,*
> *That miss the many splendoured thing.'*

Francis Thompson (paraphrased)

EPILOGUE

The characters we have met in these pages are now few and far between. Forced to eke an existence by their wits, how intimately they knew the forces from which they were sprung and how efficiently to harness them! One by one they slipped gently and quietly away with only the *bean sídhe* and a few neighbours to mourn their passing. Very few remember them, or care to. If we could somehow meet and have a chat with those old people today, as when St. Patrick met Oisín, what an interesting conversation that would be — and how enriching! A whole way of life has disappeared, swallowed up by mass culture, drowned in a sea of indifference. A very different world has replaced theirs, and we're not yet at the point of appreciating, beyond some vague sense of loss and nostalgia, just how rich and significant those lives were.

Over the years I have been fortunate to speak with many of these wise men and women and listen to their stories — of which in this book there is room for but a few. I will always be thankful to these *seanchaidhes*, for the time they gave me, for the tales they preserved, treasured and passed on: Maggie McGowan, Pat Healy, Hugh Pat G——, Bernie Kelly, Tomás B——, Mickey Mc-Groarty, Francis Crean, Paddy Leonard and many others. Some were lucky enough to have their stories recorded by broadcasters and folklore collectors; most were not.

We have space only for one last story from Pat Healy:

'One time three women from Mullaghmore went to the fair of Bellashanny to sell linen. The linen was on rolls that they carried on their backs, and they had to start out very early, long before daylight, to be in time for the fair.

As they went along the road one woman said she wanted a drink. They could see no light in any house till they came to Finner in Co. Donegal, and the woman went to the house where the light was to ask for a drink, and the other woman went with her. When they came into the house they saw a man there, and he asked them where they came from and what they wanted. When they said they came from Mullaghmore he began to ask them about people in Mullaghmore, and they wondered that a man who lived so far away should know so much about the people in Mullagh.

One of the other women said to the woman who wanted the drink that it might not be a *right* house, and she ought not to drink anything in it. You see fairies could have no power over that person if they ate or drank nothing there. So they went away, and they began talking about the man and what they had heard, and they considered it might be a house of the 'good people', the *sidhe*.

"We'll put stones here to mark the place', they said, 'and we'll see what sort of a house it is when we're coming back in daylight."
 So they made a pile of stones on the roadside to mark the place, and when they came back in the daytime they found the stones where they had put them, but there was no sign of a house there at all!'

APPENDIX A

LIFE OF MAGGIE

(1898-1997): A *Tribute*

Born in 1898 Maggie Mc Gowan spanned an era of great change in Irish life — a life re-lived by her in forceful speech and colourful phrase. A big strong-boned woman, Maggie was articulate, eloquent and persuasive. When she spoke she leaned forward in her chair, fixed the listener with a steady blue-eyed gaze and stated her views spontaneously and forcefully. Her homespun philosophy was inspiring. It exemplified her existence. A way of living only recently lost was conjured up in vivid colour as she painted earthy pictures of life in Ireland in her time.

Maggies words run like a golden thread through this book. One of the most remarkable women I have ever known, it was my good fortune to have had many conversations with her prior to her passing at almost one hundred years of age. Her words speak to us from beyond the grave. Enduring as they are relevant they are a monument to her existence, her values and her way of life. We will let her have the last say:

'A box on the ear was the punishment at school when Miss Higgins from Carns came to teach us in Breaghwy school. A full clout! But it done them all the good in the world, meself included. I got more boxes in that school it was surprising I had an ear at all. She'd draw the full shkite, she had a big hard hand, harder than me own is now. She drew it across the ear; there'd be bells in yer ear for ever so long. They had a ruler for a minor offence. I'm telling you if ye did anything much wrong ye got the sally rod. She'd go out to the garden an' pull it herself — an' they grew for spite. There'd be welts on yer hand with the beating ye'd get.

The teacher before that a Mrs. Leonard, was very good to me; if I had to stay home a day, she used to send the lessons up to the house at night to me. There was no compulsory school that time. Me father didn't go too far himself an' he thought it was good enough for me too. It was all English rule that time; people had more to worry about than education!

I hated the livin' sight of me school days. I had to do all the work in the mornin' before I left for school. An' bring two sods of turf, one under each arm; an' carry them down to the school, a slate under the other arm. No books, nothing, just a slate. Ye wrote all on the slate an' ye spitted on it an wiped it off with yer elbow. That was the teaching, an' still, they turned out the best of scholars. An' the best of children.'

Magggie was orphaned in 1914 when her mother passed away:

'Me mother was an invalid. She died young but I was sixteen at the time, old enough to have sense. They're doin' nothing now to earn a shillin'. She trained me — she knew she was going to die — to bread baking, to churning, to making up butter, making boxty on the hot coals. She died May Day 1914. I had two brothers an' me father to look after. I was keeping the house even long before that.

The hens'd have the shins et off ye waiting for their food in the morning — an' the pigs. Bran and pollard boiled and a bucket of potatoes thrown into that. Fed in a trough, the pigs. They were sold in three months an' the fatter they were the better. I saw the day changing that they wouldn't buy a fat pig at all off ye, ye had to have them lean!

We had big fields of spuds, that's what we made our living on.

Digging them and bringing them into the market and sellin' them for one shillin' a bag (cwt) — but still it was a shillin'! The hens'd get the poheens (*póirín*, small potato). James Young, beside us, the egger we used to call him, he used to send the eggs away. I'd be sent over with two tin cans of eggs, two-gallon cans they used to call them. Me father used to have to come over to carry the two cans, I wasn't fit for it. I had to wait for me turn, eggs was that plentiful that time. Mrs Foran was working in the place. She'd count the eggs and give me a docket. I'd go into the office to Sam Young an' he'd hand me three or four pounds in money. I'd pay two pounds on the book and take the rest home.

A hundred is what they called the ten dozen of eggs. There used to be more than a hundred hens around our house. We'd bring the eggs over according as we had them, ten, twelve or fourteen dozen. The hens used to lay out, we had that many of them you couldn't look after them. The hen'd go missing for a while and then land in an' mebbe she'd have ten or twelve chickens in with her. Ye could travel now to Bundoran an' ye wouldn't see a hen in a house! The hens kep' the houses long 'go, I'm tellin ye!

Taylors on the Mall is where we used to deal when me father went into town. The first thing he bought was a big bag of Indian meal, the height of that window. About two cwt., and a cwt. of bran and two cwt. of pollard. A sixteen stone bag of flour we bought; 'Purity' was written on the bags. When we had the flour all made into cakes we used to make a sheet for the bed out of two of the bags sewn together. It'd do ye fifty years. They were pure linen the loveliest stuff ever ye seen.'

An' I often had to walk into Sligo meself. Sometimes I'd get a lift from Jack Harte — his father Jim Harte had a pub in Lislarry. A jennet they had. The body of the cart used to hold six half barrels. When ye'd be leaving Sligo for home in the evening he'd be coming along at Connolly's there on the Line; he'd be half drunk but that made no differ to you whether he was drunk or sober, as long as ye got up on the cart. Ye had nothing to sit on only the barrel an' there wasn't as much as a bag under ye. An' yer basket of stuff with ye, whatever ye had. He'd draw a shkite on that poor jennet when he'd be halfway out the road to get her to gallop an' ye'd be hoppin' up an' down an' there'd be a ring on yer backside for years afterwards, the track of the barrel. But ye didn't heed that, ye got carried home anyway as far as the Cottage in Lisadell.

I was the first in the neighbourhood to get a bicycle. Paid for it out of the eggs. When I had the bike I'd share it with my friend and pal from next door. I'd start away and cycle two mile of the road, lave the bicycle up to the ditch an' she'd come along an' take it an' go on two mile more. Ye'd walk that two-mile an' hop on the bicycle then again. We were in Sligo in an hour's time. When I had to walk it, it took me three an' four hours. It was a great rest when ye came up to Tully Hill an' pull off th'oul' shoes to rest yer feet. Ye can believe that now! When times came good, we got two bicycles.

They were hard times indeed, Maggie conceded, but they weren't all bad:

'We had a garden an' it was full of carrots an' parsnips an' cabbage of every description, and turnips. For dinner we'd cut a head of cabbage an' boil it with our own bacon, ye could smell it coming into the house. It'd do yer heart good! It was the real thing in comparison to the cabbage and sponges that's goin' for bacon now! Ye had three good solid meals a day and nothing in between; they're eating all the time now but its not doing them half the good as the food we had long ago!'

APPENDIX B

MICKEY MCGROARTY

(1909-1999): *A Tribute*

No light in the window, a padlock on the door. Mickey's little house on the hill is silent, perhaps for evermore.

The rafters there once rang to the sound of the music played by Mickey on his mouth organ, his cap down over one eye shading his furrowed brow. Children once listened there to the tales he told, sometimes exaggerated with mischievous mirth, but no malice did he ever speak. Now an eerie silence shrouds his house, the little lane, those ghosts of bygone days.

Neighbouring lads watched with boyish wonder his scythe swing in graceful motion, silver edge its way through the meadow on the brae in those sunny long-agos. No clock did he need as a glance at the sun's position in the sky told him all he needed to know. A crack shot with a gun it was his delight to track hares, foxes and rabbits in the snow. A noted expert with the turfspade he could equally turn his hand to weaving handsome creels, and baskets too. The man who knew the secrets of where salmon and sea trout sheltered in the bog-brown pools of the Eanymore, who tied the flies to lure them to his reach, no longer casts his line.

Now the master of the scythe, the *slean* and the spade, storyteller, music maker, the keeper of the unwritten annals, is gone from the hill. Mickey, one of the last custodians of the wisdom of the countryside, those men who worked their few small acres with love and pride, maintaining the landscape in a patchwork of beauty in harmony with Nature, will sow and reap no more. Their likes we will never see again.

Mickey was a hard working, honourable man, generous to a fault, charitable and always helpful. No poor person ever left his door hungry. He was the Good Samaritan in every hour of need and seemed to enjoy helping his neighbours as much as working for himself. When a neighbour's last hour came it was Mickey that arrived to shave, wash and dress the body. May his soul now rest in well-deserved heavenly peace far above those fields in which during life he loved and laboured.

If there's a hereafter we can be sure the angels have put their harps aside to listen to Mickey playing *Morris Makin' Pandies* and other Donegal favourites on his beloved mouth organ!

Go gcloisfidh sé ceol na naingeal ar feadh na síoraíochta (May he hear the music of angels for all eternity)

APPENDIX C

GRANT TO HOLD A FAIR

It was once the proud boast of England that the sun never set on her Empire. Perhaps the secret of their success was an astonishing attention to detail. The writ reproduced below was a grant of permission to Lord Palmerston to hold fairs in the tiny village of Cliffoney, Co. Sligo, a remote corner of the British Empire — which market had been long established before Palmerston, or the British, came to Ireland. Similar to the policy of 'surrender and regrant', once 'permission' had been given by royal seal, taxes could be levied. The writ was produced on an illuminated scroll of heavy vellum with an elaborate seal:

George the Third by the Grace of

God of Great Britian ffrance and Ireland King Defender of the ffaith and Soforth.[37] To all unto whom these presents shall come Greeting. Whereas it appears unto us by an Inquisition taken by Virtue of our writ of Ad Inod Domnum issued in Pursuant of a Warrant given by our right Trusty and right well beloved Cousin and Counsellor ffrederick Earl of Carlisle and Lieutenant General and General Governor of our said Kingdom of Ireland on the petition of Henry Viscount Palmerston that the Granting him five ffairs to be held annually forever in or of the Town and Lands of Cliffoney in the Barony of Carbury in our County of Sligo that is to say one ffair to be held on every eighteenth day of May one other ffair to be held on every eighteenth day of June one other ffair on every ffifth day of October one other ffair on every sixth day of November and one other ffair on every fifteenth day of December As also a weekly Market to be held in or at the Town and Lands aforesaid on every Thursday forever will be no Damage Hurt or Prejudice to us or any of our subjects who now have or hold ffairs and markets in the neighbourhood of the same

[37] King of Great Britain and Ireland from 1760. Possibly suffering from porphyria, he had repeated attacks of insanity, permanent from 1811. He was succeeded by his son George IV.

Town and Lands of Cliffoney in our said County. Know ye therefore that we of our special Grant certain Knowledge and of mere
motion by and with the advice and consent of our said right
Trusty and and right well Beloved Cousin and Counsellor ffrederick Eral of Carlisle and Lieutenant General and General Governor of our said Kingdom of Ireland Have Given and Granted
and by these Presents for us our Heirs and Succefsors We Do
give and Grant unto the said Henry Viscount Palmerston his
Heirs and Afsigns full power and Authority To have and to hold
five several yearly ffairs as also a weekly market forever in or at
the said Town or Lands of Cliffoney in the Barony of Carbury in
our said County of Sligo that is to say One ffair to be held on
every eighteenth day of May One other ffair to be held on every
eighteenth day of June One other ffair on every ffifth day of October One other ffair on every sixth day of November and One
other ffair on every fifteenth day of December As also a weekly
Market to be held in or at the Town and Lands aforesaid on every
Thursday forever unlefs the said Eighteenth Day of May the said
Eighteenth Day of June the said ffifth Day of October the said
Sixth Day of November or the Said ffifteenth Day of December
happen to fall on a Sunday Then our Will is and by these Presents for us our Heirs and Succefsors We do Grant unto the Said
Henry Viscount Palmerston his Heirs and Afsigns that he the
said Henry Viscount Palmerston and every of them may have and
hold the said ffairs in or at the Town and Lands of Cliffoney
aforesaid the Monday then next following every such Sunday Together with a Court of pyepowder to be held in said Town and
Lands during the said ffair and Market And our further Will is
And by these Presents for us our Heirs and Succefsors we do
grant unto the said Henry Viscount Palmerston his Heirs and Afsigns that he the said Henry Viscount Palmerston his Heirs and
Afsigns may forever have and receive all and singular the Tolls
Customs Duties Priveleges and Immunities whatsoever for the
said ffairs and Markets and Court arising or to such ffairs Mar-

Section (from copy) of original vellum

ket and Court belonging or appertaining or by means of the same
or any of them rowing or auzning without any amount to us our
Heirs or Succefsors to be rendered for the same And our further
Will is and We strictly Injoin and Command for us our Heirs
and Succefsors that he the said Henry Viscount Palmerston his
Heirs and Succefsors may forever have and hold the said ffairs
and Markets in or at the said Town and Lands of Cliffoney aforesaid in manner and form aforesaid Together with the said court
of Pyepowder and all usual Tolls Customs Duties Privileges and
Immunities from the said ffairs Market and Court arising or to
the same of right or by Custom belonging or appertaining Yield-
ing therefore yearly to our Heirs and Succefsors the yearly rent
of one pound three Shillings and fourpence for the said ffairs
Market and Court to be paid yearly forever And our further Will
is and by these presents for us our Heirs and Succefsors we do
Grant unto the said Henry Viscount Palmerston his Heirs and
Afsigns that these our Letters patent or the enrolment thereof
shall be in all things firm good valid sufficient and effectual in
the Law against us our Heirs and Succefsors in all the Courts of
us our Heirs and Succefsors any Cause of Matter or Thing whatsoever to the contrary notwithstanding Provided always that
these our Letters patent be Enrolled in the Rolls of our Higher
Court of Chancery in our said Kingdom of Ireland and also in
the office of our Auditors General of our said Kingdom of Ireland within the space of Six Months next ensuing the date of
these presents otherwise these our Letters Patent to be void and
of None effect any thing herein contained to the contrary
notwithstanding In Witness whereof we have caused these our
Letters to be made patent Witness our aforesaid Lieutenant General and General Governor of our said Kingdom of Ireland the
fifth aux day of April in the Twentieth Year of our Reign.

BIBLIOGRAPHY

Basso, Keith H., *Wisdom Sits in Places* (University of New Mexico Press, 1996)

Breathnac, Brendán, *Folkmusic and Dances of Ireland* (Educational Company of Ireland, Dublin, 1971)

Brennan, Helen, *The Story of Irish Dance* (Brandon, Dingle, Co. Kerry, 1999)

Bulfin W, *Rambles in Eirinn* (Roberts, Dublin1907)

Carbery, Mary, *The Farm by Lough Gur* (Longmans, Green and Co. 1937)

Chambers, Ann, *At Arms Length* (New Island 2004)

Craig, David, *On the Crofters Trail* (Pimlico 1997; Jonathan Cape 1990)

Craig, Patricia, ed., *The Oxford Book of Ireland* (Oxford University Press, 1998)

Cross, Eric, The Tailor and Ansty (Devon-Adair, NY, USA, 1964)

Deane, Seamus, ed., *The Field Day Anthology of Irish Writing* (Field Day Publications, Derry 1991)

de Paor, Liam, *The Peoples of Ireland* (University of Notre Dame Press, 1986)

Dornan, Brian, *The Inishkeas* (Four Courts Press, 2000)

Dunne, Sean, (editor) *The Ireland Anthology* (Gill and McMillan, 1997)

Evans, E. Estyn, *Ireland and the Atlantic Heritage* (Lilliput Press, Dublin, 1996)

Fairley, J.S., *An Irish Beast Book* (Blackstaff Press 1975)

Feehan, John, *Farming in Ireland* (U.C.D. 2003)

Flower, Robin, *The Western Island* (Oxford University Press, Oxford, England 1992)

Flower, Robin, *The Irish Tradition* (Oxford University Press, London, England 1946)

Fogarty, Mary, *The Farm by Lough Gur* (Longmans, Green & Co., London 1942)

Frazer, Sir James, *The Golden Bough* (Wordsworth, Hertfordshire, 1993)

Freeman, Martin A., ed. by, *The Annals of Connacht* (Dublin Institute for Advanced Studies, 1996)

Gregory, Lady, *Visions and Beliefs in the West of Ireland*

Hall, Mr. and Mrs. S.C, *Hand Books for Ireland* (Virtue, Hall and Virtue 1853)

Hutton, Arthur, ed. by, *Arthur Young's Tour in Ireland* Vol. I& II (George Bell & Sons, 1892)

Irwin, Florence, *The Cookin' Woman* (Blackstaff Press, 1949)

Kavanagh, Patrick, *The Green Fool* (Penguin, 1971, St. Ives, England)

Kelly, Fergus, *Early Irish Farming* (School of Celtic Studies, 1997)

Krappe, Alexander H., The *Science of Folklore* (Methuen & Co. Ltd. 1930)

Mahon Bríd, *Land of Milk and Honey* (Poolbeg Press, 1991)

Mac Donald, Donald, *Lewis, A History of the Island* (Gordon Wright Publishing 1978)

McDonald-Douglas, Ronald The *Irish Book* (Talbot Press, Dublin 1936)

MacGill, Patrick, *Children of the Dead End* (New Island Books, 2001)

Mac Hale, Conor, *Inishcrone and O'Dubhda Country* (IRH Publications, 2003)

McGahern, John, *Memoir* (Faber and Faber 2005)

Mac Neill, Máire, *The Festival of Lughnasa* (Oxford University Press, Dublin, 1962)

Mc Glinchey, Charles, *Last of the Name* (Blackstaff Press, Belfast 1995)

Mc Gowan, Joe, *In the Shadow of Benbulben* (Aeolus Publications, 1993)

Mc Gowan, Joe, *Constance Markievicz: The People's Countess* (Markievicz Millennium Committee 2003)

Mc Gowan, Joe, *Inishmurray: Island Voices* (Aeolus 2004)

Mc Gowan, Joe, *Echoes of a Savage Land* (Mercier Press 2001)

Murphy, Pat, *Toss the Feathers* (Mercier Press, Dublin 1995)

O'Broin, Seosamh, *Plancstaí Bheacáin* (Dreolín Community Arts, Acadh Mór, 2007)

O'Connor, J.P. & Ashe, Patrick, *Irish Indoor Insects* (Townhouse & Country House Ltd. 2000)

O'Donovan, John, ed. by, *Annals of the Kingdom of Ireland*, by the Four Masters (Hodges and Smith, 1851)

Ó Duilearga, Séamus, *Béaloideas*, IML. IV UIMH. IV (Folklore of Ireland Society Dublin 1934)

Ó, hÓgáin, Dáithí, *The Sacred Isle* (Collins Press, 1999)

O'Sullivan, Patrick V., *Irish Superstitions and Legends of Animals and Birds* (Mercier Press, Cork 1991)

Oikarinen, Sari, *A Dream of Liberty* (Bibliotheca Historica 1998)

O Muirithe, Diarmaid, *A Seat Behind the Coachman* (Roberts Wholesale Books, 1972)

O'Sullivan, Maurice, *Twenty Years a-Growing* (Oxford University Press, Oxford, England, 1933)

Porter, Enid, *The Folklore of East Anglia* (B.T. Batsford Ltd., 1974)

Prendergast, John P., *The Cromwellian Settlement of Ireland* (Mellifont Press, 1922)

Raftery, Barry, *Pagan Celtic Ireland* (Thames and Hudson, 1994)

Ryan, Desmond, *Remembering Sion*

Ryan, Meda, *Biddy Earley: The Wise Woman of Clare* (Mercier Press 1978)

Ryder, Sean (Ed.), *James Clarence Mangan, Selected Writings* (University College Dublin Press, 2004)

Seymour, St, John D. *Irish Witchcraft and Demonology* (Dorset Press, 1992)

Scott, Sir Walter, *The Pirate*, 1821

Spencer, *View of Ireland*, 1596

Swords, Liam, *A Hidden Church* (The Columba Press, 1998)

Synge, J.M., *Travels in Wicklow, West Kerry and Connemara* (Maunsel and Co., 1911)

Synge, J.M., *The Aran Islands* (Oxford University Press, 1907)

Trevelyan, Marie, *Folk-Lore and Folk-Stories of Wales* (Elliot Stock 1909)

Verling, Martin, ed. by, *Beara Woman Talking* (Mercier Press, 2003)

Woodmartin, W.G, *History of Sligo* (Hodges Figgis) 1882

Yeats, W.B., *Mythologies* (Macmillan, 1934)

Periodicals

Archaeology Ireland, Volume 14, Issue No. 51, (Spring 2000)

History Ireland, Vol. 2, No. 4 (Winter 1994)
History Ireland, Vol 13 No.1 (Jan./Feb. 2005)
History Ireland, Vol. 13 No. 4 (July/August 2005)

ES2k; Earth Science 2000 Issue 10 (Autumn 2004)
The Celtic Knot Vol.1, No.1 February 1994
Ballyhaunis Parish Magazine 2006 29th edition Annagh

Pers. Comm: Daniel Giraudon, Brittany, France
Capt. Carlsen and the Flying Enterprise: **www.teesships.freeuk.com**
IFC Manuscript 1072: 185-230

GLOSSARY

Banbh	A young pig; a suckling pig
Besom	Sweeping brush made from heather
Bacóg	An armful
Báirneach	Limpet
Banc Cuirlieroidhe	Unknown
Banc Eoghainagrath	Unknown
Boothree	Boortree; elder
Bothán	A cabin; a dwelling house
Brace	Chimney breast
Breeks	Trousers
Cadger	Fishseller
Clamp	Small stack of turf
Crannach	An edible seaweed
Cunyeen	The runt of the litter
Drove	Sliver of bait for fishing
Dugges	Women's breasts
Duil	Running knot or noose; a snare
Duncle	Dunghill
Eadaíl	Dineen: 'plunder, find, jetsam'.
Elder	Udder
Farl	A cake of home-made bread
Furm	Forma: a seat, a bench, a form
Graubia	White caps (broken wave tops)
Hate	thing ('a "hate" else we could do': a "thing" else…)
Heize	Raise up
Hoke	Dig, root about
Jobber	Cattle dealer
Jook	Hide, dodge. 'Jook around him': steal around him.
Keeper	A fastening pin shaped from sally or hazel shoots.
Lochlainn	Scandinavia, Danes
Loy	A kind of spade
Poheen	Póirín, small potato
Ponjer	Porrinjer. Tin container or cup holding a pint or a quart and ususally made by tinkers
Lucks penny	A small sum agreed at the conclusion of abargain to bring good luck and seal the deal.
Porther	Stout, Guinness
Poheen	*Póirín*, small potato
seanchaí	Seanchaidh, storyteller, one versed in folklore.
Sidhe	Fairies
Scraw (*scraith*)	Earthen sod

Shkither	Diarrhoea
Sleabhac	Laver or sloke (an edible seaweed)
Slip calf	Miscarry
Taft	Seat; board running from gunwale to gunwale.
Tangler	Cattle dealer (with connotations of dishonesty)
Tinkers	Travelling tinsmiths
Whin	Gorse

Placenames translation

Alty Dubh	Black Height
Baile an tSeampaill	Town of the Church
Ben Gulban	Benbulben
Bundubh	Bunduff
Carraig Fhada	Long Rock
Carraig Ordóg	Thumb Rock
Cill Ciaróg	Church of the Beetle
Claddagh Dubh	Beach of the black stones
Clíathmhuine	Cliffoney
Cnoc na Taoisigh	Height of the Chieftains
Cromadach	Unknown: some names are so ancient they may not even be in Gaelic.
Cnoc na Tanaist	Chieftains Hill
Cruc an Gabhair	Hillock of the Goat
Cul a Chait	Bank, or reef, of the Cat
Dreimire Buidhe	Yellow ladder or steps
Geata	Gate
Leac Cam	Crooked Rock
Leac na Mealdha	Honeyed Rock
Lugashanny	Hollow of the Fox
Oilean Mór	Big Island
Poll a Ghearraidh	Inlet of the Cutting
Pollachurry (*Poll a Churraigh*)	Inlet of the Leather Boat
Poll Bréan	Stinking Hole
Poll Domhain	Deep Hole
Poll Eamonn	Eamonns Pool
Poll Ui Dhuirmuide,	Diarmuid's Pool
Poll na Weegoge	Unknown, see *Cromadach* above
Ros Caoireach	Point of the Sheep
Sean Gleann	Old Valley (*Slíabh Liag*)
Teampaill Buí	Yellow Church
TobairLeice	Flagstone Well
Tobair na Leice	Well of the Flagstones
Trágh Bundubh	Bunduff Beach

Traigh Ghearr	Short strand or beach
Tulachfinn	Tullaghan

Some placenames such as *Banc Cuirlieroidhe* and *Banc Eoghainagrath* etc
have been passed down through countless generations by word of mouth.
Consequently their translation and etymology are difficult to determine
and unknown to the author.

INDEX

ABOUT THE AUTHOR

Joe Mc Gowan is a native of Mullaghmore, Co. Sligo. Born on the family farm, he worked there in his early years until emigrating to the U.S.A. in the '60s.

Shortly after his return to Ireland in the '70's, Joe, becoming keenly aware of the accelerating pace of change in the Irish countryside, decided to record the old lore before it vanished completely. For many years he has been dedicated to preserving, visually and orally, Ireland's disappearing traditions and customs.

His books are inspired by countless nights spent listening to the stories of the older generation augmented by meticulous archival research. His short stories, cameos of Irish life both past and present, feature frequently in magazines, on local radio and on RTE. The days of the storyteller are gone but their knowledge and lore will, happily, live on in these pages.

His previous books include: *Echoes of a Savage Land*; *In the Shadow of Benbulben*; *Inishmurray: Gale Stone and Fire*; *Inishmurray: Island Voices*; *Constance Markievicz: The People's Countess*; *Sligo: Land of Destiny*; *and* A Fairy Wind CD